RECIPES FOR A
LIFE IN BALANCE

· ·

M∤RAVAL.

Author: Araxe Hajian
Recipe Author: Diane Morgan
Graphic Design: Amie Bartel
Photography: James Baigrie
Styling: Elizabeth Ann Moser

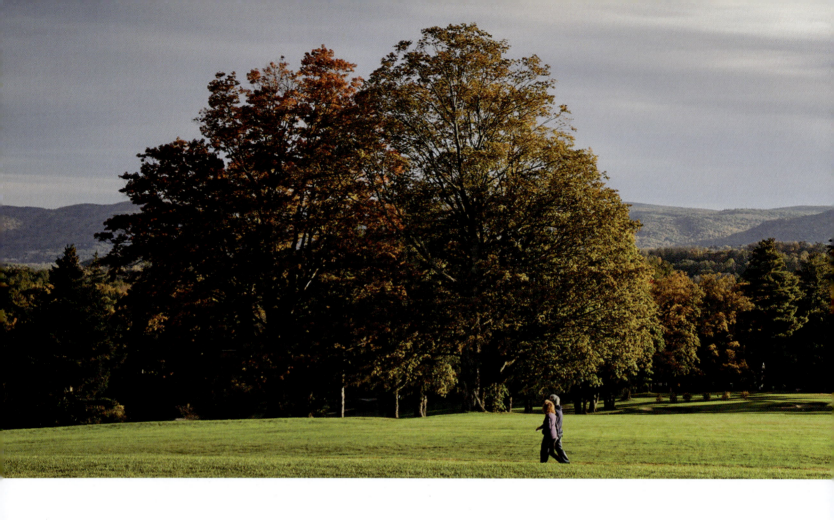

CONSCIOUS NOURISHMENT
IN THE PURSUIT OF

wellbeing

WELCOME TO OUR TABLE

Few things forge a connection to our roots as profoundly as our relationship with food. For me, that connection was woven by my father, a chef who spent decades in the bustling kitchens of the hotel industry. I recall countless hours spent watching him effortlessly transform ingredients into comforting culinary creations. His passion was palpable, and it was through his skillful hands that I learned food was more than just fuel – it was an expression of care, an invitation to connect, and a vehicle for grounding us in the present moment.

Each recipe and ritual in this book is an exploration, not only of culinary creations, but the art of mindful living. By elevating our awareness and appreciation for the world around us, we plant seeds that will grow and strengthen our collective wellbeing, allowing us to cultivate a life in balance. This cookbook is a celebration of that truth, an homage to the way a well-cooked meal has the power to transcend mere sustenance and become a symphony of flavors that nourish not just the body, but the soul.

Mindfully,
Susan M. Santiago
SENIOR VICE PRESIDENT,
MIRAVAL RESORTS & SPAS

introduction

Since 1995, Miraval Resorts has welcomed guests to create a life in balance through mindfulness. Our resorts and spas (in Texas, Arizona, Massachusetts, The Red Sea, and Southern California's Life in Balance Spa Aviara) share a common goal of bringing people together to create authentic connections. Some guests come to celebrate or reignite their purpose, while others seek transformative experiences to elevate their wellbeing. Many just need a safe space to unplug from devices and reconnect—with themselves or loved ones.

Regardless of the path that brings them here, every guest finds a celebrated seat at our ever-growing table. Guests often tell us that arriving here feels like returning to a warm, comforting kitchen—the heart of any home. At its center lies intention, the pilot light of every Miraval journey.

Our intention is to inspire each guest—and you, the reader of this book—in the pursuit of wellbeing.

Whether you have visited one of our resorts or are just learning about us through these pages, we invite you to join us at the table and explore the possibilities of the Miraval Resorts culinary experience.

This book is more than just a collection of recipes. It is a manual for cultivating knowledge and combining it with the ingredients you already have inside—authenticity, discovery, and intention—to nourish yourself and the people you love.

Dive into an ever-evolving gastronomic tale that weaves anecdotes, recipes, and techniques from Miraval specialists, chefs, colleagues, and guests into a tapestry of tastes. And—like all good stories—it invites you, the reader, to become a part of it.

HOW TO
USE THIS BOOK

This collection of recipes meets you wherever you are—from kitchen novice to home chef. Easy-to-follow recipes feature fresh, whole ingredients, and you can add your own twist and use them as a jumping-off point to create unique dishes.

Feel free to approach this book like the buffets found at Miraval Resorts, whose colors, concepts, and flavors you can explore at your own pace. Sample sections or sit down and savor it—you might discover something new about yourself, your senses, and your spirit.

Use it to create a mindful moment, meal, or meditation for yourself or someone you love. These are simple acts that can have a big impact on your wellbeing and can be repeated time and again.

Dietary Key • V | vg | gf | df | ef | nf

V • vegetarian	df • dairy-free
vg • vegan	ef • egg-free
gf • gluten-free	nf • nut-free

CHAPTER-THEMED MENUS
Recipes for a Life in Balance

We created sample menus based on each chapter's theme, including tips and timelines to guide you in preparation and serving. Use them as inspiration for pot-luck dinners, supper clubs, or gatherings with visiting family or friends. You can follow these menus as written or you can swap courses with our other recipes.

The artistic nature of our photography might present dishes that look slightly different from your creations. Each chef adds a personal flare or flourish to their plates, and we encourage you to do the same.

Our crystal pairings accompany each menu. How you use them is up to you: keep a crystal nearby as you cook or use a larger one as an energetic companion or centerpiece for your table. Smaller crystals can embellish place-settings or serve as party favors.

BRING MIRAVAL HOME
Rituals for a Life in Balance

Following the sample menus, we close each chapter with insights, tools, or practices from our resorts that highlight the chapter's theme. Use these exercises to create balance and beauty in your daily life.

Flip to the back of the book for more rituals that reflect elements of a Miraval Resorts experience.

You can discover something new—about yourself and your relationships with people, food, and the earth.

A MIRAVAL CULINARY JOURNEY

We call it a culinary journey at Miraval Resorts because it's more than one class, event, workshop, or meal. It is a curated voyage of immersive, hands-on opportunities that are as mindful, varied, and nuanced as our menus. Guests take classes, practice skills, and visit gardens, hives, and greenhouses at our resorts, and it's all part of the larger Miraval Resorts experience, guided by mindfulness.

Miraval Resorts & Mindfulness

Mindfulness is a practice based on our observance and experience of the present moment without judgment. It is process-oriented rather than outcome-driven. And in a world obsessed with outcomes and results, it can offer a different approach to how we view our lives. Mindfulness guides each of our culinary journeys and invites you to explore the natural world's wonders through knowledge, authenticity, discovery, nourishment, and intention.

Where do mindfulness and cuisine become aligned? At a common intention. Not just at one point, but with a thread that weaves a sparkling constellation of sensory delights and social connections. Integrating that alignment requires our presence. And presence is a state of being we can practice at every point of our culinary journey, with every member of our Miraval Resorts community.

When you practice mindfulness, you can rely less on external packaging and processing of yourself and your food and more on your intuition. You can discover something new—about yourself and your relationships with people, food, and the earth. Have fun with this process as you find fresh ways to combine and create moments and morsels of nourishment at the table and in your heart.

A Culinary Balance

Maybe you always wanted to grow microgreens, roll out handmade pasta, or try pickle-making or gluten-free baking. You might have held a hen at Cypress Creek Farm that produced the eggs in the Texas Breakfast Scramble at Miraval Austin. Have you ever peered into a working honeybee hive? The options and experiences are ever evolving and growing at Miraval Resorts. The chapters ahead offer a glimpse into the recipes and stories that inspire us every day.

Food can uniquely capture moments in time and take us to new landscapes. It keeps us alive and helps us evolve. It is the tangible, taste-able, and visible form of a process that encompasses so much more than consumption—eating is the last step of the long voyage your food takes to get to your fork. Food grounds us with its maker's knowledge, anchors us to our roots with authenticity, propels us into creative discoveries, and nourishes our souls.

Our culinary journey reflects the overarching intention for any Miraval Resorts stay: to gain skills and guidance for living a balanced life in the present moment.

knowledge

"*To gain knowledge is to embrace
discomfort—the tumultuous times, ugly
dishes, or off-tasting sauces. Wipe the cutting
board clean and start again. Every new day is
a foundation for learning and growing.*"

- MIRAVAL RESORTS COLLEAGUE

AWARENESS IN THE KITCHEN
Sharing Knowledge

Knowledge is one aspect of awareness—of our natural surroundings, motivations for action, relationships, and practical skills. Through experience, education, and the sharing of knowledge, we elevate our collective consciousness and overall love of cuisine.

Our resorts let people play in interactive epicurean spaces. Guests share beloved recipes, rekindle relationships with food, and connect across the table. The whole arc of the Miraval Resorts culinary journey begins with learning something new, honing skills, and developing interests that spark and spread joy—that expand our awareness.

Knowledge supports any Miraval Resorts culinary adventure in myriad ways, from helping to tame inflammation to tempering chocolate. Our pursuit of it keeps us curious and constantly tasting bites of a life that never stops teaching.

THE LIFE IN BALANCE CULINARY KITCHEN

Where Knowledge Seekers & Givers Come Together

Have you ever had a social gathering at your house and found that everyone wants to congregate in the kitchen? It's where food is made; aromas rise, textures flow, and flavors emerge. It's a warm gathering place of large knives, tiny spoons, curious coffee cups, colorful spices, and—most importantly—people.

You can stroll into someone's kitchen and know you are in a casual and safe space. It invites you to engage with others or just perch on a counter and observe someone in the act of preparation or presentation. Here, the stories surface to enrich our memories.

The kitchen calls us. It is our contemporary campfire, and its draw is inexplicable and primordial. In ancient times, the campfire was life itself, and today's kitchen beckons us with that same nascent energy. It communicates a sense of gathering.

This is why we created our state-of-the-art cooking demonstration space, the Life in Balance Culinary Kitchen. It's the Miraval Resorts campfire flame. Here, trays of newly baked fables tell stories of flavor and festivity. It's an earth oven of joy and creation where you can test new skills and practice making food together.

KNOWLEDGE
menu

Learn New Paths Toward Fulfillment

· ·

This menu comes straight from the Life in Balance Culinary Kitchen at our Miraval Arizona resort. It illustrates how you can expand your knowledge to produce delicious dishes that are nutrient-dense variations on familiar themes. You can indulge in favorites like guacamole or chocolate mousse and still feel good about staying within your nutritional goals.

Aperitif

THE CHARRED GRAPEFRUIT

Appetizer

EDAMAME GUACAMOLE &
ROASTED TOMATO SALSA

Salad

QUINOA, POTATO & PEAR SALAD

Main

BARLEY RISOTTO

Side

GOCHUJANG ROASTED
HEIRLOOM CARROTS

Dessert

MAPLE BRANDY CHOCOLATE MOUSSE

Digestif

SPARKLING CARROTS

Knowledge Menu

TIMELINE
& TIPS

The bright, satisfying flavors of this menu complement each other with inspirational roots from different parts of the world. The meal finishes with a chocolate mousse that rounds out the bold flavors and helps transition you into the rest of your evening. You may serve the suggested digestif as a lovely finale to your dinner.

3 DAYS AHEAD
Make chimichurri, edamame, and salsa and refrigerate.

1 DAY AHEAD
Make salad dressing and store in refrigerator.
Make chocolate mousse and chill in refrigerator.

IN THE MORNING
Cut and assemble crudité. Make the quinoa salad, cover, and chill until ready to serve. Prepare the ingredients for the aperitif—it can be made in a batch, if desired.

IN THE AFTERNOON
Prepare risotto ingredients and carrots, and make gochujang sauce.

1 HOUR BEFORE SERVING
Start cooking risotto.

30 MINUTES BEFORE SERVING
Roast carrots in oven.

MENU TYPE

Seated dinner served in courses.

SERVING & PLATING

Pre-set the table and portion the quinoa salad into individual bowls.

Before dinner, and while you're cooking the risotto, mingle with your guests in the kitchen. Welcome your diners by serving the citrusy aperitif with the appetizers. Mezcal's smoky flavor profile pairs well with the guacamole, but it can be replaced with lemon juice and local honey for a spirit-free alternative.

When the risotto is ready, gather around the table. Following the salad course, portion the risotto into individual shallow bowls and garnish with the chimichurri.

Place the carrots in a shallow serving bowl and pass it around with a fork for guests to serve themselves. For dessert, serve the chocolate mousse on small plates with a spoon on the side.

A LITTLE EXTRA

Take a moment with your guests before you eat to explore the "Practice Mindful Eating" section of the Trust Your Gut ritual on page 44.

CRYSTAL COMPANION

 Clear Quartz • Flourite • Lapis Lazuli

Always keep a physical distance or barrier between crystals and food or beverages.

EDAMAME GUACAMOLE

It's so handy to have a bag of frozen shelled edamame in the freezer. Here, the edamame are puréed with broccoli florets for a fresh-tasting, protein-enhanced guacamole.

1 cup frozen shelled edamame, thawed

1 cup fresh broccoli florets

1 cup chopped avocado

2 1/2 tablespoons fresh lime juice

1/2 teaspoon minced garlic

1/4 teaspoon minced jalapeño

2 tablespoons diced and seeded tomato

1 tablespoon minced red onion

1 tablespoon thinly sliced green onion

1 1/2 teaspoons chopped fresh cilantro

Fine sea salt

Freshly ground black pepper

Set up a steamer basket inside a pot and bring water to a boil over high heat. Prepare an ice bath and set aside.

Steam the edamame until tender, about 3 minutes. Using a slotted spoon transfer the edamame to the ice bath. Once cold, drain through a strainer, shaking off excess water. Blot thoroughly dry.

Meanwhile, using the same pot, steam the broccoli until bright green and tender, about 5 to 7 minutes. Transfer the broccoli to the ice bath, adding more ice, if needed. Once cold, strain, shaking off excess water and blot thoroughly dry.

In a food processor fitted with the metal blade, process the avocado, lime juice, garlic, and jalapeno until puréed. Add the edamame and process until smooth. Add the broccoli and process, scraping down the sides of the bowl once or twice to incorporate all the ingredients.

Transfer the mixture to a medium bowl and, using a rubber spatula, fold in the tomato, red and green onion, and cilantro. Season to taste with salt and pepper. Transfer the guacamole to an airtight container and refrigerate until chilled, about 1 hour. (The guacamole will keep in the refrigerator for up to 2 days.) Serve with crudités, baked tortilla chips, or baked whole-wheat pita chips.

Makes 8 servings; Serving Size: 1/4 cup

Roasted Tomato Salsa recipe on the next page

V | vg | gf | df | ef | nf

CALORIES: 60; TOTAL FAT: 4 G; CARBOHYDRATE: 5 G; DIETARY FIBER: 3 G; PROTEIN: 3 G

ROASTED TOMATO SALSA

Miraval Arizona serves a roasted salsa that brings out the bright, robust flavors of vine-ripened tomatoes, the deep spice of jalapeño chiles, and the boldness of roasted garlic. If you like cilantro, add the larger quantity suggested. Serve with toasted tortilla chips or crudités.

2 1/2 pounds vine-ripened tomatoes, cored and halved crosswise

2 jalapeño chiles, with the seeds, stem end removed

1/2 medium yellow onion, sliced

2 rounded tablespoons Garlic Confit (page 302), well drained

1/2 to 3/4 bunch fresh cilantro, leaves and tender stems

Fine sea salt

Arrange a rack in the center of the oven and heat the oven to 425°F. Spread the tomatoes, chiles, onion, and garlic on a large, rimmed sheet pan. Use 2 pans, if needed, to keep from crowding the vegetables. Roast in the oven for 20 minutes. Set aside to cool.

Working in batches, add a mixture of the roasted vegetables, along with some of the cilantro, to the workbowl of a food processor fitted with the metal blade. Pulse to coarsely chop the salsa. Transfer to a bowl. Repeat to process all the vegetables. Add salt and pepper to taste. Serve immediately, or cover and refrigerate until ready to serve. The salsa can be made up to 2 days in advance.

Makes 12 servings; Serving Size: 1/3 cup

V | vg | gf | df | ef | nf

CALORIES: 42; TOTAL FAT: 2.25 G; CARBOHYDRATE: 4 G; DIETARY FIBER: 1 G; PROTEIN: 1 G

QUINOA, POTATO & PEAR SALAD

Make this salad as a main-course lunch or to accompany a mixed grill at dinnertime. Plan ahead and have on hand a batch of homemade Vegetable Stock (page 303) as it is a key ingredient in the salad.

1 cup apple juice

1/2 cup organic white quinoa

1 cup Vegetable Stock (page 303) or store-bought vegetable broth

1 pound red bliss potatoes, quartered

1 teaspoon extra-virgin olive oil

1 tablespoon minced fresh herbs, such as thyme, rosemary, and flat-leaf parsley

1 teaspoon fine sea salt

1 teaspoon freshly ground black pepper

3 ripe Anjou pears, halved lengthwise, cored, and sliced

1/4 cup chopped green onions, including green tops

1/4 cup dark or golden raisins

1 tablespoon hazelnut oil

2 tablespoons fresh lemon juice

1/2 teaspoon ground cinnamon

1/2 teaspoon minced fresh ginger

Pea tendrils or flat-leaf parsley for garnish

Heat the oven to 350°F.

In a small saucepan, bring the apple juice to a boil, and boil until reduced by half, about 8 minutes. Set aside to cool.

Place the quinoa in a large dry sauté pan and toast over medium heat until it turns golden and is fragrant like popcorn, about 5 minutes. Add the vegetable stock and bring to a boil. Reduce the heat so the stock just simmers. Cook until all the liquid is absorbed and the grains are tender, about 10 minutes. Remove from the heat and set aside.

Meanwhile, on a large, rimmed sheet pan, coat the potatoes with the olive oil, and season with the mixed herbs, and 1/2 teaspoon each of salt and pepper. Roast the potatoes until fork-tender, about 15 minutes. Set aside to cool.

When the quinoa and potatoes are cool, toss them together in a large bowl with the pears, green onions, and raisins.

To make the dressing, whisk together the reduced apple juice, hazelnut oil, lemon juice, cinnamon, ginger, and remaining 1/2 teaspoon each of salt and pepper.

Add the dressing to the quinoa mixture and gently toss to moisten all the ingredients. Cover and chill until ready to serve. The salad can be made up to 8 hours in advance. Just before serving, garnish with pea tendrils or tender stems of flat-leaf parsley.

Makes 6 servings; Serving Size: 1 cup

V | vg | gf | df | ef

CALORIES: 210; TOTAL FAT: 3.5 G; CARBOHYDRATE: 44 G; DIETARY FIBER: 6 G; PROTEIN: 3 G

BARLEY RISOTTO
WITH WILD MUSHROOMS & CHIMICHURRI

Making risotto with toasted barley instead of arborio rice, as is traditional, delivers a nutrient-dense meal packed with dietary fiber, vitamins, and minerals. Barley has a wonderful nutty flavor that pairs perfectly with mushrooms. Choose an assortment of mushrooms or focus on just one, such as autumn's lovely chanterelles.

1 1/2 cups organic barley

1 tablespoon extra-virgin olive oil

1/2 cup finely chopped yellow onion

1 teaspoon minced fresh garlic

3 cups seasonal assorted mushrooms (shiitake, oyster, portobello, chanterelles, etc.), cut into bite-size pieces

1 bay leaf

6 to 7 cups Vegetable Stock (page 303) or store-bought vegetable broth, at room temperature

2 teaspoons chopped fresh oregano

1 teaspoon chopped fresh thyme

1 teaspoon fine sea salt

1/4 teaspoon freshly ground black pepper

1 tablespoon shredded Parmesan cheese, preferably Parmigiano Reggiano, optional

Chimichurri (page 37)

Place the barley in a dry medium sauté pan set over medium heat. Toast the barley, stirring and shaking the pan, until the barley is golden brown and is fragrant like roasted nuts, about 3 to 5 minutes. Transfer the barley to a plate and set aside.

In a large saucepan or Dutch oven set over medium heat, warm the oil and swirl to coat the bottom of the pan. Add the onions and garlic. Sauté until the onions have softened, about 2 minutes. Add the mushrooms and cook for an additional minute. Stir in the toasted barley and the bay leaf. Stir in 1/2 cup of the vegetable stock and reduce the heat to a simmer. When the barley has absorbed almost all of the liquid, add another 1/2 cup. Continue, adding stock and stirring, waiting to add more liquid until the liquid is absorbed. It will take about 40 to 50 minutes of cooking and stirring until the barley is tender. Once it is tender, stir in the oregano, thyme, salt, pepper, and Parmesan cheese, if using. Remove the bay leaf. Divide among warmed pasta bowls, add 2 tablespoons chimichurri, and serve immediately.

Makes 8 servings; Serving Size: 1/2 cup

Chimichurri recipe on the next page

V | ef | nf

CALORIES: 160; TOTAL FAT: 13 G; CARBOHYDRATE: 11 G; DIETARY FIBER: 2 G; PROTEIN: 2 G

Helpful hints: Choose an assortment of wild mushrooms to mix with aromatics.

Adding the vegetable stock in stages gives the barley a chance to absorb it at a steady pace for better consistency.

CHIMICHURRI

This fiery, herbal condiment found in Argentinian cooking is typically served with grilled meats and seafood. It is also amazing to spoon on grilled vegetables and mushrooms.

1 cup packed fresh cilantro leaves

1 cup packed fresh flat-leaf parsley leaves

3 garlic cloves

2 tablespoons red wine vinegar

Juice of 1/2 lime

1 1/4 teaspoons fine sea salt

1/2 teaspoon red pepper flakes

3/4 cup extra-virgin olive oil

In the container of a high-speed blender, combine the cilantro, parsley, garlic, vinegar, lime juice, salt, and red pepper flakes. Slowly drizzle in the oil and blend on high speed until the sauce is emulsified. Transfer to a covered container and refrigerate until ready to use. The chimichurri will keep refrigerated for up to 3 days.

Makes 10 servings; Serving Size: 2 tablespoons

V | vg | gf | df | ef | nf

CALORIES: 130; TOTAL FAT: 15 G; CARBOHYDRATE: 1 G;
DIETARY FIBER: 0 G; PROTEIN: 0 G

GOCHUJANG ROASTED HEIRLOOM CARROTS

Gochujang paste, a spicy, savory, and sweet fermented condiment, is adaptable outside its traditional Korean cooking uses. For this recipe, the chefs at Miraval Arizona pair it with high-heat-roasted carrots. Look for small, heirloom carrots with their bushy green tops still attached. They come from seeds that have been handed down—unmodified—through generations.

Gochujang Sauce

1/3 cup gochujang paste

2 1/2 tablespoons expeller-pressed grapeseed oil

1 tablespoon honey

1/4 teaspoon fine sea salt

1/4 teaspoon freshly ground black pepper

Roasted Carrots

1 1/2 pounds heirloom baby carrots, tops trimmed, scrubbed (not peeled), and cut in half lengthwise

1 tablespoon expeller-pressed grapeseed oil

Fine sea salt

Freshly ground black pepper

Arrange a rack in the upper third of the oven and heat the oven to 425°F.

While the oven is heating, make the sauce. In a small bowl or measuring cup, whisk together the gochujang paste, grapeseed oil, honey, salt, and pepper. Salt to taste and set aside.

To roast the carrots, on a rimmed sheet pan, toss the carrots with the grapeseed oil and season with salt and pepper. Spread out the carrots and roast until the tip of a sharp knife easily pierces the center, about 10 to 12 minutes, depending on the size of the carrots.

To serve, drizzle the Gochujang Sauce over the carrots and use tongs to toss the carrots, coating them completely. Transfer to a warmed serving platter and serve immediately.

Makes 6 servings

V | gf | df | ef | nf

CALORIES: 140; TOTAL FAT: 7 G; CARBOHYDRATE: 18 G; DIETARY FIBER: 3 G; PROTEIN: 1 G

MAPLE BRANDY CHOCOLATE MOUSSE

The avocado base in this recipe takes chocolate mousse to the level of delicious decadence. Avocado is generally rich in monounsaturated fats, fiber, and folate. Your family and friends will never guess that the base isn't made from whipping cream, an ingredient high in saturated fat. Dark chocolate provides plant phenols that have been found to have health benefits. Unlike traditional mousse which has little to no fiber, a serving of this treat provides 9 grams of fiber. That said, with approximately 340 calories a serving, consider this dessert a treat for a special occasion. As an added bonus, you can transform this dessert's flavor profile with additions like cayenne pepper and cinnamon.

3 ounces dark chocolate (70% cacao), finely chopped

2 cups avocado pulp (2 to 3 large ripe avocados)

1/2 cup unsweetened cocoa powder

1/2 cup plus 2 tablespoons real maple syrup

1/4 cup organic unsweetened soy milk

2 tablespoons brandy, bourbon, or cognac

2 teaspoons pure vanilla extract

1/8 teaspoon fine sea salt

1/8 teaspoon cayenne pepper, optional

1/8 teaspoon ground cinnamon, optional

In a small microwave-safe bowl, melt the chocolate, uncovered, on 50 percent power. Heat in 30 second increments, stirring each time, until the chocolate is melted. As an alternative, place the chocolate in a heatproof bowl set over a saucepan of simmering water. Stir until the chocolate melts, being careful not to let any water touch the chocolate.

In a blender, or the workbowl of a food processor fitted with the metal blade, combine the avocado, cocoa powder, maple syrup, milk, brandy, vanilla extract, and salt. Add the cayenne and cinnamon, if using. Add the melted chocolate and process until completely smooth. Transfer to a covered container and refrigerate for at least 2 hours or overnight.

Three hours before serving, spoon the mousse into 6 ramekins, or for a decorative presentation, use a pastry bag fitted with a fluted tip and pipe mousse into small dessert dishes. Refrigerate, covered, until ready to serve.

Makes 6 servings; Serving Size: 1/2 cup

V | vg | gf | df | ef | nf

CALORIES: 340; TOTAL FAT: 23 G; CARBOHYDRATE: 36 G; DIETARY FIBER: 9 G; PROTEIN: 5 G

THE CHARRED GRAPEFRUIT
WITH MEZCAL

1 1/2 ounces mezcal

1 ounce freshly squeezed grapefruit juice

1 ounce freshly squeezed lime juice

1 ounce agave nectar

Grapefruit wedges for garnish

Pour mezcal, grapefruit juice, lime juice, and agave nectar into mixing tin. Add scoop of ice into mixing tin, seal with the lid, and shake well. Strain into a martini glass and garnish with a fresh grapefruit wedge.

Makes 1 serving

CALORIES: 200; TOTAL FAT: 0 G; CARBOHYDRATE: 27 G; DIETARY FIBER: 0 G; PROTEIN: 0 G

SPARKLING CARROTS

6 large carrots - washed

6 oranges - peeled

1 bottle of sparkling wine

Run the washed carrots and peeled oranges through a juicer on medium-high speed one at a time to prepare the fresh juice. The amounts listed in the recipe should yield 24 to 32 ounces of juice, but this will vary depending on your juicer. If you do not own a juicer, use store-bought fresh orange and carrot juices. Whisk the juice to prevent separation and divide it evenly among 6 to 8 champagne flutes or glasses, leaving enough room to add the amount of sparkling wine you wish.

Garnish with washed carrot-top greens or sliced carrot circles.

Makes 6 to 8 servings

CALORIES: 150; TOTAL FAT: 0 G; CARBOHYDRATE: 14 G; DIETARY FIBER: 0 G; PROTEIN: 1 G

BRING MIRAVAL HOME
Expand Your Knowledge with Mindful Eating

At Miraval Resorts, we practice mindful and intuitive relationships with food and how it's prepared. We encourage our guests to step away from mindless eating (while driving, working, or watching screens) or eating to soothe difficult emotions. Mindful eating helps us replace distraction with knowledge, and *self*-knowledge might be your best tool in the kitchen.

Mindful eating includes being attentive to our bodies and the food we put into them; it compels us to ask questions.

- Where does our food come from?

- How does it land on the plate?

- How do we make knowledge-based choices about what and how much to eat?

When we know ourselves, we can use our intuition to differentiate between hunger for food and yearning for other kinds of fulfillment (emotional, professional, intellectual). It's subtle, but there is a difference between being full and feeling fulfilled.

Mindful eating is about being aware of and accepting our responses to food and reframing knee-jerk reactions by pausing, observing, and removing judgment. It helps us moderate and regulate how we use food to fuel our bodies, nourish our souls, and maximize our mental potential. We gain knowledge by engaging our senses and intuition.

TRUST YOUR GUT

This exercise asks you to use your intuition to learn your body's cues. By accessing your intuitive intelligence—what we sometimes call a "gut feeling"—you can tune into your emotional and physical processes that help you identify your hunger or fullness. When you understand the source, you can identify and meet your needs appropriately.

....

What You Need

1 writing utensil
(pen or pencil)

1 journal

Your intuition

Your hands

5 senses
(sight, sound, taste, smell, and touch)

Before eating, establish an intention for how to identify when you're no longer hungry. At Miraval Resorts, we often use *mudras,* or hand gestures, to channel the flow of energy. The intuition mudra* can remind you to check in with the intention of realizing when you are no longer hungry.

- *Access your Intuition*
  - Ask yourself if you are hungry for food. If the answer is no, get curious about what may be driving your hunger. Listen in for your desires or underlying intentions. Are you hungry for companionship? Creativity? Emotional support? Write down your thoughts and feelings.
  - If the answer is yes, go further. Ask about the characteristics of your hunger: Identify a taste, texture, temperature, or type of food you desire and write it down in your journal. How do you want to eat it—with a knife and fork, your hands, or a big spoon?
  - Identify nutrient-dense foods or actions that match your desires with your underlying intentions. Those could be shaped by hunger, routine, stress, or comfort.
- *Practice Mindful Eating*
  - Pay attention to what you eat and consume it with presence.
  - Explore the sensory journey in each food you eat, using all five senses, and record what you touch, taste, see, smell, and hear. Write down what the food reminds you of and how it makes you feel as you chew and swallow.
  - Practice meditation before beginning your meal to reframe your eating experience.
- *After Eating*
  - Check in with yourself to see how you feel.
  - Return to your mudra.
  - Write down your thoughts.

*For the intuition mudra, touch the tip of your thumb to the tip of your middle finger while keeping the other three fingers relaxed.

Many cultures suggest stopping eating when you are about 80 percent full to feel neither deprived nor stuffed. Your stomach takes about 20 minutes to digest your food, so you want to give your body time to catch up to your mind.

Through experience, education, and the sharing of knowledge, we elevate our collective consciousness and overall love of cuisine.

authenticity

RECLAIMING OUR ROOTS
Inspiration and the Authentic Self

What does it mean to reclaim your authentic self? At Miraval Resorts, it is a process that begins with pulling out weeds and planting seeds—in the soil and our souls.

You can go to our farms and gardens and harvest heirloom tomatoes in Austin, fresh herbs in Arizona, and forage for mushrooms in the Berkshires. Wherever you go in the Miraval Resorts ecosystem, regardless of the season or location, you will take part in the bountiful give-and-take between humans and the earth.

Every Miraval Resorts specialist guides this experience as a steward of authenticity. This is especially true when it comes to our farms, kitchens, and gardens.

The Miraval journey is all about rediscovering who we are at our roots.

Our souls, as well as our mixing bowls, are sacred vessels. What we put inside them should be measured with care and discretion. When we fill our bodies with whole foods, closest to their natural state, we inspire ourselves to add another dimension to our broader search for authenticity.

Without the extra layers imposed by society and supermarket—the additives, artificial ingredients, chemicals, and social media messaging—we have something elemental and pure. The more we move away from the processed version of ourselves and the food we consume, the closer we come to returning to our origins, to an honest, authentic person and plate.

Cultivating Authenticity

While, ideally, we would grow, hunt, or gather our food, most of us don't have the talent, tools, time, or inclination to do so. But that doesn't mean we have to forego the assurance that we are getting the food we seek at the level of quality we value.

Authenticity matters. We can't all have a 10-acre farm in our backyard like Miraval Austin's Cypress Creek Farm, but most of us are lucky to have a good farmers' market nearby instead. We can still cultivate a relationship with a community of farmers, fishers, beekeepers, and ranchers who share our values and care about food integrity.

Cultivation comes in many forms. We live in kinship with the plant world and become better custodians of ourselves when we mirror the kindness we give to our crops with self-care. Our best selves sprout from landscapes (inner or outer) that have the healthiest conditions for growth, that keep us nurtured, enriched, and hydrated. These same blooming spaces—tilled with intention from Arizona to Texas to Massachusetts—foster the foundations of Miraval Resorts.

"*Miraval ramped up our desire for healthy eating. Immediately I sought out more flax and chia seeds and added pumpkin and sunflower seeds, goji berries, and cocoa nibs to our pantry. Overnight oats became a staple in our refrigerator for weeks running.*"

— MIRAVAL AUSTIN GUEST

AUTHENTICITY
menu

Authentic Autumn in the Berkshires

···

In this part of the country, local is a synonym—
when it relates to food—for authentic. The
cartography of taste can instantly carry you to
a particular place. Ask anyone who has cracked
open a New England lobster claw—they will tell
you it's *wicked* good. This region of the country
has a distinctive flavor, and we created a menu
that highlights its spirit and transports you to
the essence of the Berkshires.

Aperitif

AUTUMN IN THE BERKSHIRES

Appetizer

BUTTERNUT SQUASH TARTINE

Salad

FENNEL & WINTER CITRUS SALAD

Main

HUDSON VALLEY DUCK BREAST

Side

VADOUVAN CAULIFLOWER

Dessert

HARVEST MOON ORANGE CAKE

Digestif

RECALIBRATOR SHOT

Authenticity Menu

TIMELINE & TIPS

This menu is a medley of dishes created by our chefs for Harvest Moon and 1894, Miraval Berkshires' main dining rooms, to reflect both dining experiences and showcase the wide range of fresh, local ingredients used in our menus. This meal leans into autumn and winter themes. You can picture sitting by a warm fire blanketed with the aroma of apples, cranberries, and spices.

ONE WEEK IN ADVANCE
Make orange cakes and freeze.

3 DAYS AHEAD
Make butternut squash caponata and cranberry agrodolce.

1 DAY AHEAD
Dry brine duck breasts, make sweet potato purée, and roast cauliflower.

IN THE MORNING
Prepare and refrigerate salad ingredients and make lemon vinaigrette and sauce vierge. Make and refrigerate coconut Chantilly and prep dessert oranges while orange cakes thaw.

45 MINUTES IN ADVANCE
Heat oven to 425°F. Cut cauliflower and arrange on sheet pans.

JUST BEFORE SERVING
Assemble butternut squash tartines. Heat sweet potato purée. Roast cauliflower wedges, sear duck breasts, and assemble dish.

MENU TYPE

Formal, seated dinner with served courses.

SERVING & PLATING

Plate the salad at the table for each place setting ahead of time and prepare aperitifs for your guests as they arrive. The aroma of freshly pressed apples transports your party into New England orchards for a drink that tastes like fall. Offer a platter of tartines for people to eat with their beverage.

Gather around the table and enjoy the salad course.

Next, serve the entrée of sliced duck, chicories, and jus, and garnish with a spoonful of agrodolce. Place the remaining agrodolce in a small serving bowl with a spoon and pass it at the table.

Place the cauliflower on the dinner plate and drizzle it with sauce. If you prefer to pass it at the table, serve the wedges shingled in a shallow serving bowl with the sauce spooned over the top.

Following the meal, serve the cake, orange wedges, and sauce, arranged on dessert plates with a fork and spoon.

A LITTLE EXTRA

The formality of this meal invites you to bring out the family china or fancy goblets and pitchers reserved for special occasions.

Consider creating a decorative centerpiece with foraged and found elements in nature that reflect the season, like autumn leaves, pine cones, and berries.

Set the tone for your evening by exploring the ritual on page 326 for creating a culinary playlist.

....

CRYSTAL COMPANION

 Citrine • Larimar • Carnelian

Always keep a physical distance or barrier between crystals and food or beverages.

BUTTERNUT SQUASH TARTINE

The chefs at Miraval Berkshires transform an Italian classic—caponata—typically made with eggplant into a vibrant fall appetizer using butternut squash instead. All the savory flavors of onion, garlic, peppers, and fennel are included in this dish that delights our guests with its elegance and simplicity. Consider sprinkling it with micro-basil to add a colorful nutritional boost.

6 thick slices artisan whole-grain bread, halved, and then griddled or toasted

1 1/2 cups Butternut Squash Caponata (recipe follows)

1/2 cup fresh burrata

8 leaves fresh basil

Red pepper flakes

To assemble each tartine, spread burrata on each toasted bread half, followed by 2 tablespoons of caponata. Garnish with a shower of basil and a few flakes of red pepper. Serve immediately.

Makes 6 servings; Serving Size: 2 half slices

V | ef | nf

CALORIES: 260; TOTAL FAT: 10 G; CARBOHYDRATE: 36 G; DIETARY FIBER: 5 G; PROTEIN: 8 G

BUTTERNUT SQUASH CAPONATA

1 1/2 pounds butternut squash, peeled, trimmed, halved, seeded, and cut into 1/2-inch dice

1/4 cup extra-virgin olive oil

Fine sea salt

Freshly ground black pepper

6 garlic cloves, minced

1 medium-large yellow onion, cut into 1/2-inch dice

1 large fennel bulb, trimmed, halved lengthwise, cored, and cut into 1/2-inch dice

1 medium red bell pepper, seeded and deribbed, and cut into 1/2-inch dice

1 rib celery, trimmed, and cut into 1/2-inch dice

2 tablespoons finely chopped fresh basil leaves

2 tablespoons red wine vinegar

2 tablespoons honey

2 tablespoons tomato paste

1/3 cup water

In a large bowl, toss the butternut squash with 2 tablespoons of the olive oil. Season with 1/2 teaspoon each of salt and pepper. Set aside.

In a large sauté pan, warm the remaining 2 tablespoons of oil over medium heat. Swirl to coat the bottom of the pan. Add the garlic, onion, fennel, bell pepper, and celery. Sauté, stirring frequently, until the vegetables are soft but not brown, 5 to 7 minutes. Add the basil and season with salt and pepper. Add the vinegar, and stir to combine, scraping up any bits clinging to the bottom of the pan. Stir in the honey, tomato paste, and water. Using a silicone spatula, add in the butternut squash.

Simmer, partially covered, until the squash is fork-tender, stirring occasionally, 12 to 15 minutes longer. Remove from the heat. The caponata can be made up to 3 days in advance. Transfer to a covered container and refrigerate.

Makes about 4 cups; Serving Size: 1/3 cup

V | gf | df | ef | nf

CALORIES: 96; TOTAL FAT: 5 G; CARBOHYDRATE: 13 G; DIETARY FIBER: 2 G; PROTEIN: 1 G

FENNEL & WINTER CITRUS SALAD
WITH TOASTED HEMP SEEDS

This salad features a mix of locally grown mesclun greens as the base for crisp fennel slices and bright-tasting oranges and grapefruit sections. There are toasted hemp seeds for crunch and a shower of lovely fresh herbs over the top. For simplicity in making this recipe, buy pre-toasted hemp seeds.

....

Lemon Vinaigrette

2 tablespoons water

1/4 cup freshly squeezed lemon juice

1/2 teaspoon fine sea salt

Freshly ground black pepper

3/4 cup extra-virgin olive oil

Salad

2 fennel bulbs, tops trimmed, halved lengthwise, cored, and cut into paper thin slices (See *Note*)

1 (5-ounce) container local mesclun mix

2 Valencia or Navel oranges

1 grapefruit

1 cup mixed fresh herbs, leaves only, chives snipped into 1/2-inch lengths (tarragon, flat-leaf parsley, chives, and the fennel fronds)

1/2 cup toasted hemp seeds

To make the dressing, put the water, lemon juice, salt, and a couple grinds of pepper in the container of a high-speed blender. With the blender running, slowly pour in the olive oil until the dressing is emulsified. Transfer to a jar with a tight-fitting lid and set aside until ready to use.

To make the salad, place the fennel slices in a bowl of ice water while you prepare the citrus. Place the mesclun mix in a large salad bowl.

To supreme the oranges and grapefruit, cut a slice from the top and bottom of each orange and grapefruit to reveal the flesh. Stand an orange upright and slice away the peel from the sides in wide strips, cutting downward, following the contour of the orange, and removing all the white pith. Use a paring knife to slice along the inside of the membranes to remove the fruit as wedges. Repeat with the second orange and grapefruit. Place the citrus in a medium mixing bowl. Capture as much of the citrus juice from the cutting board as possible and add it to the bowl with the citrus wedges. Toss with 1/4 cup of the dressing and 1/4 cup of the herbs.

Remove the fennel slices from the ice water and blot thoroughly dry with a clean kitchen towel. Put in a mixing bowl. Toss with 1/4 cup of the dressing and 1/4 cup of the herbs.

When ready to serve the salad, give the dressing a vigorous shake and then toss the mesclun mix with enough dressing to nicely coat the greens. Add half the hemp seeds and toss with the greens. Arrange on a large platter. Scatter the fennel slices and decoratively arrange the citrus over the greens. Garnish with the remaining herbs and hemp seeds. Serve immediately.

Note:
While slicing fennel into paper-thin slices is achievable with a sharp chef's knife, a handy kitchen tool is an inexpensive mandoline slicer. This is a quick way to achieve thin slices on onions, radishes, cucumbers, etc.

Makes 6 servings

V | vg | gf | df | ef | nf

CALORIES: 350; TOTAL FAT: 29 G; CARBOHYDRATE: 15 G; DIETARY FIBER: 5 G; PROTEIN: 11 G

HUDSON VALLEY DUCK BREAST
WITH SWEET POTATO PURÉE

Serving the duck with a purée of sweet potatoes, a warmly spiced cranberry sauce, and a trio of bitter greens highlights the splendors of autumn's bounty. You'll have more sauce than you need for this recipe. It will keep for several months in the refrigerator as a sauce for poultry, including turkey, for a holiday meal. This main dish is a simplified version of a classic served at Miraval Berkshires' 1894 Restaurant.

For the Duck

6 (4-ounce) duck breasts, trimmed of all fat and sinew

1 1/2 tablespoons coarse sea salt

1/4 teaspoon celery salt

1/4 teaspoon coarsely ground black pepper

1/8 teaspoon ground nutmeg

1/8 teaspoon ground ginger

1/8 teaspoon garam masala

1/2 cup warm water

1 tablespoon honey

1 tablespoon white vinegar

Cranberry Agrodolce

8 ounces fresh cranberries, picked over

1/2 cup red wine vinegar

1 cup honey

1/2 cup sherry vinegar

2 whole cloves

1 bay leaf

1/2 cinnamon stick

Sweet Potato Purée

1 pound Garnet or Jewel sweet potatoes, scrubbed

4 sprigs fresh thyme

Extra-virgin olive oil

1 to 2 tablespoons real maple syrup

Fine sea salt

2 tablespoons expeller-pressed grapeseed oil

1 tablespoon minced shallot

1 garlic clove, minced

3/4 cup dry white wine

1 tablespoon grass-fed unsalted butter

4 cups mixed radicchio, chicories, and frisée (radicchio and chicories sliced)

Fine sea salt

To dry-brine the duck, prick the duck skin all over with the tip of a paring knife or a sharp metal skewer without piercing the meat. Set aside on a plate.

Prepare a small, rimmed sheet pan with a wire rack set inside. In a small bowl, stir together the salt, celery salt, pepper, nutmeg, ginger, and garam masala. In a medium bowl, mix together the water, honey, and vinegar, making sure the honey is dissolved. Dip each duck breast in the honey mixture and place on the wire rack, skin-side up. Lightly season the skin side of each duck breast with the salt mixture. Place in the refrigerator, uncovered, for 4 to 6 hours. (At this point, the duck breasts can be rinsed, patted dry with paper towels, and covered on a plate, ready for searing. Do this entire step one day in advance, if possible.)

Meanwhile, make the cranberry sauce. In a medium saucepan set over medium heat, combine the cranberries, red wine vinegar, honey, sherry vinegar, cloves, bay leaf, and cinnamon stick. Bring to a simmer and cook, stirring occasionally, until the mixture is reduced to a light syrup consistency, about 15 minutes. Let cool for 10 minutes. Remove the cloves, bay leaf, and cinnamon stick. Purée in a high-speed blender. Set aside until ready to serve. The sauce can be made up to 5 days in advance. Cover and refrigerate. Heat before serving.

Continued on the next page

gf | ef | nf

Croquette in photo not included in recipe.

CALORIES: 340; TOTAL FAT: 15 G; CARBOHYDRATE: 46 G; DIETARY FIBER: 3 G; PROTEIN: 7 G

....

To roast the sweet potatoes, heat the oven to 350°F. Prick the skin of each sweet potato with a fork. Place each potato on a sheet of aluminum foil along with a sprig of thyme and wrap it closed. Place in the oven and roast until very soft when pierced with a knife, about 1 hour. Unwrap and set aside until cool enough to handle. Discard the thyme. Scoop the flesh of the sweet potatoes into the workbowl of a food processor. Purée until smooth, adding olive oil as needed. Add maple syrup to taste and season with salt. Keep warm until ready to serve. (The sweet potato purée can be made up to 2 days in advance. Cover and refrigerate. Heat before serving.)

When ready to cook the entrée, heat the oven to 425°F. Add the duck breasts, skin-side down, to a large, cold ovenproof skillet. Place the pan over medium heat. The duck fat from the breasts will begin to render. Continue to cook the duck breasts, without disturbing them, until the skin is browned and the skin easily releases from the pan, about 5 minutes. Using tongs, flip the breasts over and sear for 2 minutes longer. Transfer the skillet to the oven and roast until nearly medium-rare, about 3 minutes. Transfer the breasts to a warmed platter and let rest for at least 5 minutes before slicing.

Place the skillet over medium-high heat, add the shallots and garlic. Sauté 1 minute, scraping up the brown bits clinging to the bottom of the pan. Add the wine and simmer until the liquid is reduced by half, about 2 minutes. Remove from the heat and swirl in the butter.

While the wine is reducing, heat a stovetop grill pan over medium high heat, and grill the radicchio, chicories or frisée until crisp-tender and slightly charred. Do this in batches, if needed.

To serve, spoon 1/2 cup of sweet potato purée on the base of 4 warmed dinner plates. Arrange grilled radicchio and chicories over top. Slice each duck breast, crosswise, into 3 pieces. Arrange these slices over the greens on each plate. Drizzle 2 tablespoons of the cranberry agrodolce around the plate and spoon the jus from the skillet over top the duck breasts. Serve immediately.

Makes 6 servings

Helpful hints: Duck skin will do the work for you and release itself from the pan when it's ready.

Searing duck flesh-side down for two extra minutes ensures even cooking.

VADOUVAN CAULIFLOWER
WITH SAUCE VIERGE

Wedges of curry-infused roasted cauliflower make an extraordinary side dish, especially when topped with a caper, shallot, and herb sauce. This dish is ideal for a dinner party, because the cauliflower needs to steam-roast and then chill completely ahead of being sliced. Look for Vadouvan curry powder in spice shops or online and use it in any dish calling for a non-specific type of curry powder.

....

Cauliflower

1/3 cup Vadouvan curry powder

1/4 cup Miraval Oil Blend (page 304) or expeller-pressed grapeseed oil

2 heads cauliflower, base trimmed, leaves removed

Sauce Vierge

4 plum tomatoes, cored, halved, seeded, and finely diced

1/3 cup coarsely chopped flat-leaf parsley leaves

1/3 cup finely diced shallot

1/4 cup capers, drained, rinsed, and blotted dry

3 tablespoons extra-virgin olive oil

2 tablespoons red wine vinegar

1/2 teaspoon fine sea salt

Heat a convection oven to 350°F. (For a radiant oven, heat to 375°F.) Have ready a large, rimmed sheet pan and 4 long sheets of aluminum foil.

In a small bowl, stir together the curry powder and oil to make a loose paste. Place each head of cauliflower on a sheet of foil. Smear the curry paste all over the cauliflower heads, getting it into the crevices without breaking the florets. Using disposable gloves will keep your hands and nails from discoloring! Wrap the foil tightly around each head and then use the second sheet to double wrap each one. Arrange the cauliflower on the sheet pan. Bake until the cauliflower is tender, inserting the tip of a paring knife into the base to check for resistance, about 50 minutes. Set aside, still wrapped, to cool for 20 minutes and then refrigerate until cold, at least 2 hours. The cauliflower can be roasted up to 2 days in advance.

To make Sauce Vierge, in a medium bowl, combine the tomatoes, parsley, shallot, capers, olive oil, vinegar, and salt. Stir gently to combine. Set aside to allow the flavors to meld. Taste just before serving, adding more salt if needed. (The sauce can be made up to 8 hours in advance.)

When ready to assemble, heat the oven to 425°F. Have ready a 2 large, rimmed sheet pans. Remove the cauliflower from the foil. Using a sharp knife, carefully cut each head into 6 wedges. Arrange the wedges, without touching, on the sheet pans and roast until lightly browned, about 10 minutes.

To serve, shingle 2 wedges on each warmed plate and spoon some of the sauce around the plate.

Makes 6 servings

V | vg | gf | df | ef | nf

CALORIES: 264; TOTAL FAT: 18 G; CARBOHYDRATE: 23 G; DIETARY FIBER: 10 G; PROTEIN: 8 G

HARVEST MOON ORANGE CAKE
WITH COCONUT CHANTILLY

These dairy-free orange cakes are a refreshing and lovely finish to a meal. They are fanciful yet easy to make and can be made and frozen in advance—a perfect dinner party dessert. At Miraval Berkshires, they are baked in semi-sphere silicone molds. We adapted this recipe to make them in a standard muffin pan, but you can purchase silicone molds for a more sophisticated presentation. This is one of our most guest-requested desserts—even when it's not on the menu. When you make it, the whole kitchen smells like vanilla & oranges.

Cold-pressed avocado oil cooking spray

Cake Batter

1 organic orange

1 1/4 cups unbleached all-purpose flour

1 1/2 teaspoons baking powder

1/4 teaspoon baking soda

1/2 teaspoon fine sea salt

1/2 cup vegan butter, at room temperature

3/4 cup organic cane sugar

2 medium eggs, at room temperature

Soaking Syrup

1 cup confectioners' sugar

1/4 cup + 1 tablespoon fresh orange juice

Coconut Chantilly

1 can (guar free) coconut cream or coconut whipping cream, chilled overnight

3 tablespoons confectioners' sugar

1 teaspoon vanilla bean paste

3 oranges, cut supreme for garnish (See *Note*)

Arrange a rack in the center of the oven and heat the oven to 350°F. Lightly coat a standard 12-cup muffin pan with cold-pressed avocado oil cooking spray. Set aside.

To make the cake, thoroughly wash and dry the orange, and then trim off the stem end. Using the whole orange, including the peel, cut the orange into 8 chunks. Purée in a mini-chop or food processor until as smooth as possible.

In a medium bowl, sift together the flour, baking powder, baking soda, and salt. Set aside.

In the bowl of a stand mixer fitted with the paddle attachment, or in a medium bowl using a handheld mixer, cream the butter and sugar until light and creamy. Add the eggs, one at a time, mixing on medium speed, scraping the sides of the bowl after each addition. Add the puréed orange and mix well. Add half of the flour mixture and beat on low speed just until the flour disappears. Mix in the rest of the flour, scraping down the sides and bottom of the bowl once.

Continued on the next page

V | df | nf

CALORIES: 430; TOTAL FAT: 19 G; CARBOHYDRATE: 60 G; DIETARY FIBER: 1 G; PROTEIN: 5 G

....

Divide the batter among the muffin cups, filling each about 3/4 full. Bake until the cakes are puffed and golden, and a cake tester or toothpick inserted in the center comes out clean, about 25 minutes. Transfer the pan to a wire rack. Cool for 10 minutes and then unmold the cakes while still warm and set them, bottom-side up, on the wire rack.

Meanwhile, make the soaking syrup. In a small bowl, stir together the confectioners' sugar and orange juice until all the sugar is dissolved. Place a sheet pan under the wire rack that is holding the cakes. Dividing evenly, spoon some of the syrup over each cake, allowing it to run down the sides. Set aside until ready to serve. (At this point, the cakes can be frozen for up to 3 weeks. Thaw before serving.)

To make the Coconut Chantilly, in the bowl of a stand mixer fitted with the whip attachment, or in a medium bowl using a handheld mixer, combine the well-chilled coconut cream, confectioners' sugar, and vanilla bean paste. Whip on high until thickened. Cover and chill until ready to use.

To assemble the dessert, place one cake on a dessert plate, spoon a dollop of Coconut Chantilly on the side and garnish with a few orange segments. Serve immediately.

Note:
To supreme an orange, cut a slice from the top and bottom of each orange to reveal the flesh. Stand an orange upright and slice away the peel from the sides in wide strips, cutting downward, following the contour of the orange, and removing all the white pith. Use a paring knife to slice along the inside of the membranes to remove the fruit as wedges. Reserve for garnish.

Makes 12 servings

AUTUMN IN THE BERKSHIRES

4 ounces natural sparkling apple cider

1 ounce Cinnamon-Sugar Simple Syrup (recipe below)

Pour both ingredients into a mixing tin. Do not shake to avoid agitating the carbonation of the sparkling cider and making a mess. Use a metal stirrer and stir both ingredients for 15 seconds with ice. Strain in to a martini glass.

Helpful hint: create a cinnamon and sugar rim on a side plate by mixing together equal parts granulated sugar and ground cinnamon. Dip the rim of the martini glass into a shallow plate filled with leftover simple syrup. Then dip the martini glass rim into the cinnamon and sugar dry mixture. Garnish with a cinnamon stick.

Makes 1 serving

....

Cinnamon-Sugar Simple Syrup

1/2 cup granulated white sugar

1 cup water

2 tablespoons ground cinnamon

Combine the sugar and 1 cup of water in a sauce pan over high heat. Mix well until the sugar is dissolved. Add in the ground cinnamon. Mix well and remove from the heat. Refrigerate in a squeeze bottle or jar.

Makes about 1 cup

CALORIES: 110; TOTAL FAT: 0 G; CARBOHYDRATE: 27 G;
DIETARY FIBER: 0 G; PROTEIN: 0 G

RECALIBRATOR SHOT

8 ounces beet juice

1 ounce fresh ginger root juice

Several sprigs of cilantro

1/4 teaspoon ground cayenne pepper

1/2 teaspoon ground turmeric

16 drops oregano oil

Combine all the ingredients in a mixing bowl. Stir well, then strain the mixture to extract all the solid remains. Divide the mixture into a squeeze bottle or jar. Store in the refrigerator for up to 2 weeks.

To serve, pour 1 1/2 ounces of prepared beet mixture into a shot glass and add 2 drops of oregano oil.

Makes 6 servings

CALORIES: 20; TOTAL FAT: 0 G; CARBOHYDRATE: 5 G;
DIETARY FIBER: 0 G; PROTEIN: 0 G

BRING MIRAVAL HOME

Root Yourself in Authenticity by Growing Microgreens

Microgreens are ready-to-eat, tiny, aromatic, leafy versions of bigger, more mature greens. They are super convenient to grow—indoors, outdoors, in a greenhouse, or even on your windowsill. Sometimes they're called vegetable confetti because they come in assorted colors you can sprinkle over any meal. Some people add them to sandwiches and salads, juice them, or blend them into smoothies.

These mini sprouts boast a rich flavor and can pack a nutritional punch. They often have larger amounts of vitamins, minerals, polyphenols, and antioxidants than their more mature counterparts (some research points to nine times higher). Using microgreens can help get you out of what-to-nuke-for-dinner mode and into a mindset of what-to-grow-as-garnish for a healthy meal. There is also something meditative about cultivating something with your bare hands. The repetitive motion and tactile sensation can be grounding. When we place our hands into the earth, we stir up and inhale microbes that can help us feel relaxed and happier.

MASTERING MICROGREENS

Whether you visit Miraval Resorts and experience our gardening workshops or reap the benefits of sowing microgreens at home, here is a starter kit that will have you savoring homegrown greens in no time.

• •

Bi-level growing trays

Organic potting soil

Watering can

Seeds

Garden sheers

Alternatives to potting soil
Here's a great reusable option if you're looking for ease of harvesting: a reusable hydroponic jute growing pad + liquid hydroponic fertilizer.

- Set up trays and label each variety of seed.

- Wet & soak the mat. Press the seeds on top and plant as you would in soil.

- Add the fertilizer once the seeds germinate (when you see a little rootlet emerge).

- Once the greens are sprouted and harvested, remove the root matter and let the mat dry out between uses.

- Pick a spot with moderate sunshine.

- Spread the soil out in the trays and break up the clumps with your hands.

- Pack down the soil moderately with a gentle push.

- Sow your seeds. Leave about ¼ inch of space between the seeds and label each section by variety.

- The larger the seed, the deeper you plant. Small seeds don't need to be pressed as far down.

- Add a little soil on top and pat down gently (you want good seed-to-soil contact for better germination).

- Water once (conservatively).

- Wait 2 to 5 days for germination.

- Once it develops two leaves, clip and enjoy. Freeze to store for up to 6 months.

"Growing microgreens is something anyone can do at home. You can get your hands in the cycle of life, even in the middle of winter. It's a great way to start playing with plants when you have limited space and time. Microgreens allow you to feel a sense of accomplishment from breaking up a clump of dirt. You can work out some things nonverbally."
- Miraval Berkshires Colleague

As we fill our bodies with whole foods, we inspire ourselves to add another dimension to our broader search for authenticity.

discovery

"When we allow ourselves a certain joy that we might unconsciously be keeping ourselves away from, we discover things."

— MIRAVAL AUSTIN COLLEAGUE

FIND YOUR FAVORITE FLAVORS
Discovery and Dining

Imagine visiting a place numerous times and still discovering something new each time. This is what our returning guests report happening again and again at Miraval Resorts. Some guests mark their calendars quarterly to plan their visits. "Three months," says one Miraval Arizona guest, "is enough time for a habit to form and a routine to fade. So, I do my best to return every three months. It helps me rediscover my intentions."

Creativity in the kitchen extends beyond the boundaries of traditional cuisine. At Miraval Resorts, temperance and curiosity both have a place at the table. Meals cater to adventurous connoisseurs and comfort-seekers alike. The saying "Everything in moderation, including moderation," aligns with our guiding principle for creating balance and letting each guest find what is right for them. Our menus make room for indulgences on the same page as healthy choices. Tofu can share the table with toffee; kale can be a prelude to cookies.

You can consume mindfully—whether that means alcohol, caffeine, or sugar—and you can indulge a little. You can relinquish control and let a Miraval Resorts chef just cook for you or be surprised by our tasting menus. *And* you can choose every course yourself from our rotating dining options. In short, there is no right or wrong way to approach food if you bring an open mind and all your senses— including a sense of adventure.

" *When you work with food, you understand the incredible, intimate, and intricate relationship between what you are and what you consume. Because you are what you eat. Every time I eat or drink something, this is what I'm choosing to be. We always have a choice—how we behave, how we react, commit, honor our own code.* "

- MIRAVAL ARIZONA GUEST

Discovery Through Choice

The antidote to deprivation is choice. It brings our attention to abundance, to the presence of things. Our farm and garden programs teach techniques, but they also let us invest in our food. When we sink our hands into the soil or plunge our palms into a bowl of dough, we become agents of our nourishment.

You might be going through a rough time and need some comforting mashed potatoes. Or perhaps you're leaning towards lighter fare. At Miraval Resorts, we meet you wherever you are. And this book reflects our acknowledgment that wants and needs change over time and with circumstances. What stays constant is the ability to make the best choice to become our best selves in every moment.

Part of what keeps an experience fresh in our minds is the ability to choose how we combine its components. The same concept keeps us returning to the kitchen: our agency drives the adventure—culinary, spiritual, or cerebral.

Imagine opening a fully stocked refrigerator with all your favorite things next to an equal number of items you have never seen or tasted. When we realize our needs are met, we can get our nervous system to shift out of stress mode (fight, flight, freeze—all about restriction and constriction) and into a state of rest-and-digest that lets us open to new experiences. We can begin to think beyond what we need and consider what we want—we can make room for dreams and desires.

Every time people visit Miraval Resorts, they learn something new about how to make a choice. We let you stand in front of those stocked shelves with all you need in alignment with things you didn't even know you wanted. With that lineup in front of you, making healthy choices with mindful responses is easier. You have the agency to make the pairings that are perfect for you.

Allowing yourself to make conscious choices makes room for all kinds of discovery. It makes a buffet bountiful. It makes the world your own magical pantry, a regenerative garden of dining delights. It hums with the community buzz of honeybees and hens.

Let this book be the light that comes on when you open the refrigerator door.

What stays constant is the ability to make the best choice to become our best selves in every moment.

DISCOVERY
menu

A Botanical Buffet of Plant-Based Dishes

··

Just when we think the world has run out of
happy surprises, a menu can present a secret
treasure map. Dining is about the voyage we
take to discover our reactions and emotions
to consumable creations translated into new
and unexpected combinations.

Try this menu—whether you are a practicing
vegan or not—to discover the delights of
plant-based cooking.

Aperitif
GROUNDING GREEN JUICE

Appetizer
HARVEST MOON VEGAN
TOMATO BISQUE

Salad
BRUSSELS SPROUTS & PEAR SALAD

Main
HILLTOP CROSSINGS
VEGAN HEMP SEED MEATBALLS

Side
GARLIC BRAISED SPINACH

Side
GRILLED MAITAKE MUSHROOMS

Dessert
CACTUS FLOWER
PRICKLY PEAR SORBET

Digestif
PERFECT THYMING

Discovery Menu

TIMELINE
& TIPS

*Use this menu to create
something delicious inspired
by each of our kitchens
across the country. By
creating this menu, you can
bring out the marrow of
Miraval Resorts' bones and
transform it through your
personal expression.*

3 DAYS AHEAD
Make bisque, pesto, and romesco.

2 DAYS AHEAD
Make sorbet and glaze.

1 DAY AHEAD
Make Brussels sprouts, pear salad, hemp seed
meatballs, and pomodoro sauce.

IN THE MORNING
Dice kiwi for dessert and have sprigs of mint ready.

ONE HOUR IN ADVANCE
Make spaghetti squash, fry hemp seed meatballs,
and keep them warm. Prepare maitake mushrooms
and onion and garlic for spinach. Remove salad
from refrigerator.

JUST BEFORE SERVING
Sauté spinach and grill (or sear) mushrooms.
Rewarm pomodoro sauce.

MENU TYPE:
Buffet

SERVING & PLATING:
Make sure you have large serving bowls and platters on hand. Dedicate a counter or table that isn't your dining table to display your foods in a buffet-style lineup.

Serve the bisque in a soup crock (or in the Dutch oven you made it in) with a trivet and ladle. The spinach and mushrooms can go in smaller serving bowls.

Scoop the spaghetti squash onto the center of a platter, spoon the pomodoro sauce over it, and arrange the meatballs on top. Use a serving spoon for the meatballs and tongs for the squash.

When your guests have finished their meal, scoop the sorbet into individual dessert cups or martini glasses, add the glaze, and garnish with diced kiwi and a sprig of mint.

A LITTLE EXTRA:
Introduce your guests to the idea of digital mindfulness with the ritual on page 112. You can make your dinner party a device-free zone and ask your guests to reflect on the experience of disconnecting from technology to reconnect with people.

Since this meal celebrates plant-based eating, consider using botanicals and found objects in nature to create a centerpiece that complements your flora-inspired feast.

....

CRYSTAL COMPANION

Amethyst • Labradorite • Kyanite

Always keep a physical distance or barrier between crystals and food or beverages.

HARVEST MOON VEGAN TOMATO BISQUE
WITH VEGAN PESTO

This guest favorite is a vegan version of a classic tomato soup that is full of flavor, balanced, and easy to make at home. The recipe makes more than you'll need for your dinner party, but makes great leftovers.

· ·

2 tablespoons Miraval Oil Blend (page 304)

2 large onions, coarsely chopped

1 fennel bulb, tops removed, cored, and thinly sliced

2/3 cup garlic cloves, peeled

7 plum tomatoes, cored and halved lengthwise

3 carrots, trimmed, peeled, and thinly sliced

1 [28-ounce] can peeled whole tomatoes, including the juice from the can

6 large basil leaves

8 cups Vegetable Stock (page 303), or store-bought vegetable broth

Fine sea salt

Freshly ground black pepper

Vegan Pesto for garnish (page 94)

In a large soup pot, warm the oil over medium heat and swirl to coat the bottom of the pan. Add the onion, fennel, and garlic. Sauté, stirring frequently, until the vegetables are soft but not brown, about 8 minutes. Stir in the plum tomatoes, carrots, canned tomatoes (including the juice from the can) and basil leaves. Add the vegetable stock. Bring to a simmer, and then reduce the heat and simmer the soup, partially covered, until the carrots are very soft, about 25 minutes. Set aside to cool for 10 minutes.

Purée the soup in batches in the container of a high-speed blender.

To serve, ladle the soup into warmed bowls, and garnish each with a generous tablespoonful of vegan pesto. Serve immediately or set aside to cool and refrigerate in a covered container. (The soup can be made up to 4 days in advance.)

Makes about 16 cups; Serving Size: 1 1/2 cups

Vegan Pesto recipe on the next page

V | vg | gf | df | ef | nf

CALORIES: 101; TOTAL FAT: 2 G; CARBOHYDRATE: 17 G; DIETARY FIBER: 3 G; PROTEIN: 4 G

VEGAN PESTO

This nut-free and vegan pesto is a wonderful condiment. Make this as a big batch and store some in the freezer to have on hand.

4 ounces (5 3/4 cups) fresh basil leaves

4 ounces (5 3/4 cups) fresh arugula

8 garlic cloves, peeled

1/4 cup pumpkin seeds

3 tablespoons fresh lemon juice

1 teaspoon nutritional yeast

1/2 cup extra-virgin olive oil

Fine sea salt

Freshly ground black pepper

In the workbowl of a food processor fitted with the metal blade, combine the basil, arugula, garlic, pumpkin seeds, lemon juice, nutritional yeast, and 1/4 cup of the olive oil. Process until combined. With the machine running, pour the remaining 1/4 cup of oil through the feed tube until the pesto is emulsified and puréed. Season to taste with salt and pepper. Transfer to a covered container and refrigerate until ready to use. The pesto will keep refrigerated for up to 3 days or frozen up to 1 month.

Makes about 2 cups; Serving Size: 2 tablespoons

V | vg | gf | df | ef | nf

CALORIES: 76; TOTAL FAT: 7 G; CARBOHYDRATE: 2 G;
DIETARY FIBER: 0 G; PROTEIN: 1 G

BRUSSELS SPROUTS & PEAR SALAD

Add some color to your meal with this do-ahead, autumnal salad of shaved Brussels sprouts and red cabbage with the added crunch of toasted pecans and macadamia nuts.

Vinaigrette

1/4 cup extra-virgin olive oil

2 tablespoons white balsamic vinegar

2 tablespoons Dijon mustard

1 tablespoon organic raw agave syrup

1 teaspoon minced garlic

1 teaspoon fine sea salt

1 teaspoon freshly ground black pepper

1 pound Brussels sprouts, cleaned, with base cut off

1 cup shaved red cabbage

1 Anjou pear, peeled, halved lengthwise, cored, and cut into matchsticks

1/4 cup golden raisins

2 tablespoons toasted and chopped pecans

2 tablespoons chopped macadamia nuts

1 tablespoon finely chopped fresh sage

1/2 tablespoon finely chopped fresh thyme

To make the vinaigrette, in a small bowl or 2-cup glass measuring cup, whisk together the olive oil, vinegar, mustard, agave, garlic, salt and pepper until the dressing is emulsified. Set aside.

In the workbowl of a food processor fitted with the slicing disk, shave the Brussels sprouts into thin slices. Transfer them to a large bowl. Add the shaved red cabbage.

Pour the dressing over the sprouts and cabbage in the bowl. Wearing disposable gloves, toss the dressing with the salad, massaging the dressing thoroughly into the sprouts and cabbage for a couple of minutes. Add the pear, raisins, both nuts, sage, and thyme. Toss gently to combine. Cover the salad and refrigerate for at least 2 hours before serving. The salad can be made 1 day in advance.

Makes 6 servings

V | gf | df | ef

CALORIES: 210; TOTAL FAT: 13 G; CARBOHYDRATE: 22 G; DIETARY FIBER: 5 G; PROTEIN: 4 G

HILLTOP CROSSINGS VEGAN HEMP SEED MEATBALLS
WITH SPAGHETTI SQUASH

This plant-based, gluten-free take on "Spaghetti and Meatballs" is often on the menu at Hilltop Crossings Kitchen at Miraval Austin. Included with the recipe for meatballs is a recipe for roasting spaghetti squash and a basic Pomodoro Sauce. Alternatively, you can serve the meatballs with blanched spiralized zucchini or butternut squash. If desired, serve this dish with a little Vegan Pesto (page 94). The Pomodoro Sauce is quick to make, and you'll save time if you coordinate chopping the onions and garlic since both aromatics are in the meatballs and sauce.

· ·

Meatballs

Fine sea salt

2/3 cup organic white quinoa, rinsed and well drained

1 cup hulled hemp seeds

1 tablespoon unrefined avocado oil or Miraval Oil Blend (page 304), plus more for frying the meatballs

1/3 cup finely minced yellow onion

1 tablespoon minced garlic

1/2 tablespoon crushed fennel seeds

1 tablespoon fresh oregano leaves, chopped

2 to 3 tablespoons dry red wine

Freshly ground black pepper

12 fresh basil leaves, for garnish

Roasted Spaghetti Squash
(recipe follows)

Basic Pomodoro Sauce
(recipe follows)

To make the meatballs, bring 1 1/4 cups water and 1/2 teaspoon salt to a boil over high heat. Add the quinoa and stir. Reduce the heat to low, cover, and cook until the liquid is absorbed, about 15 minutes. Fluff with a fork and then transfer to a plate to cool to room temperature.

In the workbowl of a food processor fitted with the metal blade, process the cooked quinoa and hemp seeds to open up the starches and make the mixture completely sticky so it will bind together once the aromatics are added, processing for 1 minute. Scrape down the sides of the bowl and process for 1 minute longer. Try to form a ball with the mixture; if it forms a ball without falling apart then the texture is right. If it crumbles, process the mixture a little longer. Transfer to a large bowl.

In a medium sauté pan set over medium heat, warm the oil and swirl to coat the bottom of the pan. Add the onion and garlic and sauté, stirring frequently, for 1 minute. Add the crushed fennel seeds and chopped oregano. Sauté until the aromatics are soft but not brown, about 2 minutes longer. Add the red wine and deglaze the pan, scraping up any brown bits from the bottom of the pan. Season with 1/2 teaspoon of salt and 1/2 teaspoon pepper. Remove from the heat and cool for 10 minutes.

Continued on the next page

V | vg | gf | df | ef | nf

CALORIES: 340; TOTAL FAT: 24 G; CARBOHYDRATE: 17 G; DIETARY FIBER: 5 G; PROTEIN: 11 G

••

Add the sautéed aromatics to the bowl with the quinoa and hemp seeds. Mix thoroughly and taste, adding more salt or pepper, if desired. Press the mixture as if forming a meatball. It should stick together. (If not, add some gluten-free flour and a little water.) Shape into 18 (1-ounce) meatballs, each about the size of a ping pong ball. (At this point the meatballs can be arranged in a covered container and refrigerated until ready to fry. The meatballs can be made up to 1 day in advance.)

To brown the meatballs, heat a large nonstick or well-seasoned cast-iron skillet over medium-low heat. Add 2 to 3 tablespoons of avocado or Miraval Oil Blend, depending on the size of the pan, and swirl to coat the bottom of the pan. Gently add the meatballs, without crowding the pan, and fry, turning them carefully until crisply brown on all sides. Keep them warm in a 250°F oven if you need to fry the meatballs in batches. Add more oil if needed to fry the second batch.

To serve, place 1/2 cup of roasted spaghetti squash, blanched spiralized zucchini, or butternut squash in the center of a warm pasta bowl. Spoon 1/4 cup of the sauce around the squash. Arrange 3 meatballs on the sauce and garnish with basil leaves. Serve immediately.

Makes 6 servings; Serving Size: 3 meatballs

Helpful hints:
Add aromatics after
you have pulsed
the hemp seeds
and quinoa to the
desired consistency.

The best meatballs
are shaped by hand.

ROASTED SPAGHETTI SQUASH

1 spaghetti squash (about 3 pounds), halved lengthwise

Fine sea salt

Freshly ground black pepper

Pinch of cayenne pepper, optional

Heat the oven to 350°F. Scoop out the seeds and pith from the squash. Place, cut-side down, on a rimmed sheet pan and bake until tender when pierced with a fork, about 30 minutes. Remove it from the oven and set aside to cool for 10 minutes. Use a fork to scrape the squash strands from the skin and place them in a bowl. Discard the skin. Season the squash to taste with salt, pepper, and a pinch of cayenne pepper, if desired. Keep the prepared squash warm until ready to serve.

Makes 6 servings; Serving Size: 1/2 cup

V | vg | gf | df | ef | nf

CALORIES: 40; TOTAL FAT: 4 G; CARBOHYDRATE: 1 G; DIETARY FIBER: 0 G; PROTEIN: 1 G

BASIC POMODORO SAUCE

1 (14.5 ounce) can San Marzano tomatoes

1 tablespoon extra-virgin olive oil

2 tablespoons minced yellow onion

1 tablespoon minced garlic

Fine sea salt

Freshly ground black pepper

Pour the tomatoes, including the juice from the can, into a bowl. Use a potato masher, or your hands, to crush the tomatoes. Set aside.

In a medium sauté pan, warm the oil over medium-low heat. Add the onion and garlic. Sauté, stirring frequently, until the onion and garlic are soft but not brown, about 4 minutes. Add the crushed tomatoes and simmer, stirring occasionally, for 20 minutes. Season to taste with salt and pepper. Remove from the heat. Set aside until ready to use. Serve hot. The sauce can be made up to 3 days in advance. Cover and refrigerate. Rewarm before serving.

Makes 6 servings; Serving Size 1/4 cup

V | vg | gf | df | ef | nf

CALORIES: 47; TOTAL FAT: 2 G; CARBOHYDRATE: 5 G; DIETARY FIBER: 1 G; PROTEIN: 1 G

GARLIC BRAISED SPINACH

Heady with slivers of garlic and sautéed onion, a mound of fresh baby spinach cooks down to deliver a simple yet delicious and nutrient-dense side dish.

1 tablespoon Miraval Oil Blend (page 304) or unrefined avocado oil

1/2 medium yellow onion, diced

4 garlic cloves, thinly sliced

1 pound fresh baby spinach

Fine sea salt

Freshly ground black pepper

In a large nonstick sauté pan, warm the oil over medium-low heat and swirl to coat the bottom of the pan. Add the onion and garlic and sauté, stirring frequently, until soft but not brown, about 4 minutes. Add the fresh spinach by the handful, stirring with each addition, just until it wilts. When all the spinach is wilted, season to taste with salt and pepper. If there is excess liquid from the spinach, turn the heat to high and evaporate off any liquid from the bottom of the pan. Serve immediately.

Makes 6 servings

V | vg | gf | df | ef | nf

CALORIES: 40; TOTAL FAT: 2 G; CARBOHYDRATE: 4 G;
DIETARY FIBER: 2 G; PROTEIN: 2 G

GRILLED MAITAKE MUSHROOMS
WITH ROMESCO

Increasingly popular, maitake mushrooms (also known as hen-of-the-woods mushrooms) have thick fan-shaped caps and are sturdy, which makes them fabulous for grilling and high-heat roasting. This nut-free version of Romesco is a wonderful match for these robust, earthy mushrooms. To simplify timing, make the Romesco in advance and store it in a covered container in the refrigerator for up to 3 days.

1 recipe Romesco (recipe follows)

1 1/4 pounds maitake mushrooms, broken into small clumps

2 tablespoons unrefined avocado oil

Fine sea salt

Freshly ground black pepper

Store-bought balsamic glaze

6 tablespoons crumbled vegan queso fresco

Make the Romesco a couple of hours before serving, or up to 3 days ahead, so it is ready to serve.

To grill the mushrooms, prepare a medium-hot fire in a charcoal or gas grill. Alternatively, use an indoor grill pan or cast-iron skillet. Toss the mushrooms with 2 tablespoons of avocado oil and season lightly with salt and pepper. Place the mushrooms on the grate or in a grill basket and grill, turning once, until caramelized at the edges and brown, about 5 to 8 minutes.

To serve, spoon 1/4 cup of the Romesco in the center of each plate. Divide the grilled mushrooms among 6 salad plates, artfully arranging the mushrooms on top of the sauce. Drizzle a little balsamic glaze over the sauce and then scatter a tablespoon of the queso fresco over top. Serve immediately.

Makes 6 servings

V | vg | gf | ef

CALORIES: 110; TOTAL FAT: 7 G; CARBOHYDRATE: 10 G; DIETARY FIBER: 3 G; PROTEIN: 4 G

ROMESCO

3 ripe plum tomatoes, cored, halved lengthwise, and seeded

1/8 cup packed flat-leaf parsley leaves, chopped

3/4 cup roasted red bell peppers, well drained

1/2 teaspoon smoked paprika (pimentón de la Vera)

1/4 teaspoon red pepper flakes

1/2 teaspoon fine sea salt

1/2 teaspoon sherry vinegar

To make the romesco, heat the oven to 425°F. Arrange the tomatoes, cut-side up on a rimmed sheet pan. Roast until the tomatoes are soft, about 20 minutes. Set aside to cool.

In the workbowl of a food processor fitted with the metal blade, pulse the tomatoes, parsley, peppers, smoked paprika, red pepper flakes, salt, and vinegar. Process until the sauce is smooth. Transfer to a covered container and set aside until ready to use. The romesco can be made up to 3 days in advance. Cover and refrigerate until ready to use.

Makes about 1 1/2 cups; Serving Size: 1/4 cup

CALORIES: 15; TOTAL FAT: 0 G; CARBOHYDRATE: 3 G; DIETARY FIBER: 0 G; PROTEIN: 0 G

CACTUS FLOWER PRICKLY PEAR SORBET
WITH KIWI SALSA & TEQUILA GLAZE

Making sorbet or ice cream is a fun summer weekend activity, whether you are churning it in an old-fashioned hand-cranked maker or going modern with a countertop electric one. Here, the seasonal prickly pear sorbet from the Cactus Flower Restaurant at Miraval Arizona delivers a colorful dessert with Southwest flavors. Plan ahead to make this unique dessert for entertaining. Look for prickly pear purée, and other flavored purées, such as mango, in the freezer section of specialty markets.

* * *

Prickly Pear Sorbet

2 cups prickly pear purée

1/2 cup organic cane sugar

1/2 cup water

7 tablespoons fresh lime juice

Lime Tequila Glaze

1/2 cup fresh lime juice

1/4 cup tequila (see *Note*)

1/4 cup lemonade

2 tablespoons light corn syrup

2 kiwis, peeled and diced

6 sprigs fresh mint

To make the sorbet, measure the prickly pear purée into a medium-size heatproof bowl. Set aside.

In a small saucepan, combine the sugar and water. Bring to a boil, stirring until the sugar is completely dissolved. Pour the sugar syrup over the purée and stir to combine. Add the lime juice and stir to blend together. Let cool to room temperature.

Transfer the mixture to an ice-cream maker and churn according to the manufacturer's directions. Transfer the sorbet to a freezer container with a tight-fitting lid and place it in the freezer until it is solid and scoopable, about 4 hours, before serving.

Meanwhile, make the lime tequila glaze. Place the lime juice, tequila, lemonade, and corn syrup in a medium saucepan. Bring to a boil over medium-high heat, and then reduce the heat to a simmer and cook until the liquids come to a syrupy consistency, about 4 minutes. Remove from the heat and let cool to room temperature. Refrigerate until ready to use.

To assemble the dessert, place a 2-ounce scoop of the sorbet in a dessert cup or use a martini glass. Spoon a rounded tablespoon of diced kiwi over one side of the scoop. Use a small ladle to pour about 3 tablespoons of the lime tequila glaze over the top and down the sides of the sorbet. Garnish with a sprig of mint and serve immediately.

Note:
To make the glaze non-alchoholic, simply use 1 full cup of lemonade to make the glaze instead of using 1/2 cup of tequila and 1/2 cup lemonade.

Makes 6 servings; Serving Size: 1/4 cup

V | vg | gf | df | ef | nf

CALORIES: 150; TOTAL FAT: 0 G; CARBOHYDRATE: 33 G; DIETARY FIBER: 2 G; PROTEIN: 1 G

GROUNDING GREEN JUICE

4 leaves of kale (dinosaur kale recommended)

1 inch peeled fresh ginger

1 Granny Smith apple

2 celery sticks, washed and peeled

1 fresh jalapeno, diced, and unseeded

1/2 cucumber, washed, peeled, and diced

1 ounce lemon juice

Blend all the ingredients together and strain the mixture over ice. To serve it as a smoothie, add ice cubes and blend again to make this healthy, peppy, and potable treat.

Makes 2 juice or smoothie servings

PERFECT THYMING

2 ounces herbal non-alcoholic liquor

1/2 ounce thyme simple syrup (recipe below)

1/2 ounce fresh lemon juice

1/4 ounce fresh ginger juice

3 ounces sparkling water

Lemon wheel

Sprig of fresh thyme

Combine the first 4 ingredients into a mixing tin. Stir the contents and strain the mixture in to a tall glass with ice. Top with the sparkling water. Garnish with a lemon wheel and a sprig of fresh thyme.

Makes 1 serving

Thyme Simple Syrup

1 cup sugar

1 cup water

5 fresh thyme sprigs

Muddle thyme to release any extra oils. Combine the sugar, water, and thyme in a small saucepan and bring to a boil. Simmer for 5 minutes. Remove from heat. Cover the pan and cool to room temperature. Strain out solids and store in the refrigerator for up to 2 weeks.

Makes about 1 1/2 cups

CALORIES: 90; TOTAL FAT: 0 G; CARBOHYDRATE: 22 G; DIETARY FIBER: 3 G; PROTEIN: 2 G

CALORIES: 95; TOTAL FAT: 0 G; CARBOHYDRATE: 25 G; DIETARY FIBER: 0 G; PROTEIN: 0 G

BRING MIRAVAL HOME
Practice Digital Mindfulness to Discover Abundance

Few things better encapsulate the delicate balance between choice and deprivation than our digital devices. Globally, the average person spends almost seven hours staring at a screen each day. It makes you think about how much we give away our time, attention, purpose, and presence.

At Miraval Resorts, we let people practice digital mindfulness to create a device-free pause for reconnecting with what is important. It's a way to set aside sacred space. No one is asked to abandon their phones completely—we know how essential our devices are. We can purposefully step away from them, knowing they will resume their functions when *we* decide the time is right.

So, what happens when we let screens become our dinner companions? We miss out on a lot. We blunt the sensory experience of eating and miss our body's signals that tell us when we are full. We forget to chew our food thoroughly before swallowing, making it harder for our bodies to absorb its nutrients efficiently. Most importantly, we escalate the number of missed connections—with ourselves, our families, friends, or the natural world.

DIGITAL MINDFULNESS

You can maximize your culinary experience by minimizing the presence of screens. It's just easier to be present in their absence—so why not program in time every day to see what that feels like? You can still have your phone, but you can try this technique for disconnecting to reconnect, too.

....

1 smartphone

1 cellphone sleeping bag
(substitute any opaque bag)

1 intention to disconnect
from devices

1 intention to reconnect to
self, nature, or other people

- *Activate your intention to disconnect*
  - Create 3 scheduled times to be without your phone every day. Try making these times coincide with mealtimes.

  - Designate your eating space as device-free zone during mealtime.

  - At the scheduled time, silence device notifications or turn the phone off completely, place it inside the cellphone sleeping bag, and store it in a separate room if possible.

- *Activate your intention to reconnect with self, nature, or other people*
  - Make time to prepare a meal for your loved ones using your favorite recipes.

  - Have a picnic outside when the weather permits.

  - Practice a food meditation that engages your senses. Focus on what you see, hear, and smell before you eat your next meal.

When you wake up your device from its nap, consider which notifications require an immediate answer and which don't. Prioritize how you respond and record how much time you give to the screen's demands.

Each day, aim to increase your time for disconnecting to reconnect by a few minutes.

"At Miraval, you can practice giving yourself permission to make each interaction—from heart-stopping heights to subtler depths—equally deserving of your focus. Even our phones need to rest, recharge, and renew. Unplugging from our devices lets us think about other ways to connect: talk to people, commune with nature, savor the flavors of your meal, and be present with your peers."

- Miraval Austin Colleague

Like any fine art, cuisine is not static; it's an ongoing dynamic relationship between earth and kitchen, farmer and chef, plate and diner.

nourishment

> "I put love into each of my plants – and that love is a component of each one when I eat it or when anyone else is eating it. It's an act of nourishing myself as well as my community."
>
> — MIRAVAL ARIZONA COLLEAGUE

NOURISHMENT & CONNECTION
Food Prepared with Love

Nourishment is a word that describes the benefits we receive from things that sustain us. Every living thing needs certain nutrients to exist and develop in a healthy way. Nourishment at Miraval Resorts is about a human process—one that helps us absorb nutrients from food and drink but also assimilate meaning and symbolic sustenance from our experiences and interactions. It goes beyond mere survival.

The Latin root of nourishment, *nutrire,* means "to feed, nurse, or support." It implies a relationship between the source and recipient. That our connection to whomever and whatever is nourishing us is just as important as the nutrients it offers. It is an action word that is all about giving and receiving; it's about gifts and gratitude. It describes an instinct to care for and be fostered—the thing that happens in communities that converge in a shared vision for health, fulfillment, and growth.

Our senses help us decide what we like and don't like to eat, but they also give us solid cues for how to feel. The first sense to be activated when we are born is scent. It's our earliest connection to experience. Olfactory pathways lead to brain systems that control emotion and record memory. So, it's no wonder a bite, sniff, or taste of a particular food can make us feel so many feelings.

Nourishment is an action generated by feeling, and that feeling is love. You can feed people without feeling much but *nourishing* them requires something more. You might not be able to define love in your food, but you can sense, feel, and recognize it when it's there. And, in many cases, it can be the most essential ingredient in everything we do. It can be its own subtle flavor.

> "*From farm to market, kitchen to table, stovetop to dining room, love resonates as deeply and loudly as our Tibetan gongs gracing each property.*"
>
> — MIRAVAL BERKSHIRES COLLEAGUE

"The kitchen saved my life when I was a teenager," says Miraval's director of culinary experiences. *"I recognized that food was my calling. The kitchen crew used to say, 'you're joining a pirate ship,' and it's true in the sense that the glory and beauty of a pirate ship is in its celebration of all walks of life. There will always be a warm hug and safe haven for you on that ship."*

Pirate ship, pantry, recipe, or restaurant—they describe the culinary journey similarly because their point of origin and anchor is love. It's an aroma, tune, or taste that triggers the heart and mind to unleash a memory. It's the love that goes into its making that nourishes our souls.

Nourishing Circles and Community Tables

When we engage authentically with our food, we connect to a naturally nourishing world. And a big part of the natural world is other people. Our guests recognize each other as the beginning of a community, as kindred spirits coming together for a common purpose.

They realize that each piece of knowledge, each new discovery, and each genuine connection becomes a point in a circle that continues to expand. Our most loyal guests become our Authentic Circle®. And never has a name rung truer.

As our resorts grow beyond our flagship Arizona property, our circles become concentric, radiating

light from Southwest sunrises to moonlit New England nights. The shape of nourishment at Miraval Resorts is a round table; a plate, a platter, a portal to the inner self.

When you visit Miraval Resorts, you learn to explore many areas—creative expression, wellbeing, spirituality, meditation, yoga, or fitness. At the end of the day, we sit down together to share, process, and integrate those experiences. We give and receive around the table.

Many guests came to our resorts as solo travelers and found their Miraval family at our community tables. Every night, guests gather by choice to share a meal with people who are strangers, soulmates, or anything in between.

"There is such a keen sense of fellowship here. One of the first groups I ever met at Miraval Austin was a group of women who had met in Tucson years ago – they were all solo travelers who had met at the community table – now they travel annually and come together in that space."

— MIRAVAL AUSTIN COLLEAGUE

NOURISHMENT
menu

Five Elements Meet Six Tastes:
An Ayurvedic Family Meal

···

Ayurveda, the ancient healing science from India, is one lens we peer through at Miraval Resorts. It offers a unique way to think about nourishment that dovetails with Western-aligned approaches to nutrition. They converge in the idea of balance.

Ayurvedic principles say we can maintain a healthy diet by including all six tastes: sweet, sour, salty, pungent, bitter, and astringent. The six tastes are derived from the five elements (earth, water, fire, air, and space), which give them unique nutritional properties.

Aperitif
OJAS JUICE

Appetizer
BUTTERNUT SQUASH SOUP WITH CHAPATI & TRIO OF CHUTNEYS

Main
KICHARI

Side
CAULIFLOWER & POTATO SABJI

Salad
PEACH, BEET & AVOCADO SALAD

Dessert
CACAO & MEDJOOL DATE DESSERT BALLS

Digestif
GINGER ELIXIR

Nourishment Menu

TIMELINE & TIPS

Eating is a full-scale sensory experience, and this whole meal is designed to amplify and stimulate all five senses through all six tastes. Each component acts through the element of fire to take you through each step of digestion to create the most nourishing, balanced meal.

3 DAYS AHEAD
Make dessert, spice blend, and tomato chutney.

2 DAYS AHEAD
Make apple-pear chutney, butternut squash soup, and ghee.

1 DAY AHEAD
Make chapati dough and cilantro chutney and dressing.

IN THE MORNING
Prepare and measure ingredients for sabji and kichari.

TWO HOURS IN ADVANCE
Knead and form chapatis.

ONE HOUR IN ADVANCE
Remove cilantro dressing from refrigerator and begin cooking kichari. Prepare sabji with churna.

30 MINUTES BEFORE
Griddle cook chapatis and keep them warm.

JUST BEFORE SERVING
Assemble salad and sauté the cashews and coconut for kichari.

MENU TYPE:
Casual, family-style

SERVING & PLATING:
Place serving bowls and platters at the center of the table and let your guests pass them around and serve themselves.

Before sitting down, offer your guests the aperitif to spark digestion.

Add a ladle to your soup pot for serving. Place the chutneys in small bowls with teaspoons and the chapatis in a linen-draped basket.

Garnish the kichari right in the pot (or a bowl) and add a serving spoon.

The sabji and salad can go in a bowl and platter with a serving spoon for the sabji and tongs for the salad.

Invite your guests to take a dessert ball with their hands and finish the meal with the digestif poured from a pitcher or teapot into small cups.

A LITTLE EXTRA:
This menu is all about community and family coming together. Presence reigns over perfection at this meal—the combination of tastes and flavors will outrank any formality.

Flip to page 149 to teach your guests how to infuse heart-centered energy into your food. Consider beginning your evening with this ritual to honor the energy that flows from our hearts to our harvests.

. . . .

CRYSTAL COMPANION

Rose Quartz • Kunzite • Strawberry Quartz

Always keep a physical distance or barrier between crystals and food or beverages.

BUTTERNUT SQUASH SOUP

The chefs at Miraval Berkshires channel the warmth and essence of autumn with the added flavor of fresh ginger root, the bright undertone of apple cider vinegar, and the creaminess of coconut milk. Double the recipe for a bigger batch of soup to have on hand.

2 teaspoons extra-virgin olive oil

1 cup finely chopped yellow onion

2 tablespoons minced fresh ginger

1/4 cup apple cider vinegar

4 cups peeled and seeded butternut squash, cut into 1-inch chunks

2 crisp apples, cored and cut into 1-inch chunks

3 cups Vegetable Stock (page 303) or store-bought vegetable broth

1 1/2 teaspoons fine sea salt

1/4 teaspoon freshly ground black pepper

1/2 cup canned coconut milk

Roasted pumpkin seeds, for garnish

1 crisp apple, peeled, cored, and diced, for garnish

2 tablespoons snipped fresh chives, for garnish

In a soup pot or Dutch oven set over medium-low heat, warm the oil. Add the onions and sauté, stirring frequently, until soft but not brown for 5 minutes. Reduce the heat to medium-low and add the ginger. Sauté, stirring frequently, until fragrant and tender, about 2 minutes longer. Add the vinegar and stir to deglaze the pan, loosening any brown bits sticking to the bottom of the pan.

Add the butternut squash, apple chunks, and vegetable stock. Bring to a boil over medium-high heat, and then reduce the heat and simmer, covered, until the squash is very soft, about 20 minutes. Remove from the heat and add the salt, pepper, and coconut milk. Let cool for 10 minutes. Purée the soup using an immersion blender, or in batches in the container of a high-speed blender.

To serve, ladle the soup into warmed soup bowls, and garnish each with seeded roasted pumpkin, or diced apples and a teaspoon of snipped fresh chives. Serve immediately, or set aside to cool and then refrigerate in a covered container. The soup can be made up to 4 days in advance.

Makes 6 servings; Serving Size: 1 cup

V | vg | gf | df | ef | nf

CALORIES: 142; TOTAL FAT: 3 G; CARBOHYDRATE: 28 G; DIETARY FIBER: 5 G; PROTEIN: 2 G

TRIO OF CHUTNEYS

TOMATO

Make this when vine-ripened tomatoes are in season as a wonderful accompaniment to Kichari (page 137). Specialty spice stores and stores carrying Indian ingredients will carry black mustard seeds and ground fenugreek. They can also be ordered online.

2 tablespoons Ghee (page 304)

1 teaspoon minced fresh ginger

1 teaspoon minced garlic

1/2 teaspoon black mustard seeds

1/2 teaspoon cumin seeds

1/2 teaspoon ground turmeric

1/2 teaspoon ground fenugreek or ground fennel seeds

Finely chopped jalapeño

2 cups cored, seeded, and diced vine-ripened tomatoes

1 cup finely diced yellow onion

2 tablespoons dark raisins

1/4 to 1/2 teaspoon fine sea salt

Chopped cilantro and mint, for garnish

In a medium sauté pan set over medium-low heat, melt the ghee. Add the ginger, garlic, mustard seeds, cumin, turmeric, fenugreek, and jalapeño to taste. Sauté until golden and aromatic, about 1 minute. Stir in the diced tomatoes, onion, raisins and salt. Simmer until thickened, about 20 minutes. Remove from the heat and cool to room temperature. Serve garnished with cilantro, mint, or both. Store refrigerated in a covered container. The chutney will keep for approximately 3 weeks.

Makes about 2 cups; Serving Size: 2 tablespoons

V | gf | ef | nf

CALORIES: 20; TOTAL FAT: 1.5 G; CARBOHYDRATE: 2 G; DIETARY FIBER: 0 G; PROTEIN: 0 G

CILANTRO

This fresh chutney adds a vibrant herbal touch to Kichari (page 137).

1/2 cup almonds

1 teaspoon chopped fresh ginger

1 teaspoon chopped garlic

Seeded and chopped jalapeño, optional

1 cup packed cilantro leaves

1 cup packed flat-leaf parsley leaves

2 tablespoons fresh lime juice

1/4 to 1/2 teaspoon fine sea salt

1/4 cup extra-virgin olive oil

In the workbowl of a food processor fitted with the metal blade, pulse the almonds, ginger, garlic, and jalapeño (if using) until finely chopped. Add the cilantro, parsley, lime juice, and salt. Process until finely chopped. With the machine running, drizzle in the olive oil. Transfer to a bowl and serve immediately or cover and refrigerate until ready to use. The cilantro chutney can be made 1 day in advance.

Makes about 1 cup; Serving Size: 2 tablespoons

V | vg | gf | df | ef

CALORIES: 60; TOTAL FAT: 4.5 G; CARBOHYDRATE: 3 G; DIETARY FIBER: 1 G; PROTEIN: 2 G

APPLE-PEAR

A blended chutney—combining tart apples, ripe pears, and warm spices—serves as an accompaniment to Kichari (page 137).

2 Granny Smith apples, peeled, cored, and diced

2 firm but ripe Anjou or Bosc pears, peeled, cored, and diced

3/4 to 1 cup water

2 teaspoons light brown sugar

1/4 teaspoon ground cardamom

1/4 teaspoon ground cinnamon

1/4 teaspoon ground ginger

Place the fruit in a medium sauce pan and add 3/4 cup of water. Add up to 1/4 cup more water, depending on the size of the fruit. Bring to a boil over high heat, and then reduce the heat to medium-low and simmer for 5 minutes. Add the sugar, cardamom, cinnamon, and ginger. Let the mixture simmer on low heat for 15 minutes. Set aside to cool for 10 minutes and then purée in a blender or food processor. Transfer to a covered container and chill until ready to serve. The chutney can be made up to 3 days in advance.

Makes 2 1/4 cups; Serving Size: 2 tablespoons

V | vg | gf | df | ef | nf

CALORIES: 15; TOTAL FAT: 0 G; CARBOHYDRATE: 4 G; DIETARY FIBER: 1 G; PROTEIN: 0 G

CHAPATI FLATBREAD

Chapati is an everyday Indian flatbread made from the simplest ingredients—finely milled whole-wheat flour (atta), water, salt, and a little oil. It is traditionally made by hand in a large shallow pan called a paraat. Making it in a large flat pizza pan will work, as will a wide shallow bowl. Kneading can be a relaxing and therapeutic process—take the time to slow down and enjoy it.

2 cups finely-milled atta flour or finely milled whole-wheat flour

1 teaspoon fine sea salt

2 teaspoons melted coconut oil

1 cup lukewarm water

Additional flour for rolling

1/4 cup melted Ghee (page 304), to brush the tops

In a large flat pizza pan or wide shallow bowl, stir together the flour and salt. Drizzle the oil over top and mix with your fingertips. Make a well in the center and add the lukewarm water, a little at a time, while slowly pushing the flour towards the center to form a crumbly dough. Add more water as needed, and continue to knead the dough until it forms a soft smooth ball. Place the dough in a bowl, cover with a towel, and let rest for 1 hour. The dough can be made a day ahead and refrigerated in an airtight container. Let come to room temperature before using.

Knead the dough again and then divide it into 16 equal pieces. Roll each piece to form a ball slightly smaller than a ping pong ball. Dust the balls lightly with flour. Lightly dust a clean work surface with flour. Press a ball of dough between your palms to form a ½-inch-thick circle. Using a rolling pin, roll the dough into a 6-inch circle, coating with flour only as needed so it doesn't stick to the rolling pin or work surface. Repeat to form 16 chapatis. Cover with a towel.

Heat a cast-iron pan or griddle to medium-high heat for 5 minutes. Place a chapati on the hot dry griddle and cook until the dough rises, forms slight bubbles, and brown spots appear, about 1 minute. Using tongs, flip and cook the other side. Flip the chapati over again until it puffs up. Remove from the heat and brush the top with a little melted ghee. Repeat to make additional chapatis, keeping the cooked chapatis covered and warm. Serve immediately.

Makes 16 servings; Serving Size: 1 flatbread

V | vg | df | ef | nf

CALORIES: 90; TOTAL FAT: 4.5 G; CARBOHYDRATE: 11 G; DIETARY FIBER: 2 G; PROTEIN: 2 G

KICHARI
WITH CARROTS, COCONUT & CASHEWS

Kichari means "mixture," a combination of grain and legume in a warm soup. This version of Kichari is a satisfying meal any time of day. Think of this recipe as an opportunity to experiment by adding additional diced vegetables, such as zucchini, for color and texture. You could add spinach or finely chopped kale; both would wilt into the mixture.

1 cup organic white basmati rice

1/2 cup yellow mung dahl

6 cups water

1/2 teaspoon fine sea salt

2 cups (1/4-inch) diced carrots

2 tablespoons Ghee (page 304)

1 teaspoon black mustard seeds

1/2 teaspoon cumin seeds

1 teaspoon minced fresh ginger

1/2 teaspoon ground turmeric

1/2 teaspoon ground coriander

1/2 cup cashew pieces

1/2 cup unsweetened coconut flakes

Freshly chopped cilantro for garnish

Lime wedges for garnish

Place the rice and dahl in a medium bowl. Cover with cold water and swish the rice and dahl. The water will turn cloudy. Drain the water completely and then repeat the process 2 more times until the water runs clear. Drain completely.

Transfer the rice and dahl to a medium saucepan and add 5 cups of the water and the salt. Bring to a boil over high heat. Reduce the heat to low, so the water barely simmers and cook, covered, stirring occasionally, until most of the water has evaporated, and the mixture is thick like porridge, about 40 minutes. If needed, add some of the reserved water. (Cook longer if you like a thicker consistency.)

Fifteen minutes before the kichari is done cooking, stir the diced carrots into the rice mixture.

Ten minutes before serving, bloom the spices (turn on the fan over your stove top.) Heat 1 tablespoon of the ghee in a small sauté pan until smoking, and then immediately add the mustard seeds. As they begin to pop, remove the pan from the heat. Add the cumin seeds. They will brown immediately. Stir in the ginger. Reduce the heat to medium. Return the pan to the heat and stir in the turmeric and coriander until the spices are fragrant. Stir this mixture into the kichari and cook 10 minutes longer.

Just before serving, in a small sauté pan, melt the remaining 1 tablespoon of ghee over medium heat. Stir in the cashews and coconut and sauté, stirring constantly, until the coconut is toasted, about 5 minutes.

To serve, ladle the kichari into warmed bowls and garnish with the toasted cashews and coconut, chopped cilantro, and a wedge of lime.

Makes 8 servings; Serving Size: 3/4 cup

V | gf | df | ef

CALORIES: 340; TOTAL FAT: 13 G; CARBOHYDRATE: 44 G; DIETARY FIBER: 2 G; PROTEIN: 10 G

Adding spices to ghee helps them bloom.

Adjust desired consistency by adding water.

CAULIFLOWER & POTATO SABJI
WITH TRIDOSHIC CHURNA

Chopped cauliflower and potatoes are stir-fried with an aromatic mixture of black mustard seeds, ginger, garlic, and spice blend. Covered and steam-cooked until soft, this side dish is recommended as a perfect accompaniment to the Kichari (page 137). Using coconut oil and skipping the yogurt in this dish makes it vegan and dairy-free.

Tri-doshic Churna

1 tablespoon ground cumin

1 tablespoon organic cane sugar

2 teaspoons fine sea salt

2 teaspoons ground coriander

2 teaspoons ground turmeric

1 1/2 teaspoons ground fenugreek or ground fennel seeds

1 teaspoon ground cinnamon

1/2 teaspoon ground cloves

1/2 teaspoon ground cardamom

1/2 teaspoon freshly ground white pepper

Sabji

3 tablespoons Ghee (page 304) or coconut oil

1/2 teaspoon black mustard seeds

2 teaspoons finely chopped fresh ginger

1 teaspoon finely chopped garlic

1 fresh green chile, chopped, optional

4 cups cauliflower florets

2 cups peeled and diced yellow potatoes

1 cup cored, seeded, and ½-inch diced tomato

Juice of 1 lemon

1/4 cup plain lowfat yogurt, optional

Fine sea salt

Freshly ground black pepper

3 tablespoons chopped cilantro

Lemon or lime wedges, for garnish

To make the Tri-doshic Churna in a small bowl, stir together all the ingredients. Transfer to a small glass jar with a tight-fitting lid. Store in the pantry away from light and heat. The spice blend will generally keep up to 1 month.

To make the Sabji, place a wok or Dutch oven over medium-high heat. Add the ghee or coconut oil and swirl to coat the bottom of the pan. Add the mustard seeds and stir-fry until they pop and turn grey. Quickly add the ginger, garlic, 2 tablespoons Tri-Doshic Churna, and green chile, if using, and stir-fry for 1 minute. Add the cauliflower, potatoes, and tomatoes. Stir to coat the vegetables with the aromatics. Cook for 4 to 5 minutes, stirring frequently, until the vegetables are seared. Reduce the heat to medium-low and cook, covered, until the vegetables are soft, about 10 to 15 minutes. Check halfway through the cooking time to make sure the vegetables aren't sticking. Add up to 1/4 cup water if the vegetables are sticking to the pan.

Remove the pan from the heat. Stir in the juice of 1 lemon, and then stir in the yogurt or serve it on the side, if using. Season to taste with salt and pepper. Toss in the cilantro or use it as a garnish. Divide among warm bowls and serve immediately with a wedge of lemon or lime.

Makes 6 servings: Serving Size: 3/4 cup

V | gf | ef | nf

Cauliflower & Potato Sabji (with yogurt):
CALORIES: 140; TOTAL FAT: 7 G; CARBOHYDRATE: 16 G; DIETARY FIBER: 3 G; PROTEIN: 3 G

Cauliflower & Potato Sabji (without yogurt):
CALORIES: 130; TOTAL FAT: 7 G; CARBOHYDRATE: 16 G; DIETARY FIBER: 3 G; PROTEIN: 3 G

PEACH, BEET & AVOCADO SALAD

This salad is as simple to make as it sounds, yet the results are sophisticated. The peach's sweetness plays against the avocado's richness and is grounded by the beet's sweet earthiness. Colorful, flavorful, and delicious—it is a winning combination with a drizzle of cilantro dressing and a pinch of flaky natural sea salt on top.

Cilantro Dressing

2/3 bunch cilantro, washed, and stem trimmed to within 2 inches of the leafy tops

1/3 cup extra-virgin olive oil

1 1/2 tablespoons fresh lime juice

Flaky sea salt

Salad

2 large beets, roasted, skin removed, each cut crosswise into 6 thick disks (see *Note*)

2 ripe peach, blanched, peeled, and cut into 12 wedges (see *Note*)

2 ripe avocados, quartered lengthwise, pitted and skin removed

Freshly ground black pepper

To make the dressing, combine the cilantro, olive oil, lime juice, and 2 large pinches of salt in the container of a high-speed blender, or in a mini-chop food processor, and blend until the dressing is puréed. Set aside until ready to use or make up to 1 day in advance and refrigerate. Remove from the refrigerator 45 minutes before serving.

To assemble each salad, overlap 2 slices of beets in the center of each salad plate. Rest 1/4 avocado on 1 beet disk. Gently lean 2 wedges of peach onto the avocado. You may have extra avocado and peach which you can enjoy for breakfast or snacks the following day.

Drizzle each plate with cilantro dressing, spooning it both around and on top of the ingredients. Finish with a pinch of flaky sea salt and a little freshly ground black pepper. Serve immediately.

Note:

An easy way to peel peaches is to score a small "X" on the bottom of the peach and drop it into boiling water for 30 seconds. Transfer the peach to a bowl of ice water, leave for 30 seconds, and then slip the skin off the peach by hand.

To roast beets, heat the oven to 375ºF. Lay a long sheet of aluminum foil on a rimmed sheet pan. Place the beets in the center. Pierce each beet 4 to 5 times with a fork. Bring up the sides of the foil to form a tightly sealed pouch. Roast the beets on the sheet pan until fork-tender, 45 to 55 minutes, depending on the size of the beets. Remove the beets from the oven and open the pouch. Allow the beets to cool for 10 to 15 minutes. Slip the skins off the beets (best done using disposable gloves). Use as directed in the recipe.

Makes 6 servings

V | vg | gf | df | ef | nf

CALORIES: 210; TOTAL FAT: 19 G; CARBOHYDRATE: 10 G; DIETARY FIBER: 4 G; PROTEIN: 2 G

CACAO & MEJOOL DATE DESSERT BALLS

CACAO & MEDJOOL DATE DESSERT BALLS

Unlike classic tahini paste that uses hulled sesame seeds, black tahini is made from unhulled black sesame seeds. It is more intensely flavored, almost reminiscent of deeply roasted nuts. Black sesame seeds are significantly higher in iron and calcium and provide more potassium, manganese, and copper. They also contain more antioxidants and fiber. Look for organic black tahini in natural food stores or online. Use maple syrup to make these vegan. Working with black tahini is messy; use disposable gloves, if desired.

2 tablespoons toasted sesame seeds

1 tablespoon + 1/3 cup pumpkin seeds

4 Medjool dates, pitted

1/3 cup organic black tahini

3 tablespoons real maple syrup or raw honey

1 teaspoon pure vanilla extract or 1 vanilla bean, insides scraped

1/4 teaspoon fine sea salt

1/4 cup unsweetened organic cacao powder (see *Note*)

Line a rimmed sheet pan with parchment paper.

In a food processor fitted with the metal blade, pulse the sesame seeds with 1 tablespoon of the pumpkin seeds. Set aside until you are ready to roll the balls.

Put the remaining 1/3 cup of pumpkin seeds in the food processor and pulse until finely chopped. Add the dates, tahini, maple syrup or honey, vanilla, salt, and the cacao powder. Process until the mixture balls up and forms a mass around the blade.

Roll the mixture into 20 (1/2-ounce) balls, each about the size of a walnut. (Don't worry if they are a little crumbly. Press them together knowing that once chilled they will be easier to form into balls.) Arrange on the prepared pan. Chill until firm.

Once the balls are chilled, roll them between the palms of your hands until smooth and round. Dip each ball in the ground sesame mixture until evenly coated. Return the balls to the sheet pan to chill completely. Refrigerate the energy balls in a covered container for up to 10 days.

Note:
When shopping for cacao powder, look carefully at the packaging. You want to buy cacao powder, and not cocoa powder. See page 332 for details on using ceremonial cacao for a morning ritual.

Makes 10 (1-ounce) balls; Serving Size: 1 ball

V | vg | gf | df | ef | nf

CALORIES: 110; TOTAL FAT: 6 G; CARBOHYDRATE: 12 G; DIETARY FIBER: 2 G; PROTEIN: 3 G

OJAS JUICE

1 ounce fresh green apple juice

1 ounce lemongrass simple syrup (recipe below)

1 ounce fresh grapefruit juice

1 tablespoon coconut purée

2 ounces coconut water

Lemon wheel

Combine the apple juice, simple syrup, grapefruit juice, coconut purée, and coconut water in a mixing tin with ice and shake. Strain into a coup glass. Garnish with a lemon wheel.

Makes 1 serving

Lemongrass Simple Syrup

1 cup sugar

1 cup water

1 lemongrass stalk minced

Combine the sugar and water in a small sauce pan and bring to a boil. Simmer for 5 minutes. Remove from the heat and add the lemongrass. Cover the pan and cool to room temperature. Muddle the lemongrass to release any extra oils. Strain out solids and store in the refrigerator for up to 2 weeks.

Makes about 3/4 cup

CALORIES: 190; TOTAL FAT: 9 G; CARBOHYDRATE: 27 G; DIETARY FIBER: 2 G; PROTEIN: 1 G

GINGER ELIXIR

6 cups of spring water

4 thumb-size pieces of fresh ginger – peeled

3 tablespoons natural honey

3 lemons, cut in half

1 1/2 teaspoon ground turmeric

Lemon wheel

In a saucepan, bring the spring water, ginger, honey, lemons, and turmeric to a boil, then let simmer for a few minutes. Remove from the heat and let cool in the saucepan. Place the mixture in a refrigerator-safe vessel and store in the refrigerator overnight. The following day, strain the mixture through cheesecloth, a coffee filter, or a fine mesh strainer. Serve in a coupe glass with a lemon-wheel garnish.

Add a shot of your favorite bourbon for a delightful dash of sweetness and warmth.

Makes 6 servings

CALORIES: 35; TOTAL FAT: 0 G; CARBOHYDRATE: 9 G; DIETARY FIBER: 0 G; PROTEIN: 0 G

BRING MIRAVAL HOME

Infuse Your Food with Heart-Centered Nourishment

The most restorative frequencies of our subtle energy layers come from our heart center, where the energy of the earth and the heavens meet to create balance and love. We can bless our food with the power of our heart center, either directly or through our hands which naturally channel this restorative energy.

Feel the earth's energy from below and the sky's energy from above meeting in your heart center. Allow that balanced mixture of energies to move from your heart center to your arms through your hands and into your food. Sprinkle in some gratitude for this nourishment, for the hands that grew and made it, and the for chance to enjoy it fully.

Benefits of Blessing our Food

- Slowing down and becoming aware of the moment prepares us for digestion and helps to relieve stress.

- Becoming aware of the subtle energies that flow through and around us helps us receive and absorb the life force in food that nurtures our more subtle energy bodies, just as nutrients nurture our physical body.

BUILD YOUR MEAL LIKE A CAMPFIRE

We can learn from Ayurvedic practices to better balance our meals across all six tastes by imagining we are building a campfire. Because our digestive processes are influenced by the fire element, it's important to look at meal-building as an exercise in sparking, tending, and tempering the fiery aspects of our food.

....

5 elemental ingredients:

Space, Air, Fire, Water, Earth

6 taste profiles:

Sweet, Sour, Salty, Astringent, Pungent, Bitter

In Ayurvedic thought, everything from our personality type to our source of nourishment is influenced by how elements combine. These basic elements—primarily fire—also drive how we assemble a meal.

Foods feature six tastes that fuel, fan, or subdue the element of fire. Explore their connection with this exercise.

- *Build up Tinder*
  Spices and salty flavors are the tinder that prime the fire site for what follows. The aperitif in this chapter's menu ignites hearts and stomachs with a bright bump of happiness.

- *Feed the Flame*
  Following the starters, add hearty, sweet-natured foods, like root vegetables or meat, for the fire to consume and build strength. Pungent (like our trio of chutneys), salty, and sour flavors reset your palate and feed the flames.

- *Add Logs*
  Progressively layer heavier flavors of sweet (animal-based) or astringent (plant-based) proteins. This is the food equivalent of logs in the form of proteins and fats. Kichari's hearty and homey combination of lentils and grains invites us to scoop up a bowl of comfort and gather to share joys and set down our burdens for a precious moment of connection and color.

- *Leave Room for Air*
  Astringent foods give us an opportunity for space in the meal. Space lets us pause, pace ourselves, and be present.

- *Simmer*
  To close the fire, we feed it flavors that taper cravings. Serving the salad course later in the meal brings us to a slow simmer to process our food with airy, light greens and vegetables. Digestion burns a little less hot when we leave the protein behind.

- *Extinguish the Embers*
  The little embers glow at the end of a meal just enough for a small bite of something sweet like our Cacao & Medjool Date Dessert Balls. A soothing Ginger Elixir offers a warm hug at dinner's end, dousing inflammation and leaving us with the warm cinders of an evening fueled by love.

The most restorative frequencies of our subtle energy layers come from our heart center, where the energy of the earth and the heavens meet to create balance and love.

intention

"*Pay homage to your intention, whether it's a solo experience or a social engagement. That focus will make every bite and sip impactful.*"

— MIRAVAL BERKSHIRES COLLEAGUE

SETTING INTENTIONS
Through Culinary Inspiration

As soon as a guest expresses interest in visiting our resorts, we help them identify their intention. Some people know right away: eat better food, reconnect with a partner, unplug, or commune with nature. Some have no idea. A culinary journey offers us a progression through seeds of wisdom, stalks of truth, blossoms of discovery, and fruits of nourishment. It carries with it an intention of love.

When we clarify our intentions, we can adjust expected results to be achievable. We can use journaling, meditating, and reading to help us hone our intuition and gain clarity. And when it comes to food, we can create meals that reflect our greater intentions for connection and communion.

In the kitchen, intention allows forgiveness of flaws in a final plate. It turns the focus from a pursuit of perfection to a practice of presence. It will not matter if your sauce separates, your souffle falls, or your pancake won't flip. Because your intention is not attached to technical outcomes —it is guiding a process whose rewards accumulate along the way.

Lunar Cycles to Illuminate Intentions

In the quiet of the night kitchen, the evening sky's cosmic energy can nurture our intentions, aligning with celestial sparks and lunar cycles for culinary inspiration.

Balsamic Moments: The final stage of the moon's cycle, referred to as the balsamic moon, appears as a tiny slice of lunar light, winking out when the new moon cloaks us in deepest night. It is a time of retreat and quiet introspection, glowing with low, mellow energy. Like a dimmer switch in the sky, it fosters our inner luminosity and reveals tiny seeds of intentions.

What do balsamic moons and balsamic vinegar have in common? They both *feel* a certain way: soft, aged, and smooth. *Balsamic* means reposeful and restorative. The word comes from a balm produced by the balsam fir tree. A balm heals, calms, and soothes the skin—much as the balsamic moon can soothe us spiritually.

Vinegar becomes balsamic only after it has been aged, steeped, and settled to transform into something smooth and sweet. It is a heart-healthy probiotic accent to any meal, and the balsamic moon can parallel this moment of slow brewing in our lives. It is a sliver in time for going easy and making rest a priority.

If we are not paying attention to ourselves in this time of germination, we might miss our sprouting spaces where ideas prosper. Fertile fields don't rise from depleted ground. It's a perfect time to practice self-care.

Benefits of Balsamic Vinegar

- Full of antioxidants that may help lower cholesterol
- Supports healthy weight goals
- Can improve your skin's appearance
- May help with hypertension

For a recipe that uses balsamic vinegar, see Blistering Shishitos (page 231).

New Moon Dreams to Open Possibilities

On the night of a new moon, the moon and sun conjoin in the sky, generating a new cycle of light. Here, we recharge so we can rev up again in sync with the energy-building of the waxing moon.

New moons are tremendous opportunities for fresh starts and setting intentions. With a dreaming pillow (see page 334 for a dreaming pillow ritual), we can plant the seeds of something that inspires us. We can mix it into the realm of sleep and slow-cook our hopes and desires to fruition with the future arrival of a full moon.

INTENTION
menu

Intentions Under Starry Texas Skies

....

This meal was created at Miraval Austin for the
Libra full moon, which rises in spring and reminds
us to connect with our hearts and communicate
with others. The Aries sun joins forces with the
Libra full moon to produce a social, romantic, and
close-knit vibe. Libra is the sign of beauty and
love, so run with it and make your décor delightful
and delectable. From sprouting peas to spring
strawberries, this menu highlights the fresh start
that comes with the season.

Aperitif

ROSEMARY PALOMA FIZZ

Soup

CHILLED CORN SOUP

Appetizer

KING TRUMPET MUSHROOM TARTINE

Main

SPRING PEA GNOCCHI

Side

GRILLED OKRA

Dessert

FRESH STRAWBERRY TART

Digestif

BLACK & BASIL

Intention Menu

TIMELINE & TIPS

At Miraval Austin, Celestial Suppers are a regular event. Our astrologer sets the scene and intention for the evening, while our chef and sommelier pair and serve food and drinks that celebrate the night sky's themes. This menu takes you on a journey of colors, flavors, and textures.

2 DAYS AHEAD
Make soup, pickled onions (optional), and pistachio romesco.

1 DAY AHEAD
Make pea pesto and brown butter for gnocchi. Make mushroom stock and gravy for tartines and refrigerate.

IN THE MORNING
Prepare and bake tart pastry and make chocolate ganache. Prepare strawberries and dip baked pastry triangles in chocolate ganache.

4 HOURS AHEAD
Prepare, cut, and boil gnocci, make Asiago frico, fry prosciutto, and prepare okra.

1 HOUR AHEAD
Assemble tart, rewarm mushroom gravy, and prepare and sauté mushrooms for tartine.

JUST BEFORE SERVING
Prepare and toast bread and assemble mushroom tartines. Grill okra and sauté gnocchi.

MENU TYPE:
Semi-formal, coursed, and seated meal

SERVING & PLATING:
Share the aperitif with your guests and inhale the fragrance of rosemary—an herb that grows year-round at the Cypress Creek Farm at Miraval Austin.

Serve the soup in individual bowls.

Use a separate plate for the tartine. Offer your guests a fork and butter knife, but this tartine is great finger food and can be eaten with your hands.

Spoon the gnocchi into a dinner plate or shallow bowl and garnish creatively.

Place the okra in a medium-sized bowl or plate and serve with a fork.

Plate the desserts individually and serve the digestif. Made with fresh blackberries, this is a sophisticated sip without the alcohol. The mild sweetness of the dessert's berries pairs with bubbles and lime juice to complete an elegant evening.

A LITTLE EXTRA:
Invite your guests to take a moment before the meal to share their intentions for the evening or for where they are in their lives. Set the scene with candles or soft lighting.

This meal was created for the Libra full moon. However, you can tailor the décor and accessories to match any full moon throughout the year by consulting the chart at the end of the chapter on pages 190-194.

· ·

CRYSTAL COMPANION

Tourmalinted Quartz •
Rutilated Quartz •
Aquamarine

Always keep a physical distance or barrier between crystals and food or beverages.

CHILLED CORN SOUP

Make this summery chilled soup when fresh corn is in season. It's quick to make and deliciously refreshing.

4 1/2 cups fresh corn kernels

2 cups Vegetable Stock (page 303) or store-bought vegetable broth

1 cup organic cultured lowfat buttermilk

1 teaspoon fine sea salt

Microgreens or cilantro leaves for garnish

Place half of the corn in a large dry skillet over medium-high heat. Toast the corn, stirring constantly, until golden in spots, 4 to 5 minutes. Transfer to a bowl. Repeat with the remaining corn. Set aside ½ cup of the toasted corn for garnish.

In the container of a high-speed blender, combine the corn and vegetable stock. Blend until smooth. Transfer to a covered container and gently stir in the buttermilk and salt. Refrigerate until cold, at least 1 hour. The soup can be made up to 2 days in advance.

Serve the soup in small soup bowls, garnishing each, as pictured, with the reserved toasted corn and either microgreens or cilantro leaves.

Makes about 6 cups; Serving Size 3/4-cup

V | gf | ef | nf

CALORIES: 70; TOTAL FAT: 1 G; CARBOHYDRATE: 14 G; DIETARY FIBER: 1 G; PROTEIN: 3 G

KING TRUMPET MUSHROOM TARTINE
WITH GOAT CHEESE

The King Trumpet mushroom, also called King Oyster mushroom, has a wonderful meaty texture and complex umami flavor. Unlike some mushrooms, the stems of these mushrooms are tender and tasty. Cutting them in half and searing them in olive oil brings out all their goodness. Seek an artisan bakery that makes whole-wheat sourdough bread for these tartines. Use the leftover mushroom gravy for another meal, or as a topping for cooked vegetables, pasta, or whole grains.

Vegan Mushroom Gravy

1/4 cup extra-virgin olive oil

1/3 cup chopped yellow onion

1 garlic clove, finely chopped

1/4 pound cremini mushrooms, wiped clean, thinly sliced

1 sprig fresh thyme

3 cups plus 1 tablespoon Vegetable Stock (page 303) or store-bought vegetable broth

1 teaspoon tapioca flour or starch

Fine sea salt

Freshly ground black pepper

Tartine

6 large King Trumpet mushrooms (about 1 pound)

Fine sea salt

1/2 cup extra-virgin olive oil

6 slices (about 1 ounce each) of whole-wheat sourdough bread

3/4 cup soft goat cheese

6 sprigs fresh thyme for garnish

1/3 cup Pickled Onions (page 260)

Zest of 1 lemon

To make the mushroom gravy, set a medium saucepan over medium-high heat, add the oil and warm it, swirling to coat the bottom of the pan. Add the onions and garlic and sauté, stirring occasionally, until soft and just beginning to turn golden, about 3 minutes. Add the mushrooms and sauté, stirring frequently, until the mushrooms turn beautifully brown and begin to caramelize, about 6 minutes.

Add the sprig of thyme and 3 cups of the vegetable stock and bring to a boil. Reduce the heat so the liquid gently simmers and cook until the liquid is reduced by half, about 10 minutes.

Remove the pan from the heat. Pluck the sprig of thyme out of the pot and discard. Set the mixture aside to cool for 10 minutes.

Transfer all of the mushroom mixture to the container of a high-speed blender. Clean the pan and set it aside. Blend the mixture on low speed for 10 seconds, and then increase the blender speed to high and purée the ingredients to make a smooth gravy.

Continued on the next page

V | ef | nf

CALORIES: 370; TOTAL FAT: 26 G; CARBOHYDRATE: 27 G; DIETARY FIBER: 3 G; PROTEIN: 9 G

• •

Transfer the gravy back to the saucepan and set over medium heat. Bring to a simmer. In a small bowl, stir together the tapioca flour (or starch) and the remaining 1 tablespoon of vegetable stock to make a smooth slurry. While whisking the gravy, slowly stir in the slurry and simmer for 2 minutes, whisking constantly, until the gravy is thickened and smooth. Season to taste with salt and pepper. Remove from the heat and keep warm until ready to serve.

To prepare the mushrooms, slice each King Trumpet mushroom in half lengthwise. Using a paring knife, cut a cross hatch design into the inside of each mushroom half (the flat portion). Rub some salt into each cross-hatched marking.

In a large sauté pan set over medium heat, warm 1/4 cup of the olive oil. Add the mushrooms, cut-side down, and cook until golden brown, about 4 minutes. Set the mushrooms aside while you toast the bread.

In a second large sauté pan, heat the remaining 1/4 cup of oil over medium-high heat. Arrange the bread in the pan, cook in batches if needed, and toast the bread on one side until golden brown. Remove the bread from the pan and spread the toasted side of each piece with 2 tablespoons of goat cheese. Place 2 halves of the trumpet mushrooms, flat-side up, on top of the goat cheese. Spoon 1/4 cup of the Mushroom Gravy over each tartine. Garnish with a sprig of fresh thyme, pickled onions, and fresh lemon zest.

Makes 6 servings

SPRING PEA GNOCCHI
WITH PROSCIUTTO, PEA PESTO & ASIAGO FRICO

Light and airy pillows of potato and pea goodness, these gnocchi are easier to make than they seem. They can be made, cut, and boiled up to 2 hours in advance. Cover the gnocchi, leave at room temperature, and sauté it just before serving. The Asiago frico and pea pesto can also be made in advance. The dish comes together quickly with all the components ready.

Gnocchi

2 pounds russet potatoes

1 cup cooked English peas (use fresh or frozen peas)

1 large egg, beaten

1/2 cup freshly grated Parmesan cheese, preferably Parmigiano-Reggiano

1/2 teaspoon fine sea salt

1 3/4 cups all-purpose flour, plus more for flouring the pan

1/4 cup grated Asiago cheese

4 slices prosciutto, cut crosswise into thin slices

3 to 4 tablespoons brown butter (see *Note* on page 178)

1 cup frozen peas, thawed

2 cups baby spinach

1/2 cup Pea Pesto (page 179)

Freshly grated Parmesan cheese, preferably Parmigiano-Reggiano, for serving

Fresh pea tendrils for garnish, optional

To make the gnocchi, position a rack in the center of the oven and heat the oven to 425°F.

Prick each potato several times with a fork and place them on a sheet pan. Bake the potatoes until they are tender enough to be easily pierced with a paring knife, about 1 hour. Remove the potatoes from the oven and set them aside until they are just cool enough to handle but still very hot, 5 to 10 minutes. Cut the potatoes in half lengthwise and scoop the flesh from the skins. Discard the skins. Pass the flesh through a food mill or ricer into large bowl. Measure the potatoes and use just 2 cups. Save any remaining potato for another use. Again, using the food mill or ricer, set it over the bowl of potatoes, and mash and push through the cooked peas. To this mixture, stir in the egg, Parmesan, and salt. Mix gently to combine.

Fold in the flour, about 1/2 cup at a time, just until the flour disappears and the dough comes together. Using your hands, shape the dough into a large ball, adding more flour if it seems too moist; the dough should be slightly tacky but not sticky (it should stick more to itself than to your hands).

Transfer the dough to a floured work surface. Lightly flour a rimmed sheet pan. Cut off a baseball-size hunk of dough and roll it between your hands to form a ball. Then, using your palms, roll the ball back and forth on the floured surface into a skinny log, 3/4 inches in diameter and about 15 inches long. Cut the log crosswise into pieces about 1 inch long and place the pieces on the floured sheet pan. Cover the sheet pan with plastic wrap so the gnocchi do not dry out while you roll and cut the remaining dough the same way.

Continued on page 178

V | nf

CALORIES: 460; TOTAL FAT: 19 G; CARBOHYDRATE: 56 G; DIETARY FIBER: 6 G; PROTEIN: 15 G

Use any tool with a fine mesh surface, such as a food mill, potato masher, or even two forks.

Follow the recipe steps in sequence for a smoother dough texture.

Use a bench knife or butter knife to cut the log crosswise.

Optional - roll across a gnocchi board to achieve signature-looking grooves.

• •

Fill an 8- to 10-quart stockpot two-thirds full of water, add a pinch of salt and bring to a rolling boil over high heat. Add the gnocchi and stir gently once or twice so they don't stick together. After 1 or 2 minutes, the gnocchi will bob to the surface; wait for 1 minute longer and then, using a slotted spoon, transfer the gnocchi to a large platter.

To make the Asiago frico, prepare a plate lined with a paper towel. Heat a small nonstick pan over medium heat. Place 1 tablespoon of the Asiago cheese in the pan and gently spread it out flat like a cracker. Toast on 1 side until golden brown. Use a silicone spatula to lift it out and place on a paper towel. Repeat to make 3 more. Set aside. Wipe the pan clean.

Using the same pan, sauté the prosciutto until crisp, Set aside.

To sauté the gnocchi, in a large sauté pan, melt the browned butter over medium heat and swirl to coat the pan bottom. Add the gnocchi; they should fit in a single layer without crowding; otherwise do this in batches. Sauté, turning as needed, until the gnocchi are golden brown on all sides, about 4 minutes. Toss in the peas and spinach. Sauté, stirring constantly, until the spinach is wilted and the peas are heated through, about 2 minutes. Remove from the heat.

To serve, spread a generous spoonful of pesto on the bottom of each warmed pasta bowl. In each bowl, arrange 9 gnocchi on top. Sprinkle crisp pieces of prosciutto around and shower with Parmesan. Crumble each Asiago frico and sprinkle over the top along with the pea tendrils, if desired. Serve immediately.

Note:

To make brown butter, melt a stick of butter in a medium skillet over medium-low heat. Cook slowly until the butter becomes light brown and smells nutty. Swirl the pan gently, the butter will foam and then subside. Watch closely as you'll see brown bits on the bottom of the pan. Remove the pan from the heat when the butter is beautifully browned. Set aside until ready to use or refrigerate to have on hand for sautéing fish or spooning over vegetables as a sauce.

Makes 6 servings; Serving Size: 9 gnocchi

PEA PESTO

2 cups English peas, fresh or frozen

1 garlic clove

3 tablespoons extra-virgin olive oil

1/4 cup freshly grated Asiago or Parmesan cheese, preferably Parmigiano Reggiano

1/4 cup toasted sunflower seeds

1 tsp fine sea salt

If using fresh peas, cook them in boiling salted water until tender but still bright green. Immediately transfer them to an ice bath to cool. Drain and blot completely dry. If using frozen peas, thaw them and blot them dry.

In the workbowl of a food processor fitted with the metal blade, process the peas, garlic, oil, cheese, sunflower seeds, and salt until coarsely smooth like a basil pesto would be in texture. Transfer to a covered container. Set aside until ready to use or refrigerate if making ahead. The peas pesto can be made up to 1 day in advance.

Makes about 1 1/4 cups; Serving Size: 2 tablespoons

V | gf | ef | nf

CALORIES: 90; TOTAL FAT: 7 G; CARBOHYDRATE: 5 G;
DIETARY FIBER: 2 G; PROTEIN: 2 G

GRILLED OKRA

GRILLED OKRA
WITH PISTACHIO ROMESCO

In our opinion, the best way to cook okra for a crisp-tender texture is to grill it or sear it in a hot pan. This side dish works well with either cooking technique. The pistachio romesco is a delightful accompaniment. The recipe calls for roasted peppers; using well-drained, jarred roasted red peppers works equally well.

· ·

Pistachio Romesco

3 ripe plum tomatoes, cored, halved lengthwise, and seeded

1/2 cup shelled pistachios

1/8 cup packed flat-leaf parsley leaves

3/4 cup roasted red bell peppers, well drained

1/2 teaspoon smoked paprika (pimentón de la Vera)

1/4 teaspoon red pepper flakes

1/2 teaspoon fine sea salt

1/2 teaspoon sherry vinegar

1 1/2 pound fresh okra, sliced in half lengthwise

3 tablespoons unrefined avocado oil

Fine sea salt

To make the pistachio romesco, heat the oven to 425°F. Arrange the tomatoes, cut-side up on a rimmed sheet pan. Roast until the tomatoes are soft, about 20 minutes. Set aside to cool.

In the workbowl of a food processor fitted with the metal blade, pulse the pistachios and parsley until finely chopped. Add the tomatoes, peppers, smoked paprika, red pepper flakes, salt, and vinegar. Process until the sauce is relatively smooth. Transfer to a covered container and set aside until ready to use. (The romesco can be made up to 3 days in advance. Cover and refrigerate until ready to use.)

To prepare the okra, toss the okra with the oil and season with salt. Using a grill pan inside on a stovetop, or on an outdoor grill, grill the okra over high heat until crisp-tender and lightly charred in spots. Serve the grilled okra hot accompanied with the pistachio romesco.

Makes 6 servings

V | vg | gf | df | ef

CALORIES: 170; TOTAL FAT: 12 G; CARBOHYDRATE: 14 G; DIETARY FIBER: 5 G; PROTEIN: 4 G

FRESH STRAWBERRY TART
WITH CHOCOLATE GANACHE

Make this fabulous chocolate ganache tart when strawberries are in season and at the peak of flavor. While the description is long, the steps are easy and can be done in stages. Dipping baked pastry triangles in ganache, as a garnish for the tart, gives the dessert an elegant finish. If you want to simplify this dessert, you could skip dipping the baked pastry triangles in the chocolate and save them for nibbling later.

For this recipe, you will need a couple of specialty kitchen items that not every baker has on hand. Please read through the recipe completely before starting. This dessert requires a 9-inch tart pan with a removable bottom, plus several sheets of parchment paper to roll out and bake the pastry. In addition, you'll need 2 large, rimmed sheet pans; both the same size.

Pastry

2 cups whole-wheat pastry flour

1 teaspoon fine sea salt

1 cup grass-fed unsalted butter, frozen

About 1/2 cup ice water

Ganache

1 3/4 cups heavy (whipping) cream

1 cup bittersweet baking wafers or chunks (not chips)

About 26 evenly sized ripe strawberries (approximately 2 pints)

Sweetened whipped cream, for serving

To make the pastry, in a large bowl, toss together the flour and salt. Using the large holes on a 4-sided cheese grater, grate the butter right onto the flour. Working quickly and gently, use your fingers to massage the butter into the flour. Sprinkle the dough with the ice water. Using a fork, gently mix the water into the dough until it is evenly distributed. Turn the dough onto a lightly floured work surface. Gather the dough into a thick disk, wrap it in plastic wrap, and then flatten it a bit more. Refrigerate the dough for 30 minutes.

Arrange a rack in the center of the oven and a second rack in the lower third. Heat oven to 375°F. Have ready a 9-inch tart pan with a removable bottom, plus 2 sheet pans of the same size that can nest together. Line one of the sheet pans with parchment paper. Have two more pieces of parchment ready, along with pie weights (dried beans or rice work too).

When the dough is well chilled, cut it in half, with one portion slightly larger than the other. Roll the smaller portion into a circle slightly larger than the bottom of the tart pan. Use the pan as guide to trace a neat circle of dough. Place this smaller piece of pastry on the sheet pan lined with parchment. Use a pizza cutter or paring knife to cut the pastry into 10 wedges. Place a sheet of parchment over the pastry and then place the second sheet pan on top, sandwiching the pastry so it doesn't rise during baking. Refrigerate the sheet pan with the dough while you roll the second portion.

Roll the slightly larger portion of dough into a 10 1/2-inch circle. Slide the bottom of the tart pan under the dough, fold the excess loosely inwards, and then drop the bottom into the pan. Unfold the dough and fit it into the pan, pressing up the sides and trimming the top. Use a fork to prick small holes in the pastry all over the bottom. Line the crust with parchment and then fill it with pie weights.

V | ef | nf

Continued on the next page

CALORIES: 460; TOTAL FAT: 37 G; CARBOHYDRATE: 32 G; DIETARY FIBER: 5 G; PROTEIN: 5 G

Fresh Strawberry Tart continued

....

Bake both pieces of pastry for 25 minutes. Remove the parchment with the pie weights from the tart pan, as well as the top sheet pan and top sheet of parchment. Continue to bake the pastry until golden, about 15 minutes longer. (Since this is a fully baked crust, you want a deeply colored pastry so it stays crisp on the bottom. Set aside on wire racks to cool.

To make the ganache, in a small saucepan set over medium heat, heat the cream to 200°F. Remove from the heat, add the chocolate, and allow it to melt for a few minutes. Whisk thoroughly until the mixture is smooth and emulsified.

While the ganache is cooling prepare the strawberries. Select the most perfectly ripe ones without any blemishes or soft spots. Remove the stems, wash the berries, and blot them completely dry. Trim the stem end so they will have a flat base when placed on the tart.

To assemble the dessert, line a sheet pan with parchment paper. Dip each baked wedge of pastry halfway lengthwise into the ganache. Carefully set each on the parchment. Refrigerate to set the chocolate. Using the remaining ganache, pour it into the tart pan, filling it 3/4 full. Stud the ganache with the prepared berries, arranging the berries pointed-side up. Start at the outer rim and make concentric circles to the center, nestling the berries close together. Refrigerate the pie so the ganache sets up.

To serve, remove the sides from the tart pan. Cut the tart into 10 slices. Place each slice on a dessert plate. Garnish with 1 chocolate-dipped pastry triangle. Serve with a dollop of whipped cream.

Makes 10 servings

ROSEMARY PALOMA FIZZ

2 ounces rosemary simple syrup (recipe below)

1 ounce fresh grapefruit juice

1/2 ounce fresh lime juice

3 ounces seltzer water

Sprig of rosemary

Combine the first 3 ingredients in a mixing tin. Shake and then pour the mixture into a tall glass over ice. Top with seltzer water and garnish with a sprig of rosemary.

Makes 1 serving

Rosemary Simple Syrup

1 cup sugar

1 cup water

4 sprigs of fresh rosemary

Combine the sugar, water, and rosemary in a small pot and bring to a boil. Simmer for 5 minutes. Remove from the heat. Cover the pan and cool to room temperature. Strain out the solids and store in the refrigerator for up to 2 weeks.

Makes 1 1/2 cups

CALORIES: 160; TOTAL FAT: 0 G; CARBOHYDRATE: 42 G; DIETARY FIBER: 0 G; PROTEIN: 0 G

BLACK & BASIL

6 ounces blackberry shrub (recipe below)

6 ounces lemon juice

3 ounces black pepper simple syrup (recipe below)

24 ounces sparkling water

6 basil leaves

Combine the first 3 ingredients in a mixing tin. Stir and strain the mixture over ice into a coup glass. Top with sparkling water and garnish with a basil leaf.

Makes 6 servings

Blackberry Shrub

1 cup fresh blackberries

1 cup granulated sugar

1 cup apple cider vinegar

In a mixing bowl, mash the fresh blackberries with the sugar. Let the result sit for 15 minutes to allow the fruits to expel their juices. Slowly stir in the apple cider vinegar. Cover and let steep in the refrigerator for 2 to 3 days. Strain out the solids and store in the refrigerator until ready to use or for up to 1 month.

Black Pepper Simple Syrup

1/3 cup water

1/3 cup sugar

3 tablespoons ground black pepper

Place the sugar, water, and pepper in a small sauce pan and bring to a boil. Simmer for 5 minutes and let cool. Store in the refrigerator for up to 2 weeks.

CALORIES: 110; TOTAL FAT: 0 G; CARBOHYDRATE: 29 G; DIETARY FIBER: 0 G; PROTEIN: 0 G

BRING MIRAVAL HOME

Pair Your Intentions with Celestial Suppers

The waxing moon's journey culminates in the spark that ignites each month's full moon, a time of action, exhibition, and illumination. You can use this momentum to gather around the table, share a meal together, and celebrate and honor the intentions you set at the new moon.

This is a peak in the lunar month and an opportunity to enjoy the night sky, bring people together, and share what is going on in your life. When we look at the zodiac signs and how they affect our lunations throughout the year, it's important to remember that the sun and moon are always on an axis. New moons will be in the same sign as the sun, while full moons will rise in the sun's opposite sign.

Full moons radiate the 180-degree energy of celestial bodies and people coming together. A sign and its opposite join forces to generate a cosmic vibe that unifies polarities and helps us moderate opposites. It can heighten and enhance how we pair people, foods, music, art, or any other element of expression and connection.

FULL MOON FESTIVITIES & CELEBRATIONS

Try out our Intention Menu on page 163 or use the celestial inspiration on the following pages to frame how you would present a celestial supper during any of the year's 12 full moons.

Season	Dates	Sun Sign	Full-Moon Sign	Themes for Food & Décor Choices
	March 21 – April 19	ARIES	LIBRA	Present sophisticated food and stunning decor elegantly and gracefully. This is a perfect time for a social and romantic meal with close friends and partners.
SPRING	April 20 – May 20	TAURUS	SCORPIO	These earth and water signs combine to create sensual, rich, and indulgent food. Keep your surroundings comfortable and nature-oriented with flowers, herbs, and fresh, delectable fare.
	May 21 – June 20	GEMINI	SAGITTARIUS	Be playful and experiment with exotic foods from other cultures. Create an adventurous, jovial mood and decorate your space with a sense of humor.

Season	Dates	Sun Sign	Full-Moon Sign	Themes for Food & Décor Choices
	June 21 - July 22	CANCER	CAPRICORN	This is the season of family gatherings and ancestral eats. Stick to traditional summer meals like BBQ or tried-and-true recipes. It's a practical time that has no patience for fuss or fancy. Hang up some hammocks and be happy to be outside.
SUMMER	July 23 - August 22	LEO	AQUARIUS	Show off a little with glitter, glamor, and original displays. Feature summer fun, ripe fruits, and s'mores while you network, gather with friends, and engage in stimulating conversations. Impress your guests with unusual presentations of familiar foods and visual formats.
	August 23 - September 22	VIRGO	PISCES	A creative, artistic axis heralds dreamy, imaginative, and strong emotional energy. Beckon fairies and sprites with stardust and inspiration. Health-oriented Virgo presents simple, creatively comforting food in a fanciful, magical way. If Aries is the beginning of everything, Pisces ends all cycles and evolves with unclouded insight and fluid intuition.

Season	Dates	Sun Sign	Full-Moon Sign	Themes for Food & Décor Choices
	September 23 - October 22	LIBRA ♎	ARIES ♈	This is a bold, spicy lunation where action is big! Pair your meal with an activity or sports viewing. Serve arousing, spicy foods with focused, bold, in-your-face colors, flavors, and décor.
FALL	October 23 - November 21	SCORPIO ♏	TAURUS ♉	Return to luxury with rich, indulgent, and luxurious foods. Play up sensuality and leave your guests feeling pampered with fancy fare.
	November 22 - December 21	SAGITTARIUS ♐	GEMINI ♊	This whimsical, festive menu brings witty conversation and playfulness to a less traditional holiday vibe. Riff off convention; amuse guests with curious combinations and presentations of varied cultures and flavors.

Season	Dates	Sun Sign	Full-Moon Sign	Themes for Food & Décor Choices
	December 22 – January 19	CAPRICORN	CANCER	Present sophisticated food and stunning decor elegantly and gracefully. This is a perfect time for a social and romantic meal with close friends and partners.
WINTER	January 20 – February 18	AQUARIUS	LEO	Drama, costumes, and a fun-loving theme shape this lunation's outgoing, showy energy. Add flair to your menu and take a cue from the Gilded Age in this axis of royals and lions. This kind of joy compounds itself with companionship and creates a social energy that seeks an audience. It wants a full-on festival!
	February 19 – March 20	PISCES	VIRGO	Hearty, fortifying, and balancing foods anticipate spring in this healthiest axis of signs. But healthy does not mean boring. Virgo's gifts of perception meet Pisces's imagination and illuminate all the feelings Pisces makes us feel. Sprinkle twinkling lights, microgreens, or fresh sprouts to make this meal airy and bright.

In the quiet of the night kitchen, the evening sky's cosmic energy can nurture our intentions, aligning with celestial sparks and lunar cycles for culinary inspiration.

THE DINING EXPERIENCE

Take a tour through the Miraval Resorts culinary spaces and learn more about where our experiences unfold.

Miraval Arizona Cactus Flower Restaurant

This sunny, spacious gathering place is a bright light of epicurean adventure. Modern décor and comfortable seating invite guests to break bread—or tortillas—together. Surprise your tastebuds with home-baked local tacos wrapped in flatbreads made with amaranth flour and ground mesquite pods. Here, you can discover curious pairings like chocolate and chiltepín peppers—wild, native chiles that also flavor our salsas with their mellow, smooth spice. Picture windows and wrap-around patios reveal stunning views of the Santa Catalina Mountains, which host the many hives nurtured by our resident beekeeper; they produce enough honey to supply the kitchen's needs and provide a variety of local honey that reflects the flora of the Sonoran Desert sprouting all around us.

Miraval Austin Hilltop Crossings Kitchen

From an enormous indoor fireside table to a sweeping outdoor deck overlooking Lake Travis, you can dine by warm flames or under the cool shade of Miraval Austin's regal cedar trees. Austin's robust farming community and our own Cypress Creek Farm celebrate local ingredients that rise from this lush, rich land. Foods reflect local Texas fare and incorporate new combinations that range from tastes of top-notch Texas steaks to delicious plant-based creations that make it easy to shift your palate to include more colorful and nutritious vegetables on your plate.

Miraval Berkshires 1894

Fine Dining at 1894 unfurls a fantastic fairy tale with the language of food at Miraval Berkshires' historic Wyndhurst Mansion. Its 1894 dining room has served lavish, luxurious feasts for over 100 years. Built as a summer "cottage," it emerged in the glimmering Gilded Age of the late 1800s and early 1900s, that opulent period of excess, extremes, and extraordinary characters. It was a time of dazzling dinners and tea parties in a region steeped in culture. A tasting menu transports you to another century and offers an interactive sampling of a sensory tale, traveling through tureens of time and paired with fine wines.

Miraval Berkshires Harvest Moon

The Harvest Moon Restaurant at Miraval Berkshires pays homage to the many rustic barns that dot the hilly New England landscape surrounding the resort. Roughly hewn exposed rafters and vaulted ceilings are lit by impressive, copper-ensconced lanterns, casting a starry glitter across the sturdy, galvanized tables and other metallic details. Like the space itself, the food served at Harvest Moon finds a comfortable balance between healthy staples and luxuriant treats, all vibrant and nourishing.

MORE RECIPES & RITUALS
For a Life in Balance

Have you ever come home after a long day and wished someone would magically make you a perfect meal? At Miraval Resorts, we created an entire experience based on this feeling and called it Just Cook for Me.

Because one of the best ways to feel cared for is when someone intentionally prepares a delightful feast just for you. It delivers a feeling of pure joy at a table prepared with love. That feeling captures the essence of the culinary experience at Miraval Resorts.

What if we could flip that script? What if we could take the time to cook a delicious, healthy meal for ourselves and the people we love, and in the process, nourish our bodies, minds, and spirits?

With this book in your hand, you can cook for your family and friends and recreate the spirit of Just Cook for Me. Use the tips, techniques, recipes, and rituals throughout the remainder of this book to embark on your own culinary journey.

It can become your way of saying to your loved ones, *let me just cook for you.*

FOUNDATIONS
For Mindful Cooking

INGREDIENTS

Always aim for seasonal, local, organic, and fair-trade foods whenever possible that are minimally modified from how they appear in nature. Focus on freshness, quality, and sustainability.

If you find yourself overwhelmed by foods claiming to be organic and safe, there are several online resources that help rate food categories and make it easier to make conscious choices about the foods you buy (e.g., The Cornucopia Institute, Monteray Bay Aquarium Seafood Watch).

TERMS & TECHNIQUES

Gluten-Free
Has no gluten-containing grains (including wheat, barley, rye, and triticale) or products made with them.

Non-GMO
Contains no genetically modified organisms. All USDA Organic Certified food is non-GMO. Bioengineering is the same as genetic modification. For more information, refer to the shopping section (page 209).

Organic
Prohibits the use of synthetic chemical inputs (fertilizer, pesticides, antibiotics, food additives, etc.), irradiation, and the use of sewage sludge. We strive to purchase according to the "Dirty Dozen" and "Clean 15" lists by the Environmental Working Group (www.ewg.org) when prioritizing organic purchases. Consuming organic food can reduce your pesticide residue ingestion, which current research shows can help support a healthy gut.

Plant-Based Diet
Contains foods derived from plants, including vegetables, whole grains, nuts, seeds, legumes, and fruits, but few or no animal products.

Prebiotics and Probiotics
Probiotic-containing foods (e.g. yogurt, kefir, kombucha, and naturally fermented sauerkraut and kimchi) help support healthy gut flora and digestion. Prebiotics are carbohydrates that resist digestion, like fiber, in the small intestine and feed the gut bacteria.

Regenerative Farming
Many farmers practice regenerative agriculture, which is the process of restoring degraded soils using techniques (adaptive grazing, no-till planting, minimal use of pesticides and synthetic fertilizer, etc.) based on ecological principles.

Vegan
A lifestyle choice that avoids eating foods or wearing products derived from animals, including consuming honey, eggs, or dairy, or wearing leather.

KNIFE SKILLS

- STAY SHARP: Knives should be used with safety and care in mind. Dull knives are likely to cause more injuries than sharp ones. Buy a sharpening steel for home use. Watch a video online for safe ways to sharpen knives at home. Find a local store that sharpens knives and have them professionally sharpened every six months or at least once a year.

- PAY ATTENTION: Focus on your cutting board, knife, non-cutting hand, and food. Do not be distracted by conversations, children, pets, or devices.

- USE A KNIFE FOR ITS INTENDED PURPOSE: Do not use it to cut string, boxes, bones, metal, or paper, as these materials will dull or break the blade, and may increase odds of knife-related injuries.

- USE A CUTTING BOARD: Do not use a knife if the cutting board is not stable on your work surface. Help keep it from slipping or moving on your work surface with a damp towel or anti-slip mat underneath.

- HAND-WASH KNIVES IN HOT SOAPY WATER: Wash with care and handle the knife only by the handle, never the blade. Never put them in the dishwasher, as high heat and caustic detergents can corrode blades and swell handles.

- STORAGE: A magnetic knife rack or knife block is best. If you use a drawer, keep a separate knife compartment.

AS YOU'RE COOKING

- Prepare your workstation: set the oven temperature and clean utensils and surfaces.

- Mise en place, French for *set in place*, is a method of preparation professional chefs use.
    - Know your recipe, including ingredients, cookware, and baking times, before starting.
    - Prepare your ingredients: wash, chop, marinate, etc.
    - Arrange your ingredients and tools and position them sequentially.

- Plan efficiently and prepare ahead: make whole dishes or components in advance whenever possible.

- Go easy on the seasoning. You can always add more before serving.

- Keep a bowl near your workspace for compost or freeze it for later use in soup stock.

HELPFUL TIPS

Add fresh and dried herbs to your preparations for stronger aromas and more pronounced flavors. Dried herbs have more concentrated flavors than fresh ones, so add them to a recipe first. Add fresh herbs at the end of the recipe, as their flavors are more delicate, and their aromas fade quickly.

Egg-white omelets tend to stick to the pan during cooking. To cut the need for extra oil or butter in their cooking, precook the egg whites in a microwave-safe bowl in the microwave until they rise and become fluffy (about 45 seconds). The whites can then be combined with steamed vegetables and cooked in a small sauté pan for a perfect omelet.

When cooking mixed vegetables, add the firmer varieties to the pan or steamer first to ensure even cooking and the increase nutritive values. For instance, carrots may take longer to cook than squash or asparagus and should be added to the pan first. Toss the cooked vegetables in a bowl with one or two squirts of olive oil or Miraval Oil Blend (page 304), a dash of kosher salt, and finely chopped fresh herbs for a satisfying and easy side dish or pasta topping.

Appearance goes a long way toward making food more appealing.

- Dress up your plates by piping mashed potatoes from a pastry bag with a star tip into the center of the plate, garnish with fresh herbs, and drizzle with reduced vinegars, herb oils, or small diced vegetables.

- Pack cooked grains into a small cup and then invert the cup onto the plate. Gently lift away the cup and arrange vegetables around the pile, keeping height in mind. Add fresh herb sprigs as a garnish.

STOCKING THE KITCHEN

- Invest in the best kitchen equipment and appliances you can afford; good-quality pots, pans, and knives can last a lifetime with proper use and upkeep.

- Avoid buying kitchen tools designed for a single purpose, like an avocado knife. The more versatile the tool, the more valuable it is.

- As you'll see, the recipes in this cookbook use specialty tools and equipment. These tools make cooking so much easier:
  - Food processor and mini chop
  - High-speed blender
  - Immersion blender
  - Kitchen scale
  - Stand mixer or hand-held mixer
  - A set of mixing bowls
  - Good quality cutting and carving boards, large and small
  - Silicone spatulas
  - Small and large whisks
  - Rimmed sheets pans (quarter sheet pan; half sheet pan)
  - Dutch oven (6-quart)
  - Food thermometer
  - 9-inch tart pan with removable bottom

SHOPPING

- Seek excellent vendors in your area. A farmers market usually has the best seasonal produce; local butchers, fishmongers, and cheese shops typically offer service and selections you may not find in your supermarket.

- DECIPHERING LABELS
    - Look for the labels from several organizations that certify certain foods and brands as following guidelines and standards to ensure quality (e.g. USDA Certified Organic, Non-GMO Project Verified).
    - Watch out for GMO/Bioengineered labels: A GMO is a genetically modified organism made in a laboratory using genetic engineering, which is not the same as traditional crossbreeding methods. Bioengineered labeling is now required on foods with 5% or more genetically modified material.

Fruits & Vegetables

- Always look for fresh, seasonal fruits and vegetables that are unblemished, firm, and not wrinkled.

- Frozen vegetables and fruits are a great option for out of season produce.

- Ensure that the stem ends of vine-ripened fruits and vegetables are fresh looking, green, and not moldy.

- Fresh herbs should look full, bright, and vibrant—never wilted.

- When choosing juices, seek fresh, low-sodium, unsweetened varieties.

Plant Protein

- We suggest adding plant-based foods to your diet as often as you can. You can help support your health and wellbeing—and the planet's— by making even one of the 21 meals you eat in a week full of minimally processed, plant-based proteins like tofu, tempeh, soybeans, or seitan surrounded by plant-exclusive sides.

- Beware of packaged "fake" meats and meat-replacement products that are so highly processed that they negate the benefits of their plant-based origins.

Non-Plant Protein

- BEEF, LAMB, PORK, AND DAIRY: In addition to USDA Certified Organic meats, look for local, hormone- and antibiotic-free, Certified GrassFed, and Humanely Raised meats.

- EGGS: Seek Omega-3-enhanced pasture-raised eggs (if not available, look for free-range)

- FISH AND SEAFOOD: Look for Marine Stewardship Council-labeled seafood (MSC). This ensures you are buying from sustainably managed fisheries dedicated to ending overfishing. The Aquaculture Stewardship Council (ASC) identifies aquaculture farms independently assessed and certified as environmentally and socially responsible. Monterey Bay Aquarium Seafood Watch is a great resource to help you identify where you can buy sustainable and ethically raised fish.

- POULTRY: USDA Certified Organic means the feed is free of pesticides, herbicides, and additives, and the chicken is antibiotic-free and free-range. Pasture-raised and Certified Humane Raised are ideal.

Dairy & Dairy Substitutes

- In general, try to avoid antibiotics or growth hormones. Strive to buy organic, grass-fed milk products, if possible.

- BUTTERS: Unsalted butter is typically fresher than salted butter and you can control how much salt is added.

- MILKS: Try to avoid additives and emulsifiers like carrageenan, as they that can be inflammatory.
  - Organic reduced-fat milk
  - Organic soy milk (typically has higher nutritional value and lower environmental footprint, but if you have an allergy or intolerance, switch to oat milk).
  - Organic oat milk.
  - Organic almond milk (consider using alternatives since almond milk has lower nutritional content and a more negative environmental impact on bees and water).

- ORGANIC YOGURT: Try to choose plain yogurt—you can add fruit and other items yourself.

Beans & Legumes

- Use organic and locally sourced when possible.

- Transfer bags of beans and legumes to sealed containers and store in a pantry away from heat and light.

- Keeping a pantry stocked with canned beans and legumes is helpful in an emergency, and these can be go-to ingredients for nourishing meals in a pinch.

Flours & Grains

- Use organic, unbleached, and locally milled or sourced if available.

- Transfer bags of flour and grains to sealed containers and store in a pantry away from heat and light.

- If you have freezer space, store whole-wheat flour in the freezer to help keep it fresh.

Herbs & Spices

- Look for spices in the bulk section of grocery stores; buy small quantities at a time to keep them fresh. Buying spices in the bulk section is often less expensive.

- Replace spices and other pantry items yearly, as they lose their flavor over time. Red spices such as cayenne, paprika, crushed red pepper, and chile powders will last longer in the refrigerator.

Oils & Fats

The best oils to stock in your kitchen are:

- Extra-virgin olive oil (EVOO) for salad dressings, sauces, and low-temperature cooking.
- Organic, expeller-pressed canola oil for high-temperature cooking.
- Refined avocado oil for high-temperature cooking; unrefined can be used in place of EVOO.
- Organic expeller-pressed grapeseed or safflower oil.
- Toasted sesame oil.
- Cold-pressed avocado oil cooking spray
- Use less often: Coconut oil, butter, cultured butter, ghee, or vegan butter.

Buy and use a spray bottle for oils instead of pouring oil directly from the bottle to control amounts better. A spray of oil typically dispenses 1/8 to 1/4 teaspoon quantities.

Oil should never smoke when cooking. If it does, let the oil cool to room temperature before discarding and begin again.

Raw, Unsalted Nuts & Seeds

- Nuts and seeds typically have a short shelf life due to the natural oils in them; roasting them can reduce it even more.

- If you have room, store nuts, such as almonds, walnuts, etc., and seeds, such as sesame seeds, in the freezer in tightly sealed, freezer-strength bags. They may stay fresh for months compared to storing them at room temperature.

- Store hemp seeds in a sealed container in the refrigerator.

Salts

The best salts to stock in your kitchen are:

- Fine sea salt
- Coarse and flaky sea salt
- Specialty salts such as Himalayan, black lava, smoked salts, etc.
- Authentic kosher salt without additives—read the label before purchasing. Kosher salt typically has about 30 percent less sodium than iodized salt.

Sweeteners

- Where possible, use unprocessed sweeteners (molasses, honey, maple syrup, or date syrup).

- Minimize your use of other processed sweeteners (agave or rice syrup, turbinado, cane, or coconut sugar).

- Today, most agave sweeteners are treated with heat and enzymes that destroy any potential health benefits and create a highly refined syrup. If a recipe calls for agave syrup, we recommend that you use organic raw agave syrup.

breakfast & breads

MAKE YOUR OWN SMOOTHIE

Great smoothies have a good proportion of carbohydrates, protein, and fat. Many are too high in sugar due to fruit juice, added sugar, and fruit. Here's a terrific mix-and-match recipe to suit your mood and taste preferences.

....

1/2 cup unsweetened liquid

1/2 cup primary protein

1/2 cup fresh or fresh fruit

1/2 cup fresh or frozen fruit

1 big handful of veggies

1 fat

1 carbohydrate

A touch of pizzazz

A touch of sweetness

Place all the specific ingredients you have chosen in the container of a high-speed blender. Blend until smooth. Enjoy.

Makes 1 serving; Serving Size: 12 to 16 ounces

Unsweetened Liquid	*Primary Protein*	*Fresh or Frozen Fruit*	*Vegetables*
4 GRAMS OF PROTEIN	Organic Tofu	FRESH	FRESH
Kefir	Plain Greek Yogurt	Apple, with peel	Greens
Soy Milk	Cooked Lentils	Banana	Spinach
Protein Nut Milk		Grapes	Kale
0 TO 1 GRAM OF PROTEIN		Berries	FROZEN
Brewed Green Tea		Kiwi	Spinach
Almond Milk		Pear	Zucchini
Pure Water		FROZEN	ADD COLOR
Coconut Water		Banana Slices	Beets
Rice Milk		Berries	Carrots
Hemp Milk		Pitted Cherries	Red Bell Pepper
		Mango Chunks	Canned Pumpkin
		Peach Slices	
		Pineapple Chunks	

Fat	*Carbohydrate*	*Pizzazz*	*Sweetness*
1/2 Avocado	2 tbsp Rolled Oats	Vanilla	2 Dates
2 tbsp Nut Butter	1/4 cup Cooked Whole Grains	Cinnamon	1 tbsp Real Maple Syrup
1 ounce Seeds		Ginger	
1 ounce Nuts		Cardamom	1 tsp Honey
		Cocoa Powder	

CHOCOLATE SMOOTHIE

Following the mix-and-match formula on the previous page, this recipe makes a generous 16-ounce portion packed with protein, fiber, and plant nutrients. The chia seeds add satisfying fat and fiber.

1/2 cup organic unsweetened soy milk

1/2 cup plain nonfat Greek yogurt

1/2 ripe Bosc pear, with peel, cored

1/2 cup frozen mixed berries

A large handful (1-ounce) fresh spinach leaves

1/4 red bell pepper, seeded, deribbed, cut into chunks

2 tablespoons chia seeds

2 tablespoons gluten-free old-fashioned rolled oats

1 tablespoon unsweetened cocoa powder

1/2 teaspoon ground cinnamon

1/2 teaspoon pure vanilla extract

Place all the ingredients in the container of a high-speed blender. Blend until smooth.

Make-Ahead Tip

For a quick breakfast, you can put all the ingredients, except the frozen fruit, in the container of the blender and refrigerate overnight. Add the frozen fruit just before processing.

Makes 1 serving; Serving Size: 16 ounces

V | gf | ef | nf

CALORIES: 430; TOTAL FAT: 14 G; CARBOHYDRATE: 59 G; DIETARY FIBER: 24 G; PROTEIN: 26 G

BIRCHER MUESLI

Muesli is a favorite for a quick breakfast. This makes a batch perfect for a family or having it on hand for several days. Top this basic recipe with additional fresh fruit, nuts, cinnamon, or maple syrup.

8 ounces quick-cook steel cut oats

3 cups organic grass-fed 2% milk

1 cup plain nonfat yogurt

1/4 cup honey

1/2 tablespoon hazelnut flour

1/2 large Granny Smith apple, grated on the large holes of a box grater

1 small banana, peeled and sliced

In a large container with a lid, stir together the oats, milk, yogurt, honey, hazelnut flour, and grated apple. Carefully stir in the sliced banana. Cover and refrigerate for at least 1 hour and up to 4 days.

Stir before serving and add a bit more yogurt or milk if it has gotten too thick.

Makes 6 servings; Serving Size: 1 cup

V | ef

CALORIES: 280; TOTAL FAT: 5 G; CARBOHYDRATE: 49 G; DIETARY FIBER: 5 G; PROTEIN: 11 G

NO-BAKE FIBER BAR

Here's an easy-to-make oatmeal protein bar recipe that is perfect as a grab-and-go option for breakfast or refueling after a workout.

2 cups gluten-free old-fashioned rolled oats

1/4 cup flax seeds

1/4 cup chia seeds

1 cup almond or cashew butter

1/2 cup organic unsweetened oat or soy milk

2 teaspoons honey

In a medium bowl, toss together the oats, flax and chia seeds.

In a medium saucepan, combine the almond or cashew butter, soy or oat milk, and honey. Warm over medium-low heat until the nut butter is melted. Fold in the oat mixture and stir until well combined.

Press the mixture firmly and evenly into a square baking dish. Let sit until cooled and slightly hardened before cutting into 12 bars.

Makes 12 servings; Serving Size: 1 small bar

V | gf | df | ef

CALORIES: 240; TOTAL FAT: 16 G; CARBOHYDRATE: 19 G; DIETARY FIBER: 6 G; PROTEIN: 8 G

PALM COURT CAFÉ ENERGY BITES

These small energy bites can help fuel you when you need a burst of nutrition. Keep a batch in the refrigerator for you and your family.

2 cups honey

1 cup cashew butter

1 cup organic unsweetened oat or soy milk

3/4 cup hemp protein powder

2 cups chia seeds

2 cups flax seeds

10 cups gluten-free old-fashioned rolled oats

5 cups dried cranberries

Have ready a 9-by-13-inch rimmed baking pan (quarter sheet pan).

In a very large bowl, stir together the honey, cashew butter, and almond milk until smooth. Stir in the hemp protein powder, and then the chia and flax seeds. Finally, for your upper body workout, stir in the oats and cranberries. Press the mixture evenly into the pan. Refrigerate for at least 1 hour before cutting into rectangles approximately 1-by-1 1/2-inch in size. Store between layers of parchment or waxed paper in a covered container in the refrigerator for up to 2 weeks or freeze up to 2 months.

Makes 72 (1-by-1 1/2-inch) servings;
Serving Size: 1 bite

V | gf | df | ef

CALORIES: 51; TOTAL FAT: 1 G; CARBOHYDRATE: 9 G; DIETARY FIBER: 1 G; PROTEIN: 2 G

MIRAVAL
OVERNIGHT OATS

Having a healthy breakfast ready to go is key to a nutritious diet. We can avoid muffins and bagels more easily when the refrigerator contains flavorful fiber-packed overnight oats with enticing bites of banana chips, raisins, sunflower seeds, and goji berries. For those who tolerate dairy and want a breakfast that delivers more protein per serving, stir in 1/4 cup of nonfat Greek yogurt before serving. You'll need 4 jars or containers with lids holding at least 8 ounces.

1 cups gluten-free old-fashioned rolled oats

1 teaspoon ground cinnamon

1/4 teaspoon fine sea salt

1 teaspoon real maple syrup

1 teaspoon honey

2 cups unsweetened organic soy or oat milk

3/4 teaspoon pure vanilla extract

1/4 cup goji berries

1/4 cup sunflower seeds

1/4 cup dark or golden raisins

1/4 cup banana chips

Arrange a rack in the center of the oven and heat the oven to 375°F.

In a large mixing bowl, toss together the oats, cinnamon, salt, maple syrup, and honey. Spread the mixture out on a large rimmed sheet pan and bake until lightly toasted, 8 to 10 minutes. Set aside to cool.

Using the same large bowl, stir together the milk, vanilla, goji berries, sunflower seeds, and raisins. Add the oats and stir to combine. Scoop 8 ounces of the overnight oats into each jar and seal with a tight-fitting lid. Refrigerate for up to 5 days. When ready to eat, stir in a rounded tablespoon of banana chips to add a nice crunch.

Makes 4 servings; Serving Size: 1 (8-ounce) container

V | gf | df | ef | nf

CALORIES: 280; TOTAL FAT: 10 G; CARBOHYDRATE: 39 G; DIETARY FIBER: 5 G; PROTEIN: 11 G

BERRY ACAI BOWL

With a little planning, you can make a tasty berry acai bowl. The suggested toppings offer a nutritious mix of color and crunch, but you can make it your own with seasonal fruits, nuts, and seeds.

2 (3-ounce) portions Acai Granita (recipe follows)

1/2 cup Toasted Seeds (recipe follows)

1/3 cup fresh berries

1/2 banana, thinly sliced

6 tablespoons goji berries

Drizzle of honey

To make the acai bowls, place a 3-ounce portion of the granita in each bowl. Let the granita sit at room temperature to thaw slightly. Scatter 1/4 cup of toasted seeds on top of each serving. Divide berries, sliced banana, and the goji berries over each serving. Drizzle honey over the top and serve immediately.

Makes 2 servings; Serving Size: 1 bowl

V | gf | df | ef | nf

CALORIES: 460; TOTAL FAT: 25 G; CARBOHYDRATE: 57 G; DIETARY FIBER: 6 G; PROTEIN: 11 G

ACAI GRANITA

3 1/2 ounces thawed acai purée (approximately 6 standard-size packets)

1 cup fresh blueberries

1 cup 100% pomegranate juice

1/2 cup water

1/4 cup honey

In the container of a high-speed blender, combine the acai purée, blueberries, pomegranate juice, water, and honey. Blend until smooth. Divide among 6 (3-ounce) containers. Cover tightly and freeze until ready to serve.

Makes 6 servings; Serving Size: 3 ounces

CALORIES: 160; TOTAL FAT: 6 G; CARBOHYDRATE: 27 G; DIETARY FIBER: 1 G; PROTEIN: 1 G

TOASTED SEEDS

1 cup assorted seeds, such as pumpkin seeds, sunflower seeds, flax seeds, sesame seeds (black and white varieties)

Heat the oven to 300°F. Spread a mix of seeds of your choice on a rimmed sheet pan, scattering them evenly. Bake, stirring occasionally, until fragrant and golden brown, 8 to 12 minutes. Check often as they roast. Set aside to cool. Store at room temperature in a container with a tight-fitting lid.

VEGAN CINNAMON STREUSEL COFFEE CAKE

Here's our vegan take on the classic sour cream coffeecake we all know and love—laced with a cinnamon and brown sugar filling and topped with a nubby streusel covering. We added whole-wheat flour and used vegan yogurt to replace the dairy.

Vegan butter for greasing the pan

Streusel Topping

1/4 cup + 2 tablespoons unbleached all-purpose flour

1/4 cup + 2 tablespoons whole-wheat flour

2/3 cup light brown sugar

1/4 teaspoon fine sea salt

1/2 cup vegan butter, at room temperature

Filling

3/4 cup light brown sugar

1 1/2 tablespoons ground cinnamon

1/4 cup vegan butter, melted

Cake

1 cup unbleached all-purpose flour

1 cup whole-wheat flour

1 teaspoon baking powder

1/2 teaspoon baking soda

1/2 teaspoon ground cinnamon

3/4 teaspoon fine sea salt

1 1/2 cups vegan yogurt

1 cup organic cane sugar

2/3 cup organic expeller-pressed canola oil

1 teaspoon pure vanilla extract

1/2 teaspoon white vinegar

Arrange a rack in the center of the oven and heat the oven to 350°F. Grease a 9-by-13-inch baking pan with vegan butter, and then line the bottom of the pan with parchment paper. Set aside.

To make the streusel topping, in a medium bowl, use your fingers to crumble together the flours, sugar, salt, and butter until the texture of coarse sand. Set aside.

To make the filling, in a small bowl, stir together the brown sugar and cinnamon. Stir in the melted butter until evenly combined. Set aside.

To make the cake batter, in a medium bowl, sift together the flours, baking powder, baking soda, cinnamon, and salt.

In a large bowl, whisk together the yogurt, sugar, oil, vanilla, and vinegar until it is smooth and creamy like pudding. Using a rubber spatula, fold in half of the flour mixture until the flour disappears. Add the remaining flour mixture and mix just until combined. Finish by gently scraping down the sides and bottom of the bowl with a rubber spatula.

Spread the batter evenly in the prepared pan. Sprinkle the filling over the top and use a fork to dimple the filling into the batter. Top with the streusel mixture, spreading it lightly so it adheres to the batter. Bake the coffee cake until the top is browned and a toothpick inserted into the center of the cake comes out clean, 40 to 50 minutes. Transfer to a wire rack to cool. Cut into 2-inch squares.

Makes 24 servings; Serving Size: 1 (2-inch) square

V | vg | df | ef | nf

CALORIES: 241; TOTAL FAT: 12 G; CARBOHYDRATE: 32 G; DIETARY FIBER: 1 G; PROTEIN: 2 G

VANILLA ALMOND PANCAKES

Make these delicious, gluten-free pancakes on the weekend for your family or friends with toppings like mixed berries, sliced peaches, almonds, or real maple syrup.

....

1 2/3 cups white rice flour

1/2 cup almond flour

3/4 teaspoon baking powder

3/4 teaspoon baking soda

1 cup + 2 tablespoons unsweetened almond milk

3 1/2 tablespoons apple cider vinegar

1 tablespoon unrefined avocado oil, plus more for greasing the pan

1 teaspoon pure vanilla extract

1/4 teaspoon pure almond extract

2 large eggs, beaten

In a large bowl, whisk together the rice flour, almond flour, baking powder, and baking soda.

In a separate bowl, whisk together the almond milk, vinegar, oil, vanilla and almond extracts, and the eggs. Using a rubber spatula, stir the wet ingredients into dry ingredients just until the flour disappears. Let the batter rest for 10 minutes before making the pancakes. At this point the batter can transferred to a covered container and refrigerated for up to 2 days.

To make the pancakes, preheat a griddle or heavy 12-inch skillet over low heat for 5 minutes. Increase the heat to medium and brush the bottom of the pan with just enough oil to glaze it. Ladle in the pancake batter. (About half of a standard soup ladle makes a 4-inch pancake.) Don't crowd the pan—it is hard to flip pancakes that have run together. When little holes form on top of the pancakes, lift up just a little of the side to check for browning. If nicely browned, then flip the pancakes, and cook on the other side until nicely browned. Transfer to a warmed plate and serve immediately.

Makes 10 servings; Serving Size: 2 (4-inch) pancakes

V | gf | df

CALORIES: 320; TOTAL FAT: 11 G; CARBOHYDRATE: 45 G; DIETARY FIBER: 2 G; PROTEIN: 8 G

FARM EGG OMELET
WITH WILD MUSHROOMS, ARTISAN CHEESE & HERBS

The chefs at Miraval Berkshires use a sharp cow's milk cheese to fold into the breakfast omelets with wild mushrooms and fresh herbs.

....

3 large eggs

1 1/2 tablespoons Ghee (Clarified Butter, page 304)

6 ounces assorted wild mushrooms, wiped clean and sliced

1 teaspoon finely diced shallot

Fine sea salt

Freshly ground black pepper

2 ounces sharp cow's milk cheese, thinly sliced

1 tablespoon chopped fresh herbs, such as chives and chervil

Flaky sea salt

In a medium bowl, beat the eggs with a fork until fluffy. If desired, pass the eggs through a fine-mesh strainer.

In an 8-inch nonstick skillet set over medium-high heat, melt 1/2 tablespoon of the ghee. Swirl to coat the bottom of the pan. Add the mushrooms and sauté, stirring frequently, until the mushrooms are golden brown. Add the shallots and sauté until soft, about 1 minute. Season to taste with salt and pepper. Transfer the mushroom mixture to a warm plate.

Wipe out the pan and return to the heat. Add the remaining ghee. Once it is sizzling, add the eggs. Using a silicone spatula stir the eggs constantly, catching the sides and folding inwards, similar to making scrambled eggs. Lower the heat and tilt the pan so the eggs run and cover the bottom of the pan. Once the eggs begin to set, they will look like an open-faced omelet but still undercooked. Turn off the heat.

Place the slices of cheese in the center of the eggs. Lay the mushroom mixture on top. Roll the omelet by tilting the pan away from you, and gently running the spatula underneath the eggs, in order to create 3 folds. Transfer the omelet to a warm plate. Garnish with the fresh herbs and sprinkle with flaky sea salt. Serve immediately.

Makes 2 servings

V | gf | nf

CALORIES: 330; TOTAL FAT: 26 G; CARBOHYDRATE: 4 G; DIETARY FIBER: 1 G; PROTEIN: 18 G

TURKEY SAUSAGE & EGG WHITE FRITTATA

Aged Gouda cheese melts to compliment the sausage in this frittata. Refrigerate the extra caramelized leeks and use them in an omelet or as a garnish to roasted potatoes, vegetables, or grilled meats. At Miraval Arizona, this frittata sits under a breakfast salad, shaved radishes, and edible flowers.

....

1 1/2 tablespoons Ghee (Clarified Butter, page 304)

1 leek, white, and light green part only, cut into 2-inch julienne

2 ounces bulk turkey sausage

1 small garlic clove, minced

1 teaspoon peeled and minced fresh ginger

3 large egg whites, beaten

Fine sea salt

Freshly ground black pepper

1 teaspoon minced fresh thyme leaves

1 ounce aged Gouda, grated

Heat the oven to 400°F.

In an 8-inch nonstick skillet with a heatproof handle, set over medium heat, melt 1 tablespoon of the ghee. Swirl to coat the bottom of the pan. Add the leeks and sauté, stirring frequently, until caramelized, about 5 minutes. Using a slotted spoon, transfer the leeks to a plate, leaving any remaining fat in the pan.

Add the remaining 1/2 tablespoon of ghee to the pan. When melted, add the sausage and sauté, breaking up the chunks with the side of a spatula, until nicely browned, about 3 minutes. Add the garlic and ginger and sauté, stirring constantly, for 1 minute. Stir in 1 tablespoon of the caramelized leeks. Pour the beaten egg whites over top. Season with salt and pepper. Tilt the pan to cover the filling with the eggs. Sprinkle the thyme over the top and scatter half of the cheese over the frittata. Place in the oven and bake just until the eggs are set and the cheese is melted, about 4 minutes.

To serve, top the frittata with the remaining cheese. Using a silicone spatula, slide the frittata out of the pan and onto a warmed dinner plate.

Makes 1 serving

gf | nf

CALORIES: 500; TOTAL FAT: 38 G; CARBOHYDRATE: 11 G; DIETARY FIBER: 1 G; PROTEIN: 28 G

VEGAN TEXAS SCRAMBLE

A little advance planning gets you breakfast in no time. Having a batch (or a double batch) of Tofu Scramble (recipe below) in the refrigerator gives you an easy way to make a nutritious, protein-rich breakfast. The chefs at Miraval Austin reach for already diced tomatoes and bell peppers to toss into this scramble, and you can do the same with some preparatory steps.

2 teaspoons expeller-pressed grapeseed oil

1/2 cup cored, seeded, and chopped plum tomatoes

1/2 cup seeded, deribbed, and diced bell peppers

2 teaspoons chipotle seasoning

1/2 cup drained and rinsed black beans

1 recipe Tofu Scramble, (recipe follows)

4 tablespoons grated vegan cheese, for topping

Warm the oil in a large skillet over medium heat. Add the tomatoes and peppers and sauté, stirring frequently, until softened, about 2 minutes. Add the chipotle seasoning and give the vegetables a quick stir. Add the black beans and stir to heat through. Add the Tofu Scramble and toss gently to heat through and combine. Serve on warm plates garnished with vegan cheese.

Makes 2 servings

V | vg | gf | df | ef | nf

CALORIES: 410; TOTAL FAT: 23 G; CARBOHYDRATE: 22 G; DIETARY FIBER: 6 G; PROTEIN: 26 G

TOFU SCRAMBLE

2 teaspoons expeller-pressed grapeseed oil

1 [14-ounce] container firm tofu, drained, blotted dry, and crumbled

2 tablespoons nutritional yeast

2 teaspoons ground turmeric

1 teaspoon garlic powder

2 tablespoons organic unsweetened oat milk

Warm the oil in a large skillet over medium heat. Swirl to coat the bottom of the pan. Add the crumbled tofu and cook, stirring occasionally, until all the water is gone, about 3 minutes. Add the nutritional yeast, turmeric, and garlic powder. Cook, stirring frequently, for 5 minutes longer. Add the oat milk and stir until heated through. Remove from the heat. Serve on warm plates.

Makes 2 servings

V | vg | gf | df | ef | nf

CALORIES: 259; TOTAL FAT: 14 G; CARBOHYDRATE: 11 G; DIETARY FIBER: 5 G; PROTEIN: 21 G

LAMB
SHAKSHUKA

Shakshuka, a popular North African dish, is essentially eggs poached in a tomato-pepper sauce. There are many variations, and this guest favorite at Miraval Austin is made with lamb, caraway, and smoked paprika. Shop for a good-quality Italian-style tomato purée, often called passata. Make this savory egg dish for a weekend brunch or on a weeknight when you feel like having breakfast for dinner. Serve with grilled flatbread on the side.

....

4 tablespoons unrefined avocado oil

1 pound boneless leg of lamb, trimmed of excess fat and cut into 1-inch cubes

1 tablespoon caraway seeds

2 teaspoons smoked paprika (pimentón de la Vera)

1 teaspoon ground cumin

1 medium yellow onion, diced

1 red bell pepper, seeded, deribbed, and diced

4 garlic cloves, minced

6 ripe plum tomatoes, halved lengthwise, cored, seeded, and diced

1 1/2 cups tomato purée (passata)

2 cups Vegetable Stock (page 303) or low-sodium chicken stock

6 leaves lacinato kale, deribbed, cut crosswise into ribbons

Fine sea salt

Freshly ground black pepper

4 large eggs

1 tablespoon minced fresh cilantro

1 tablespoon minced fresh flat-leaf parsley

In a deep, 10-inch sauté pan, heat 2 tablespoons of the oil over medium-high heat. Add the cubed lamb and sauté, stirring frequently until browned on all sides, about 5 minutes. Using tongs, or a slotted spoon, transfer the lamb to a plate.

Add the remaining 2 tablespoons of oil to the pan, swirl to coat the bottom of the pan. Add the caraway seeds, smoked paprika, and cumin. Cook, stirring constantly, until the spices are fragrant and the caraway seeds crack in the pan for 30 seconds. Reduce the heat to medium and then add the onion, bell pepper, and garlic. Sauté, stirring frequently, until the vegetables are soft but not brown, about 5 minutes.

Add the tomatoes, tomato purée, stock, and the reserved lamb. Bring to a simmer. Lower the heat and cook, uncovered, at a slow simmer, stirring occasionally, until the lamb is fork-tender, about 50 minutes. Stir in the kale ribbons, and then add salt and pepper to taste. Cook until the kale is soft, about 2 minutes.

Using the back of a large spoon, make 4 depressions in the sauce and crack an egg into each depression. Cover the skillet and poach the eggs until the whites are set and the yolks are runny, about 4 minutes. Cook a little longer if you like your eggs more set, 5 to 7 minutes. Sprinkle the minced cilantro and parsley over the top. Serve immediately.

Makes 4 servings

gf | df | nf

CALORIES: 571; TOTAL FAT: 35 G; CARBOHYDRATE: 31 G; DIETARY FIBER: 6 G; PROTEIN: 34 G

BASIC FLATBREAD DOUGH

This dough comes together quickly using a stand mixer with the dough hook attachment but is easily made by hand, letting you enjoy the quiet rhythm of kneading.

1 cup warm water, not above 110°F

1 tablespoon active dry yeast

1/4 cup extra-virgin olive oil, plus 1 teaspoon for greasing the bowl

1/4 cup honey or organic raw agave syrup

2 cups whole-wheat flour

1 1/2 cups semolina flour

3/4 teaspoon fine sea salt

In the bowl of a stand mixer fitted with the dough hook, mix together the water, yeast, 1/4 cup of oil, and the honey. Let the mixture stand until foamy, about 5 to 10 minutes.

Meanwhile, stir together the whole-wheat flour, semolina, and salt.

With the mixer on low speed, add the flour to the yeast mixture, 1/2 cup at a time. After all the flour has been added, continue to mix the dough on low speed for 5 minutes.

Use the remaining 1 teaspoon of oil to grease a large bowl. Place the dough in the bowl. Cover loosely with plastic wrap and let sit in a warm spot until it doubles in size, about 1 to 2 hours (timing will depend on how cool or warm your kitchen is—ideally about 72°F).

Turn out the dough onto a lightly floured work surface and divide it into 12 equal portions. (A kitchen scale comes in handy here; otherwise eyeball the portions.) At this point the dough is ready to use. Alternatively, place the balls in a covered container and refrigerate for several hours or up to 2 days. Remove from the refrigerator 1 hour before you plan to stretch the flatbreads.

To make the flatbreads, one at a time, roll out each portion to 1/4-inch thick, making sure the center is not stretched too thin. The flatbreads "tighten" as they cook, so making sure they are rolled very thin will help. Use as directed in the recipes on page 240 and 241.

Makes 12 servings; Serving Size: 1 flatbread

V | vg | df | ef | nf

CALORIES: 170; TOTAL FAT: 4 G; CARBOHYDRATE: 29 G; DIETARY FIBER: 3 G; PROTEIN: 5 G

appetizers & soups

APPETIZERS

SOUPS

ROASTED BABAGANOUSH

Use the globe variety of eggplant, which are the big purple-black ones you often see in the market. Look for eggplants that are firm, feel heavy for their size, and have a glossy skin that is neither shriveled nor has brown spots. Serve this dip with crudités or with toasted whole-wheat pita chips.

1 large eggplant [about 1 1/4 pounds]

1/8 cup peeled garlic cloves

1/2 teaspoon fine sea salt, plus more as needed

1/3 cup tahini (sesame seed paste)

1/3 cup fresh lemon juice

2 1/2 tablespoons extra-virgin olive oil

Freshly ground white pepper

Arrange a rack in the center of the oven and heat the oven to 425°F. Have ready a rimmed sheet pan lined with aluminum foil. (See **Note**)

Prick the eggplant all over with the tines of a fork. Place the eggplant on the prepared sheet pan and roast the eggplant until it collapses when you press the top and is fork-tender, about 45 minutes. Let cool for 15 minutes before scooping out the pulp. Discard the skin and stem end of the eggplant.

In the workbowl of a food processor fitted with the metal blade, process the garlic with 1/2 teaspoon of salt until minced. Add the eggplant pulp along with the tahini and lemon juice. Add the olive oil and process until smooth. Add pepper to taste, along with additional salt, if needed. Transfer to a serving bowl and serve immediately or cover and refrigerate until ready to serve. (The dip can be prepared up to 2 days in advance.)

Note:
As an alternative, to add a smokier flavor to the babaganoush, you can roast the eggplants on a charcoal or gas grill. Prepare a medium-low fire in the grill. Prepare the eggplant as directed above, but grill-roast it, covered, directly on the grill rack until completely fork-tender, about 30 minutes. Turn the eggplant every 10 minutes so the skin chars evenly. Remove from the grill and cool for 15 minutes before scooping out the pulp.

Makes 8 servings; Serving Size: 1/4 cup

V | vg | gf | df | ef | nf

CALORIES: 70; TOTAL FAT: 6 G; CARBOHYDRATE: 4 G; DIETARY FIBER: 1 G; PROTEIN: 2 G

BLISTERING SHISHITOS

Miraval Austin's Cypress Creek Farm produces Shishito peppers every summer and the kitchen prepares them in a searing hot pan or on the grill. These peppers are sneaky because they can vary in heat level—sometimes mild, sometimes hot—and about one in every five can make your eyes water. Serve them as an appetizer or on the side of an entrée.

1/2 pound Shishito peppers, washed and blotted dry

2 tablespoons unrefined avocado oil

1 teaspoon flaky, natural sea salt

1 to 2 teaspoons store-bought balsamic glaze

In a large bowl, toss the peppers with 1 tablespoon of the oil. Sprinkle with salt and toss again.

Heat a large cast-iron skillet over medium-high heat. Add the remaining tablespoon of oil and swirl to coat the bottom of the pan. Scatter the peppers in the pan and sear, stirring frequently or shaking the pan, until the skins blister and the peppers are crisp-tender, about 2 minutes. (If grilling the peppers, use a perforated grill pan.)

Transfer the peppers to a serving bowl, drizzle with a touch of balsamic glaze, and serve hot.

Makes 4 servings

V | vg | gf | df | ef | nf

CALORIES: 81; TOTAL FAT: 7 G; CARBOHYDRATE: 5 G; DIETARY FIBER: 0 G; PROTEIN: 0 G

HARVEST MOON HUMMUS

With a food processor, making hummus at home is not only delectable and fresher tasting than store-bought varieties, but also easy to make. It takes about one minute of whizzing to create this guest favorite at the Harvest Moon Restaurant at Miraval Berkshires. Serve with a selection of crudités or toasted whole-wheat pita chips.

1 garlic clove

1/2 teaspoon fine sea salt, plus more as needed

1/4 teaspoon freshly ground white pepper, plus more as needed

1 [15oz] can chickpeas, drained and rinsed

1/4 cup extra-virgin olive oil

1/4 cup tahini (sesame seed paste)

2 tablespoons fresh lemon juice

Ground sumac for garnish

In the workbowl of a food processor fitted with the metal blade, process the garlic, salt, and pepper until the garlic is finely minced. Add the chickpeas, olive oil, tahini, and lemon juice. Process the mixture until smooth and puréed. Add water, a tablespoon at a time, if needed, to make the hummus creamy and the right consistency for dipping. Season to taste with salt and pepper.

Transfer to a serving bowl. Cover and refrigerate for 2 hours before serving to meld the flavors. Garnish the hummus with a sprinkling of ground sumac before serving. The hummus can be made up to 3 days in advance.

Makes about 2 cups; Serving Size: 1/4 cup

V | vg | gf | df | ef | nf

CALORIES: 170; TOTAL FAT: 14 G; CARBOHYDRATE: 10 G; DIETARY FIBER: 3 G; PROTEIN: 4 G

BEET HUMMUS

*Vividly colored and deeply delicious, beet hummus is a delightful appetizer for entertaining. Serve the hummus with a selection of crudités or toasted whole-wheat pita chips. Plan ahead and roast beets (as directed in the **Note** below) several hours or 1 day before making the beet hummus. This way the beets are cooked and ready to purée. You'll need 2 cans of chickpeas and will end up with about 1/3 cup leftover. Save them to sprinkle on salads.*

2 garlic cloves

1 teaspoon fine sea salt

2 cups drained and rinsed canned chickpeas

1/2 cup tahini (sesame seed paste)

1/4 cup plus 2 tablespoons extra-virgin olive oil

1/4 cup puréed roasted beets (see **Note**)

Juice of 1 lemon, or more, if needed

1 tablespoon paprika

In the workbowl of a food processor fitted with the metal blade, process the garlic and salt until the garlic is finely minced. Add the chickpeas, tahini, olive oil, beets, lemon juice, and paprika. Process the mixture until smooth and puréed. Add water, a tablespoon at a time, if needed, to make the hummus creamy and the right consistency for dipping. Season to taste with additional lemon juice and salt, if desired.

Transfer to a serving bowl. Cover and refrigerate for at least 2 hours before serving to allow the flavors to meld. The hummus can be made up to 3 days in advance.

Note:
To roast beets, heat the oven to 375°F. Scrub the beets and then trim the tops and tail of each beet. Lay a long sheet of aluminum foil on a large rimmed sheet pan. Place the prepared beets in the center. Drizzle the olive oil over top. Season the beets with the salt and a few grinds of pepper. Toss the beets with the oil. Pierce each beet 4 to 5 times with a fork. Bring up the sides of the foil to form a tightly sealed pouch. Roast the beets on the sheet pan until fork-tender, 45 to 55 minutes, depending on the size of the beets. Remove the beets from the oven and open the pouch. Allow the beets to cool for 10 to 15 minutes. Slip the skins off the beets, using a paper towel to help scrub off any tough-to-remove skins. (This is best done wearing disposable gloves.) Purée one beet for this recipe and measure out 1/4 cup. The remaining beets can be refrigerated and then sliced or quartered for salads.

Makes about 2 cups; Serving Size: 1/4 cup

V | vg | gf | df | ef | nf

CALORIES: 110; TOTAL FAT: 5 G; CARBOHYDRATE: 14 G; DIETARY FIBER: 2 G; PROTEIN: 4 G

AUTUMN BEETS
WITH SHERRY VINAIGRETTE & BUCKWHEAT TUILE

This artful salad embraces all the seasonal produce of late summer and early autumn—baby beets, fresh figs, and a shower of bitter greens and herbs. Dressed with a lovely sherry vinaigrette and topped with a buckwheat tuile, this composed salad's components can be made ahead of time. You won't need to use all of the dressing; refrigerate the rest and use it for any fresh salad.

Sherry Vinaigrette

1 cup expeller-pressed grapeseed oil

1/2 cup extra-virgin olive oil

2 teaspoons Dijon mustard

2 teaspoons minced shallots

1/2 cup sherry vinegar

4 teaspoons fresh lemon juice

1 teaspoon honey

1 teaspoon orange zest

Fine sea salt

Freshly ground black pepper

1 teaspoon minced fresh rosemary

1 teaspoon snipped fresh chives

Salad

8 baby red beets, trimmed and scrubbed

8 baby golden beets, trimmed and scrubbed

8 baby candy striped beets, trimmed and scrubbed

2 tablespoons extra-virgin olive oil

1/2 teaspoon fine sea salt

Freshly ground black pepper

12 ounces good-quality feta cheese

1/2 cup full-fat Greek yogurt

8 ounces frisée lettuce, washed and dried

4 Brown Turkey figs, cut into quarters

4 kumquats, thinly sliced

4 ounces fresh chives, snipped into 1/2-inch lengths

4 ounces fresh chervil

4 ounces baby sorrel leaves

4 Buckwheat Tuiles, optional, (recipe follows)

To make the vinaigrette, whisk together the grapeseed and olive oil in a 2-cup measuring cup. In the container of a blender or using an immersion blender, combine the mustard, shallots, vinegar, lemon juice, honey, and orange zest. Slowly pour in the oil mixture and blend to form an emulsified dressing. Add salt and pepper to taste. Stir in the rosemary and chives. Transfer to a covered container and set aside until ready to use, or refrigerate for up to 5 days.

To roast the beets, heat the oven to 375°F. Lay a long sheet of aluminum foil on a large rimmed sheet pan. Place the prepared beets in the center. Drizzle the olive oil over top. Season the beets with the salt and a few grinds of pepper. Toss the beets with the oil. Pierce each beet 4 to 5 times with a fork. Bring up the sides of the foil to form a tightly sealed pouch. Roast the beets on the sheet pan until fork-tender, 45 to 55 minutes, depending on the size of the beets.

Remove the beets from the oven and open the pouch. Allow the beets to cool for 10 to 15 minutes. Slip the skins off the beets. This is best done wearing disposable gloves. Use a paper towel to help scrub off any skin from the beets that is tough to remove. Cut the beets into 1-inch squares and place in a medium bowl. (There is no need for perfection here; just bite-size squares of beets.) Toss the beets with 1/3 cup of the dressing. Allow to marinate 1 to 2 hours at room temperature, or cover and refrigerate up to 24 hours.

V | gf | nf

CALORIES: 540; TOTAL FAT: 30 G; CARBOHYDRATE: 56 G; DIETARY FIBER: 15 G; PROTEIN: 18 G

Combine the feta cheese and yogurt in a food processor. Pulse until blended and is light and fluffy, about 30 seconds. Transfer to a covered container and refrigerate until ready to use.

To assemble the salad, select 4 large salad plates. Spread a generous 1/4 cup of the whipped feta in a circle at the center of each plate. Divide the beets evenly and arrange artistically in a circle on each plate. Lightly dress the frisée with some of the vinaigrette. Divide among the plates scattering it about. Divide the figs and kumquats among the 4 plates. And then scatter the chives, chervil, and sorrel randomly on each plate. To finish, rest one of the tuiles on top. Serve immediately.

Makes 4 servings

BUCKWHEAT TUILE

1 large egg white, at room temperature

3 1/2 tablespoons buckwheat flour

2 tablespoons water

2 tablespoons Clarified Butter (page 304)

1 teaspoon honey

1 teaspoon fine sea salt

1/4 teaspoon freshly ground white pepper

In a small bowl, whisk together the egg white, flour, water, clarified butter, honey, salt, and pepper.

Heat an 8-inch nonstick omelet pan over medium heat. Pour about 2 tablespoons of the batter into the pan to create a thin crepe-like tuile. Allow to set on one side, about 2 minutes, and then gently flip it over using a silicone spatula or fork and cook all the way through, about 2 minutes longer. Remove from the pan to a wire rack. Repeat to make the remaining tuiles. To keep them crisp, allow them to dry at room temperature. Store in an airtight container at room temperature for up to 2 days.

Makes 4 tuiles

CALORIES: 88; TOTAL FAT: 7 G; CARBOHYDRATE: 6 G;
DIETARY FIBER: 1 G; PROTEIN: 2 G

CRISPY BRUSSEL SPROUTS
WITH SHIITAKE "BACON"

The Brussels sprout, a cute but unremarkable vegetable on its own, takes on big flavors and terrific texture when high-heat-roasted until slightly charred and crisp. The chefs at Miraval Berkshires give this appetizer a Korean flavor profile with "shiitake bacon" and a vinaigrette that includes Korean gochujang paste. Look for this spicy, savory, and sweet fermented condiment in specialty stores or order it online. While we call the shiitake mushrooms "bacon," think of them as "shiitake jerky," a flavor-packed, dried, and chewy version of the mushrooms.

4 cups (about 1 pound) Brussels sprouts, trimmed and halved

2 tablespoons extra-virgin olive oil

Fine sea salt

Freshly ground black pepper

1 cup Shiitake Bacon (recipe follows)

1/2 cup Gochujang Vinaigrette (recipe follows)

2 tablespoons toasted white sesame seeds

Arrange a rack in the center of the oven and heat the oven to 425°F. Have ready a large, rimmed sheet pan (if you have a convection oven, use it for roasting the Brussels sprouts).

Toss the sprouts with the oil and season lightly with salt and pepper. Roast until crisp-tender and beautifully browned at the edges, about 10 minutes. Set aside to cool completely. The sprouts can be roasted up to 2 hours in advance.

When ready to serve, scatter the shiitake bacon over the pan of roasted sprouts and return it to the hot oven until crisp and heated through, 5 to 7 minutes longer. Divide the sprouts and bacon among 4 warmed salad plates. Drizzle a generous spoonful of the vinaigrette over each portion, adding more, if desired. Sprinkle 1/2 tablespoon of sesame seeds over the top. Serve immediately.

Makes 4 servings

V | gf | df | ef | nf

CALORIES: 460; TOTAL FAT: 25 G; CARBOHYDRATE: 45 G; DIETARY FIBER: 9 G; PROTEIN: 18 G

SHIITAKE "BACON"

2 tablespoons Miraval Oil Blend (page 304) plus more to grease the sheet pan

2 tablespoons gluten-free soy sauce

2 tablespoons organic cane sugar

1 tablespoon smoked paprika (pimentón de la Vera)

1 1/2 teaspoons unsulfured dark molasses (not blackstrap)

1/2 teaspoon freshly ground black pepper

1/4 teaspoon celery salt

1 pound shiitake mushrooms, stems removed, wiped clean with a damp paper towel, caps very thinly sliced

Heat the oven to 350°F. If you happen to have a convection oven or air fryer, use that, and set the temperature to 325°F. Have ready a rimmed sheet pan lightly greased with oil.

In a large bowl, whisk together the oil, soy sauce, sugar, paprika, molasses, pepper, and celery salt until the sugar dissolves. Add the mushrooms and toss until well coated. Spread the mixture out on the prepared pan and roast the mushrooms until they have dried out, about 15 to 20 minutes in a convection oven, but closer to 30 minutes in a radiant oven. Check frequently after the 15 minute mark to check for dryness and "chewiness." Set aside to cool. The mushrooms can be prepared up to 3 days in advance. Store refrigerated in a covered container. Bring to room temperature before using in the salad.

Makes about 1 cup; Serving Size: 1/4 cup

CALORIES: 220; TOTAL FAT: 8 G; CARBOHYDRATE: 26 G; DIETARY FIBER: 5 G; PROTEIN: 13 G

GOCHUJANG VINAIGRETTE

3 tablespoons rice wine vinegar

2 tablespoons honey

2 tablespoons gochujang paste

1 teaspoon finely minced fresh ginger

2 garlic cloves, minced

2 tablespoons toasted sesame oil

In a small bowl, whisk together the vinegar, honey, gochujang paste, ginger, and garlic. Slowly pour in the oil, whisking constantly until the dressing is emulsified. Set aside until ready to use, or transfer to a glass jar with a tight-fitting lid and refrigerate for up to 3 days.

Makes a generous 1/2 cup; Serving Size: 2 tablespoons

CALORIES: 110; TOTAL FAT: 9 G; CARBOHYDRATE: 9 G; DIETARY FIBER: 0 G; PROTEIN: 0 G

TEXAS SHRIMP & ARTICHOKE

At Miraval Austin, the chefs love to feature Texas artichokes in springtime. They are in season then, but the season is short. To make the most of them, they steam them to open like a flower on a plate. Tarragon aioli is spooned into the center and sautéed shrimp gingerly hang on the edges. The artichokes and aioli can both be made up to 1 day before serving.

4 large artichokes, stem end cut close to the base

Tarragon Aioli

2 garlic cloves

1 teaspoon lemon zest

1 large egg yolk

3 teaspoons fresh lemon juice

1/2 cup expeller-pressed grapeseed oil

1/2 cup extra-virgin olive oil

2 tablespoons finely chopped fresh tarragon

2 tablespoons unrefined avocado oil

16 jumbo (10 to 12 per pound) gulf prawns, peeled with the tails left on, and deveined

Fine sea salt

Freshly ground black pepper

1/4 cup micro greens, for garnish

To steam the artichokes, place them, bottom sides up, in a steamer basket over 2 to 3 inches of boiling water. Cover and steam until the bottoms feel tender when pierced with a paring knife, 35 to 45 minutes. Check the water level halfway through and add water, if needed. Drain and cool. Spread open the center petals carefully so you can see into the middle of the artichoke. Using a soup spoon, gently scrape and remove the purple prickly leaves and the thistle fuzz that protects the artichoke heart. Twist if needed to remove all of the center leaf grouping, exposing the artichoke heart. Repeat with the remaining artichokes. For presentation, gently open up each artichoke so it looks like a little bowl with the surrounding leaves as the walls of the bowl. Set aside. (The artichokes can be prepared up to this point and refrigerated in a cover container until ready to serve. Remove from the refrigerator 2 hours before serving.)

While the artichokes are steaming, make the aioli. In the container of a high-speed blender, combine the garlic, 2 teaspoons of lemon juice, and the egg yolk. Blend to mince the garlic. Slowly add the oils and blend until the sauce is emulsified. Transfer the aioli to a small bowl and fold in the remaining 1 teaspoon of lemon juice, lemon zest, and tarragon. Refrigerate until ready to serve.

Just before serving, sauté the shrimp. Warm 2 tablespoons of oil in a large skillet set over medium heat. Add the shrimp, season with salt and pepper, and sauté, stirring frequently, until they turn pink and are cooked through, 4 to 5 minutes.

To serve, place a tablespoon of aioli into the center of each artichoke. With the prawn tails pointed downward, hang 4 prawns on each artichoke, spacing them evenly around the sides. Garnish the center of each artichoke with a tablespoon of micro greens. Serve immediately.

Makes 4 servings; Serving Size: 1 artichoke

gf | df | nf

CALORIES: 260; TOTAL FAT: 18 G; CARBOHYDRATE: 18 G; DIETARY FIBER: 9 G; PROTEIN: 11 G

GRILLED FLATBREAD
WITH BLUE CHEESE, DATES & CARAMELIZED ONIONS

In our opinion, the best strategy for making flatbreads at home is to make the dough and refrigerate it, either a day in advance or on the morning of the day you serve them. Caramelizing onions in advance can make this appetizer a breeze to assemble. The flatbreads pick up a lightly charred, smoky quality if made on a grill. Slick the grill grates with a little unrefined avocado oil before baking.

4 portions Basic Flatbread dough (page 227)

1 cup Caramelized Onions (page 306)

1 cup blue cheese crumbles

16 Medjool dates, quartered lengthwise and pitted

Balsamic glaze, store-bought

Arrange a rack in the center of the oven and heat the oven to 400°F.

Lightly flour a clean work surface. Stretch the dough by hand or use a rolling pin to form a flatbread that is approximately 1/4-inch thick, being careful not to stretch it too thin at the center. These do not need to be perfect circles, but making sure they are very thin helps them get crisp when griddled.

Place a wide frying pan, preferably cast iron, over medium-high heat. Carefully place the flatbread in the pan and cook until it bubbles and toasts on one side, about 3 minutes. Flip and cook the other side until bubbly, crisp, and brown, about 2 minutes longer. Repeat to griddle the remaining flatbreads.

Spread 1/4 cup of caramelized onions on each griddled flatbread. Sprinkle 1/4 cup of the cheese over top. Stud the tops with 8 pieces of dates. Bake the flatbreads on a pizza stone or large sheet pan until the cheese has melted. Drizzle balsamic glaze over the top and serve immediately.

Makes 4 servings

V | ef | nf

CALORIES: 470; TOTAL FAT: 20 G; CARBOHYDRATE: 58 G; DIETARY FIBER: 4 G; PROTEIN: 17 G

GRILLED FLATBREAD
WITH WHITE BEAN SPREAD & MUSHROOMS

Flatbreads are hugely popular at Miraval Resorts. The dough bubbles and crisps up as it hits the hot pan or grill, creating the perfect base for a myriad of toppings. For this recipe, a protein-rich, vegan white bean spread is spooned over the flatbread and then topped with sautéed mushrooms, artichoke hearts, roasted red peppers, and cheese. Use vegan cheese, if desired. Make your own roasted red peppers, if so inclined, or buy a jar of roasted red peppers. They are a terrific pantry staple.

4 portions Basic Flatbread dough (page 227)

1/2 cup White Bean Spread (recipe follows)

1/2 cup chopped shiitake mushrooms, sautéed

8 canned artichoke hearts, quartered

1/2 cup jarred roasted red peppers, thinly sliced

1/4 cup shredded mozzarella cheese

V | ef | nf

Arrange a rack in the center of the oven and heat the oven to 400°F.

Lightly flour a clean work surface, and stretch the dough by hand to form a flatbread that is approximately 1/4-inch thick, being careful not to stretch it too thin at the center. These do not need to be perfect circles.

Place a wide frying pan, preferably cast-iron, over medium-high heat. Carefully place the flatbread in the pan and cook until it bubbles and toasts on one side, about 3 minutes. Flip and cook the other side until bubbly, crisp, and brown, about 2 minutes longer. Repeat to griddle the remaining flatbreads.

Spoon 2 tablespoons of the bean spread evenly over each flatbread. Layer 2 tablespoons of the sautéed mushrooms on top. Scatter 8 pieces of artichoke on each one, along with 2 tablespoons of the peppers. Sprinkle a tablespoon of cheese over the top. Arrange on a large, rimmed sheet pan and bake until heated through and the cheese is melted. Serve immediately.

Makes 4 servings

CALORIES: 260; TOTAL FAT: 8 G; CARBOHYDRATE: 38 G; DIETARY FIBER: 6 G; PROTEIN: 11 G

....

WHITE BEAN SPREAD

1/2 cup cooked white beans

1/2 cup extra-firm tofu

1/4 teaspoon minced garlic

1/3 cup fresh spinach, packed

2 teaspoons rice wine vinegar

Pinch fine sea salt

Pinch freshly ground black pepper

In the workbowl of a food processor fitted with the metal blade, purée the beans, tofu, garlic, spinach, vinegar, salt, and pepper until puréed and smooth. Cover and refrigerate until ready to use.

Makes 1 cup; Serving Size: 1/4 cup

V | vg | gf | df | ef | nf

CALORIES: 53; TOTAL FAT: 2 G; CARBOHYDRATE: 5 G; DIETARY FIBER: 2 G; PROTEIN: 4 G

ROASTED BONE BROTH

Talk to your butcher and plan ahead so you have the quantity and type of beef bones needed to make this nutrient-dense beef bone broth. It makes a big batch of broth, but you could cut the recipe in half if desired. Follow all the creative variations at the end of the recipe to turn this roasted bone broth into other delicious sipping broths.

1 large yellow onion, cut into eight wedges

3 pounds beef bones, knuckles and legs

Fine sea salt

Freshly ground black pepper

1 tablespoon unrefined avocado oil

1 carrot, trimmed and coarsely chopped

1 rib celery, trimmed and coarsely chopped

3 garlic cloves, peeled

3 bay leaves

1 sprig fresh flat-leaf parsley

1 sprig fresh thyme

1 1/2 teaspoons fennel seeds

1/2 teaspoon black peppercorns

3 whole cloves

3 quarts [12 cups] water

Arrange an oven rack 6 inches from the broiler and turn on the broiler. Arrange the onions on a rimmed sheet pan and broil until charred at the edges, flipping once to char both sides. Set aside. Move the oven rack to the center of the oven and heat the oven to 400°F.

Arrange the beef bones in a large roasting pan or on a large, rimmed sheet pan. Season on all sides with salt and pepper. Roast for 20 minutes. Set aside.

Have ready a 6-quart stock pot, or one large enough to hold the beef bones and 3 quarts of water. Place the stock pot over medium heat and add the oil. Swirl to coat the bottom of the pot. Add the charred onions, carrots, and celery. Sauté, stirring frequently, until the vegetables are soft but not brown, about 5 minutes. Add the garlic cloves, bay leaves, parsley, thyme, fennel seeds, peppercorns, and cloves. Give the ingredients a stir, and then use tongs to lay the browned beef bones on top. Add the water and bring to a boil. Reduce the heat to low, partially cover the pot, and simmer for 6 to 8 hours.

Using tongs, remove the beef bones from the pot and discard. Strain the roasted beef broth through a fine-mesh strainer or through a colander lined with cheesecloth into a large container. Discard the solids. Cool to room temperature and then ladle the mixture into quart-size jars with tight-fitting lids. Refrigerate for up to 4 days or freeze for up to 2 months.

Makes about 10 cups; Serving Size: 3/4 cup

gf | df | ef | nf

CALORIES: 30; TOTAL FAT: 0 G; CARBOHYDRATE: 0 G; DIETARY FIBER: 0 G; PROTEIN: 5 G

Afternoon Sipping Broth Variations:

MISO MUSHROOM:

To 2 quarts (8 cups) of basic bone broth, add one (3-inch) piece kombu and 3 dried shiitake mushrooms. Simmer the broth for 20 minutes and then use a slotted spoon to remove the kombu and mushrooms. Stir in 1 1/2 cups shiro miso. Simmer the broth, without letting it boil, for 20 minutes.

BAY LEAF AND CLOVE:

To 2 quarts (8 cups) of basic bone broth, add 4 bay leaves and 3 whole cloves. Simmer the broth for 20 minutes and then use a slotted spoon to remove the bay leaves and cloves.

GINGER TURMERIC:

To 2 quarts (8 cups) of basic bone broth, add 1/2 cup roughly chopped fresh ginger, 1/2 cup peeled garlic cloves, juice of 1/2 lemon, and 2 tablespoons of ground turmeric. Simmer the broth for 20 minutes. Pour through a fine-mesh strainer.

FIRE CIDER BOOST:

To 2 quarts (8 cups) of basic bone broth, add 1/4 teaspoon cayenne pepper, 1/4 teaspoon ground cinnamon, 1-ounce fresh oregano leaves, and 1/2 cup fire cider raw vinegar. Simmer the broth for 20 minutes. Pour through a fine-mesh strainer.

VEGETARIAN MINERAL BROTH

Here's a weekend cooking project if you love to make nutrient-dense broths and stocks. The recipe could easily be cut in half if you don't have a big stockpot or want to make it in a large slow cooker. Keep quarts of this in the freezer for quick meals. Look for dried kombu, a member of the kelp family and used widely in Japanese cooking, in the Asian foods section of most supermarkets. It adds an umami flavor to the mineral broth.

· ·

3 carrots, trimmed and scrubbed

1 yellow onion, coarsely chopped

1 leek, white and light green part only, coarsely chopped

1/2 fennel bulb, including the tops, bottom trimmed, halved and coarsely chopped

1/2 bunch celery, bottom end removed, ribs coarsely chopped (include leafy tops)

2 leaves of kale, including stem, coarsely chopped

1/2 bunch flat-leafy parsley

3 sprigs fresh thyme

6 garlic cloves, peeled

1 1/2-inch piece fresh ginger, peeled, cut into thin slices

1 strip kombu

6 black peppercorns

2 juniper or allspice berries

1 bay leaf

4 quarts (16 cups) water

Fine sea salt

In a 6-quart stock pot, combine the carrots, onion, leek, fennel, celery, kale leaves, parsley, thyme, garlic, ginger, kombu, peppercorns, juniper or allspice berries, and bay leaves.

Add the water. Bring to a boil over high heat, and then reduce the heat to low and simmer, partially covered, for 6 to 8 hours. At this point all the deep vegetable flavors and nutrients will be extracted.

Remove from the heat and let cool for 30 minutes, and add salt to taste.

Strain the vegetable mineral broth through a fine-mesh strainer or through a colander lined with cheesecloth into a large container. Discard the solids. Cool to room temperature and then ladle the mixture into quart-size jars with tight-fitting lids. Refrigerate for up to 5 days or freeze for up to 2 months.

Makes about 10 cups; Serving Size: 3/4 cup

V | vg | gf | df | ef | nf

CALORIES: 36; TOTAL FAT: 0 G; CARBOHYDRATE: 8 G; DIETARY FIBER: 2 G; PROTEIN: 1 G

ASPARAGUS POTAGE

In the spring, when asparagus is fresh in the garden and available at farmers markets, the chefs at Miraval Arizona make this velvety soup. Asparagus has such a short season that enjoying it as an appetizer, salad, accompaniment to a main dish—and here, as a soup—takes full advantage of this glorious vegetable.

6 tablespoons grass-fed unsalted butter

1 leek, white and light green part only, chopped

1 medium yellow onion, halved and cut crosswise into thin slices

1 large garlic clove, coarsely chopped

1 small shallot, sliced

1 Yukon Gold potato, peeled and diced

6 cups water

1 3/4 pounds fresh asparagus, tough woody bottoms snapped off, spears cut crosswise into 1-inch pieces

3/4 cup heavy (whipping) cream

4 ounces baby spinach

1 tablespoon truffle oil

1/8 teaspoon cayenne pepper

Fine sea salt

Freshly ground black pepper

Generous pinch freshly grated nutmeg

In a large soup pot set over medium heat, melt the butter. Add the leeks, onion, garlic, and shallot. Sauté, stirring, frequently, until the onion mixture is soft but not brown, about 8 minutes. Add the diced potatoes and water. Bring to a boil and then reduce the heat and simmer, partially covered, until the potatoes are tender, about 20 minutes. Add the asparagus, bring back to a simmer, and cook until the asparagus is tender and bright green, about 3 to 5 minutes longer, depending on the thickness of the spears. Remove from the heat. Add the cream and spinach. Let cool 10 minutes.

In the container of a high-speed blender, process the soup in batches until puréed. Return the soup to the pot. Add the truffle oil, cayenne pepper, and season to taste with salt, pepper, and a generous pinch of nutmeg. Serve immediately or set aside to cool and refrigerate in a covered container. The soup can be made up to 3 days in advance.

Makes 8 cups; Serving Size: 1 cup

V | gf | ef | nf

CALORIES: 224; TOTAL FAT: 18 G; CARBOHYDRATE: 11 G; DIETARY FIBER: 3 G; PROTEIN: 4 G

JACKFRUIT POZOLE

This recipe is an innovative twist on classic pozole, which is traditionally made with pork. Jackfruit, typically full of nutrients and fiber, takes on a meaty texture in this vegan version. To best concentrate the flavors, make it 1 day ahead of serving.

1 1/2 dried guajillo chiles, stemmed and seeded

1 dried ancho chile, stemmed and seeded

1 dried chile de árbol, stemmed and seeded

4 cups Vegetable Stock (page 303) or store-bought vegetable broth

1 1/4 cups (10-ounces) drained, cooked white hominy

1/3 white onion, diced, with more reserved for garnish

2 garlic cloves

1 tablespoon Miraval Oil Blend (page 304)

2/3 cup (3 1/2 ounces) drained jackfruit

Fine sea salt

Freshly ground black pepper

1 small zucchini, ends trimmed, diced

3 tablespoons chopped cilantro leaves

4 radishes, trimmed and thinly sliced

6 wedges of lime

Put the guajillo, ancho, and chile de árbol in a small saucepan and add 2 cups of water. Bring to a simmer over medium-high heat and simmer the chiles for 10 minutes. Set aside to cool.

Meanwhile, in a large saucepan set over medium heat, bring the vegetable stock and hominy to a simmer. Reduce the heat to low, partially cover the pan, and cook at a bare simmer while you prepare the chiles.

Drain the chiles in a strainer set over a bowl. Reserve 1/2 cup of the water you cooked the chiles in and discard the rest.

In the container of a high-speed blender, combine the simmered chiles, onion, garlic, and the reserved chile water. Blend until smooth. Set aside.

In a medium sauté pan set over medium heat, warm the oil and swirl to coat the bottom of the pan. Add the jackfruit and brown on both sides. Pour the blended chile sauce over the jackfruit and reduce the heat to low. Simmer for 10 minutes, using a fork to shred the jackfruit as it cooks down. Season lightly with salt and pepper.

While the jackfruit is simmering, ladle 1 cup of the hominy-stock mixture into the blender and blend until smooth. Pour this mixture back into the pot with the remaining stock and hominy. Add the shredded jackfruit with all the sauce from the pan into the pot with the pozole. Add the diced zucchini, and simmer until the zucchini is tender, 6 to 8 minutes longer. Season to taste with additional salt and pepper.

Cool the soup to room temperature and then transfer to a covered container and refrigerate for at least 8 hours, preferably overnight, to allow the flavors to meld. Heat before serving. Ladle into warmed soup bowls and garnish with chopped cilantro, diced onion, and sliced radish, if desired. Serve immediately with wedges of lime.

Makes 6 servings; Serving Size: 1 cup

V | vg | gf | df | ef | nf

CALORIES: 130; TOTAL FAT: 4 G; CARBOHYDRATE: 19 G; DIETARY FIBER: 2 G; PROTEIN: 3 G

LEMON CHICKEN SOUP

This comforting bowl of chicken soup combines the brightness of lemon, a hint of ginger, cumin, turmeric, and the hearty addition of chickpeas and rice.

....

1 teaspoon ground turmeric

1 teaspoon ground cumin

1 teaspoon freshly ground black pepper

1/2 teaspoon fine sea salt

2 pounds boneless, skinless chicken breasts

4 tablespoons Miraval Oil Blend (page 304)

1 1/2 cups finely chopped yellow onion

1/3 cup finely chopped celery

1 teaspoon minced garlic

1 teaspoon minced fresh ginger

6 cups homemade or store-bought low-sodium chicken broth

2 bay leaves

2 strips zested lemon peel

1/3 cup basmati rice

1 [15oz/425g] can chickpeas, drained and rinsed

2 tablespoons fresh lemon juice

Mix together the turmeric, cumin, pepper, and salt. Season the chicken all over with the spice mixture.

In a large skillet set over medium-high heat, warm 2 tablespoons of the oil and swirl to coat the bottom of the pan. Add the chicken and sauté until lightly browned on one side, and then flip and brown the other side, 5 to 7 minutes. The chicken will be seared on both sides but not completely cooked through. Set aside on a clean plate to cool slightly. Cut the chicken into 1-inch dice.

In a soup pot or Dutch oven, heat the remaining 2 tablespoons of oil over medium heat. Add the onion, celery, and garlic. Sauté, until soft and lightly browned, about 4 minutes. Add the ginger and sauté 1 minute longer. Add the chicken, broth, bay leaves, and lemon peel. Bring to a simmer and cook for 15 minutes. Add the rice, chickpeas, and lemon juice. Bring back to a simmer and cook until the rice is tender, about 20 minutes longer. Remove the bay leaves and lemon peel. Season to taste with salt and pepper. Serve immediately.

Makes 10 servings; Serving Size: 1 cup

gf | df | ef | nf

CALORIES: 200; TOTAL FAT: 8 G; CARBOHYDRATE: 14 G; DIETARY FIBER: 2 G; PROTEIN: 25 G

salads & sides

SALADS

SIDES

ROASTED CORN & BLACK BEAN SALAD

The chefs at Miraval Arizona offer 2 tips to ensure the success of this often-requested salad. While this salad can be served at room temperature as soon as it is made, we find it tastes best when served chilled. This way, the raspberry vinegar has a chance to marry with the other ingredients for an hour. We also suggest using fresh corn, as the flavor and texture is difficult to replicate with frozen kernels.

1 teaspoon chili powder

1 teaspoon ground coriander

1 teaspoon ground cumin

1 cup fresh corn kernels

1 teaspoon extra-virgin olive oil

1 1/3 cups Basic Black Beans (page 307) or canned black beans, rinsed and drained

1/4 cup diced red onion

1/4 cup diced red bell peppers

2 tablespoons finely chopped fresh cilantro

1 1/2 tablespoons raspberry vinegar

Heat the oven to 400°F.

In a small bowl, combine the chili powder, coriander, and cumin. Add the corn and oil. Toss to coat. Transfer to a small rimmed sheet pan and roast until fragrant, 10 to 12 minutes. Let cool to room temperature.

In a medium bowl, combine the black beans, red onion, peppers, and cilantro. Add the cooled corn, raspberry vinegar, and stir. Cover and refrigerate for 1 hour before serving.

Makes 4 servings; Serving Size: 1/2 cup

V | vg | gf | df | ef | nf

CALORIES: 130; TOTAL FAT: 2 G; CARBOHYDRATE: 23 G;
DIETARY FIBER: 6 G; PROTEIN: 6 G

CHARRED BROCCOLI & FARRO SALAD

This hearty salad created by the team at Miraval Berkshires is a great alternative to a leafy green salad with the addition of farro a source of protein. Add your own flourishes to this salad by topping it with toasted almonds or crumbled ricotta salata. Use whole instead of peeled farro if you want the added fiber of the bran layer covering the grain.

1 cup pearled farro

2 heads broccoli, including the tender stems, cut into long florets

2 green onions, including green tops, ends trimmed

1 tablespoon Miraval Oil Blend (page 304)

Fine sea salt

Freshly ground black pepper

1 cup cherry tomatoes, halved

2 tablespoons finely chopped flat-leaf parsley

1 tablespoon finely chopped fresh tarragon leaves

Lemon Vinaigrette

1/2 cup fresh lemon juice

1/2 cup expeller-pressed grapeseed oil

1/2 cup extra-virgin olive oil

1 tablespoon Dijon mustard

1 teaspoon honey

Fine sea salt

Freshly ground black pepper

Bring 4 cups of lightly salted water to a boil in a medium saucepan. Add the farro and cook, stirring, frequently, until tender but still a bit chewy, about 20 minutes. Drain the farro, transfer to a large bowl, and keep warm while you prepare the vegetables.

Heat a grill pan or an outdoor grill to medium. Toss the broccoli and green onions lightly with the Miraval Oil Blend and season with salt and pepper. Grill the broccoli until crisp-tender and lightly charred. Grill the green onions until wilted and lightly charred. Set the vegetables aside.

To make the vinaigrette, in a medium bowl or 2-cup glass measuring cup, whisk together the lemon juice, oils, mustard, and honey. Add salt and pepper to taste.

To assemble the salad, toss the farro with the cherry tomatoes, parsley, and tarragon. Cut the grilled green onions into 1-inch lengths and add them to the bowl. Give the dressing a stir and add 1/2 cup of it to the farro mixture. Toss gently until the grains are well coated. In another bowl, toss the grilled broccoli with 1/2 cup of the vinaigrette. Add additional dressing, if needed, otherwise refrigerate the remaining dressing and save for another use. Divide the farro mixture among 6 large salad plates and artistically lay the grilled broccoli over the top. Serve immediately.

Makes 6 servings

V | df | ef | nf

CALORIES: 350; TOTAL FAT: 16 G; CARBOHYDRATE: 45 G; DIETARY FIBER: 4 G; PROTEIN: 12 G

TOASTED BARLEY & APPLE SALAD

One way to bring out barley's nutty quality is to toast it in a dry skillet before cooking it. This can be an easy step, and richly rewards you with a more robust flavor to the grain. This is a guest-favorite salad offered at Miraval Arizona.

2 cups barley

5 cups Vegetable Stock (page 303) or store-bought vegetable broth

1/2 cup chopped flat-leaf parsley

1/2 cup chopped fresh mint leaves

1 crisp, red apple, cored, and sliced

1 Granny Smith apple, cored, and sliced

Vinaigrette

1/3 cup rice wine vinegar

1/4 cup fresh lemon juice

1/4 cup unsweetened apple juice

1 tablespoon honey

2 teaspoons extra-virgin olive oil

1/4 teaspoon fine sea salt

1/8 teaspoon freshly ground black pepper

Place the barley in a large dry sauté pan and toast over medium heat, stirring constantly, until it turns golden and fragrant like roasted nuts, about 2 minutes. Add the vegetable stock and bring to a boil. Reduce the heat so the stock just simmers, cover and cook until the barley is tender, about 25 minutes. Remove from the heat and drain through a fine-mesh strainer. Transfer to a large bowl and set aside to cool to room temperature.

To make the vinaigrette, whisk together the vinegar, lemon juice, apple juice, honey, olive oil, salt, and pepper.

To finish the salad, add the parsley, mint, and slices of both apples to the bowl with the barley. Pour the vinaigrette over the top and gently toss to combine. Serve immediately or cover and set aside at room temperature for up to 2 hours.

Makes 6 servings; Serving Size: 1 1/2 cups

V | df | ef | nf

CALORIES: 180; TOTAL FAT: 1.5 G; CARBOHYDRATE: 40 G; DIETARY FIBER: 5 G; PROTEIN: 3 G

BEEF & GLASS NOODLE SALAD
WITH SPICY PEANUT SAUCE

Choose this recipe when you have time to savor the process of creating it. Look for glass noodles, often labeled "rice sticks" or "rice vermicelli" in the Asian section of well-stocked grocery stores. Lemongrass, also readily available, requires a sharp knife to remove the fibrous bottom quarter-inch from the stem. Pulling away the tough outer layers reveals the soft inner core, which is what you want to use in this recipe.

. . . .

2 ounces glass noodles

1 teaspoon sriracha sauce

1 teaspoon minced garlic

1 teaspoon fresh lime juice

1 teaspoon toasted sesame oil

1 teaspoon low-sodium gluten-free soy sauce

8 ounces beef steak, such as sirloin or New York strip

1 teaspoon finely chopped lemongrass

1/4 teaspoon + 1 tablespoon Miraval Oil Blend (page 304)

1 ripe Anjou or Bosc pear, peeled, cored, and thinly sliced

1/2 cup rice wine vinegar

1 tablespoon Vegetable Stock (page 303)

1/2 cup peeled carrot, cut into 3-inch julienne strips

1/2 cup red bell pepper, cut into 3-inch julienne strips

1 teaspoon chopped fresh cilantro, plus 8 sprigs for garnish

4 tablespoons Spicy Peanut Sauce (recipe follows)

Place the noodles in a medium bowl and cover with warm water. Set aside to soak at room temperature until softened and the strands are easy to separate, 20 minutes. Drain and set aside.

In a medium bowl, combine the Sriracha, garlic, lime juice, sesame oil, and soy sauce. Add the steak and turn to coat evenly. Let marinate for 20 minutes at room temperature, turning occasionally. The meat can be marinated, covered, and refrigerated for up to 4 hours. Bring to room temperature before cooking.

To make the dressing, heat a medium skillet over high heat. Add the lemongrass and cook until fragrant, 45 seconds. Add 1/4 teaspoon of the oil and reduce the heat to medium. Add the pears and cook, stirring gently, until caramelized on all sides, 3 to 4 minutes. Add the rice vinegar and reduce the heat to low (the vinegar will boil aggressively). Cook until the mixture is slightly reduced, about 3 minutes. Transfer to the bowl of a blender and add the Vegetable Stock and remaining tablespoon of oil. Blend on high speed until smooth.

Prepare an ice bath in a medium bowl.

Fill a medium saucepan 2/3 full of water and bring to a boil. Add the soaked noodles and cook just until tender, 3 minutes. Quickly transfer the noodles to the prepared ice bath to cool for 2 minutes. Drain well in a colander, shaking off all the excess water. Transfer to a large bowl.

gf | df | ef | nf

CALORIES: 250; TOTAL FAT: 11 G; CARBOHYDRATE: 22 G; DIETARY FIBER: 3 G; PROTEIN: 16 G

Add the carrots, bell peppers, and chopped cilantro to the noodles and toss with the dressing to coat evenly. Set aside.

To cook the steak, heat a medium skillet, preferably cast iron, over high heat. Place the meat in the hot pan and cook until seared on the first side, 1 minute. Reduce the heat to medium-high and cook for 2 minutes longer. Flip and cook the other side, 3 minutes. Using tongs, hold the meat so the sides touch the hot pan and sear the sides, about 2 minutes (for a total cooking time of 8 minutes for rare, or cook to desired doneness). Remove from the pan and let rest for 4 minutes before cutting crosswise into 8 slices.

To serve, spoon 1 tablespoon of the Spicy Peanut Sauce on the bottom of each of 4 serving plates. Divide the noodles evenly among the plates and arrange 2 slices of steak on each serving. Garnish each plate with 2 cilantro sprigs.

Makes 4 servings; Serving Size: 3/4 cup

SPICY PEANUT SAUCE

Whether you are preparing a flavorful dish for a relaxing evening for two or inviting friends to share a meal, take the time to prepare this sauce—it is a culinary keeper. Double it to have on hand, as it is delicious with grilled or broiled chicken, beef, or shrimp.

1/3 cup rice wine vinegar

1 tablespoon low-sodium soy sauce

1 teaspoon sriracha sauce

1 teaspoon toasted sesame oil

1/4 cup creamy, old-fashioned peanut butter

In the container of a blender, or in a mini-chop food processor, combine the vinegar, soy sauce, sriracha, and sesame oil. Blend until smooth. Add the peanut butter and blend until evenly combined, scraping down the sides of the bowl as needed. Serve immediately, or transfer to an airtight container and refrigerate for up to 1 week.

Makes 1/2 cup; Serving Size: 1 tablespoon

V | vg | gf | df | ef | nf

CALORIES: 62; TOTAL FAT: 5 G; CARBOHYDRATE: 2 G;
DIETARY FIBER: 1 G; PROTEIN: 2 G

SMOKED SALMON POTATO SALAD

A colorful medley of potatoes pairs with cold-smoked salmon, crisp greens beans, a touch of onion and a creamy mustard dressing—ideal for lunch or brunch any time of year.

4 ounces (2 medium) Red Bliss potatoes

4 ounces (1 medium) Yukon Gold potato

4 ounces (1 medium) Peruvian Purple potato

2 ounces very thin fresh green beans (haricots verts), stem ends trimmed

1/2 cup cold-smoked salmon, roughly chopped

1/4 cup thinly slice red onion

Pinch fine sea salt

Pinch freshly ground black pepper

2 tablespoons Vegetable Stock (page 303)

2 tablespoons mascarpone cheese

1 tablespoon red wine vinegar

1 1/2 teaspoons extra-virgin olive oil

1/2 teaspoon Dijon mustard

1/2 teaspoon honey

Heat the oven to 400ºF. Roast the potatoes in a baking pan until fork-tender, about 1 hour. Set aside to cool to room temperature.

Meanwhile, bring a small pot of lightly salted water to a boil. Prepare an ice bath. Add the green beans to the pot and lightly blanch for 2 minutes. Transfer the beans to the ice bath to cool for 2 minutes. Blot dry and transfer to a large bowl.

Cut each potato into 8 wedges and add them to the bowl with the green beans. Add the salmon, red onion, and a pinch of salt and pepper. Toss lightly to combine, being careful not to break the potatoes.

To make the dressing, in a small bowl whisk together the Vegetable Stock and mascarpone cheese until smooth. Add the vinegar, oil, mustard, and honey. Whisk until combined. Toss the dressing with the potato mixture until evenly coated. Serve immediately.

Makes 4 servings; Serving Size: 1/2 cup

gf | ef | nf

CALORIES: 140; TOTAL FAT: 6 G; CARBOHYDRATE: 18 G; DIETARY FIBER: 2 G; PROTEIN: 5 G

ITALIAN CHICKPEA SALAD

Like an antipasto in a bowl, this wholesome salad includes chickpeas and the leafy crunch of romaine hearts.

Salad

1 1/2 cups chopped romaine hearts

1 [15oz/425g] can chickpeas, drained and rinsed

6 ounces canned artichoke hearts, drained and chopped

1/2 cup grape tomatoes, halved

1/2 cup chopped cucumber

1/2 cup cubed salami

1/2 cup diced provolone cheese

1/4 cup mini pepperoni

1/4 cup thinly sliced green onions, including the green tops

1/4 cup pepperoncini peppers

Dressing

1/4 cup red wine vinegar

1 tablespoon honey

1 teaspoon minced garlic

1/2 teaspoon Dijon mustard

1/2 teaspoon dried Italian herbs

1/4 cup extra-virgin olive oil

Fine sea salt

Freshly ground black pepper

In a large bowl, toss together the lettuce, chickpeas, artichoke hearts, tomatoes, cucumber, salami, cheese, pepperoni, and green onions. Set aside.

To make the dressing, whisk together the vinegar, honey, garlic, mustard, and herbs. Slowly drizzle in the olive oil until the dressing emulsifies. Season to taste with salt and pepper.

Add the dressing to the salad in the bowl and gently toss to evenly coat the ingredients. Transfer to a serving bowl and top with the pepperoncini peppers. Serve immediately.

Makes 8 servings; Serving Size: 1/2 cup

gf | ef | nf

CALORIES: 140; TOTAL FAT: 8 G; CARBOHYDRATE: 11 G; DIETARY FIBER: 3 G; PROTEIN: 8 G

FORBIDDEN RICE SALAD

This salad is chock-full of colorful vegetables and the big flavors of chili oil, sriracha sauce, ginger, and lime. Forbidden rice, an antioxidant-rich whole grain loaded with iron and fiber, adds a wonderful texture and nutty flavor. Note that we make the chili oil optional. Use as much as you like to add an extra kick of heat beyond the sriracha sauce.

1/2 cup forbidden black rice

1 1/2 tablespoons gluten-free soy sauce

1 tablespoon fresh lime juice

1 teaspoon toasted sesame oil

1/4 to 1/2 teaspoon chili oil, optional

1/2 teaspoon sriracha sauce

2 tablespoons minced fresh ginger

1 1/3 cup shredded carrots

1 cup diced red bell pepper

2/3 cup shelled edamame

1/4 cup sliced green onions, including the green tops

8 ounces mixed salad greens

1 cup roasted cashews

Follow the package directions for cooking the rice. Once cooked spread it out on a plate to cool.

Meanwhile, in a large bowl, whisk together the soy sauce, lime juice, sesame oil, chili oil (if using), sriracha, and ginger until smooth. Set aside. Prepare the rest of the vegetables while the rice is cooking.

To assemble the salad, add the rice to the bowl with the dressing, along with the carrots, bell pepper, edamame, and green onions. Give the salad a toss to evenly coat the ingredients with the dressing. Add the salad greens and toss gently. Divide evenly among 4 salad plates. Top with cashews and serve immediately.

Makes 6 servings; Serving Size: 1 1/2 cups

V | vg | gf | df | ef

CALORIES: 290; TOTAL FAT: 13 G; CARBOHYDRATE: 36 G; DIETARY FIBER: 3 G; PROTEIN: 9 G

SMASHED CUCUMBER SALAD

This salad has a bold amount of garlic but marinating it in the vinaigrette tames the rawness and delivers a flavor punch. There is something cathartic and fun about whacking the cucumbers as directed in the recipe; this technique allows the bruised cucumbers to absorb even more of the dressing than just chopping them. If you like heat, add more red pepper flakes or chile crisp to the salad.

....

Vinaigrette

1/4 cup rice wine vinegar

1/4 cup honey

1/4 cup toasted sesame oil

1/2 teaspoon red pepper flakes

1/3 cup finely chopped garlic

Salad

4 to 5 English cucumbers

4 ripe plum tomatoes, cored, seeded, and julienned

2 cups Shishito peppers, stems removed, cut crosswise into 1/4-inch-thick rounds

1/2 cup chopped green onions, including green tops

1/2 cup chopped fresh cilantro

Fine sea salt

Freshly ground white pepper

Toasted sesame seeds

To make the vinaigrette, in a large bowl, whisk together the vinegar, honey, toasted sesame oil, and chili flakes. Add the garlic and let the garlic marinate in the dressing while you prepare the other ingredients.

Trim the stem end of each cucumber. Using the flat heel of a knife, or a small heavy saucepan, firmly whack the whole cucumbers along their entire length so they split at the sides. Now, quarter each cucumber lengthwise. Cut the cucumbers into 1/2-to-3/4-inch dice. Add to the bowl with the vinaigrette, along with the tomatoes, peppers, and all but 2 tablespoons each of the green onions and cilantro. Toss together until evenly coated with the dressing. Season to taste with salt and pepper. Set aside at room temperature for 1 hour to allow the flavors to meld.

To serve, transfer to the mixture individual salad plates or to a serving bowl and garnish with the remaining green onions and cilantro. Sprinkle sesame seeds over the top. Serve immediately.

Makes 6 servings

V | gf | df | ef | nf

CALORIES: 200; TOTAL FAT: 11 G; CARBOHYDRATE: 20 G; DIETARY FIBER: 4 G; PROTEIN: 3 G

GIARDINIERA & PICKLED ONIONS

*Here is Miraval Austin's spin on classic giardiniera, punctuated with heat from the jalapeños, heady with garlic, and spiced with fennel and coriander seeds—a magnificent accompaniment to flatbreads, an antipasto platter, and grilled foods. **To make pickled onions**, pack peeled baby onions or wedges of white or red onion into a quart-size jar. Make a quarter batch of the Pickling Brine and pour it over the onions, following the same directions.*

2 large carrots

2 ribs celery, trimmed, and cut on an angle into 1/4-inch-thick slices

1 red bell pepper, seeded, deribbed, and julienned

1/2 head cauliflower, cut into small florets

1 red onion, julienned

1 jalapeño, stem removed, seeded, and cut into thin rings

12 whole garlic cloves, peeled

Pickling Brine

6 cups water

4 cups red wine vinegar

2 cups organic cane sugar

1 tablespoon black peppercorns

1/2 tablespoon fennel seeds

1/2 tablespoon coriander seeds

Trim and peel the carrots. Using a serrated peeler, press hard and shave long thin ribbons from the carrots. Combine the carrots, celery, bell pepper, cauliflower, onion, jalapeño, and garlic in a 1-gallon container. (Alternatively, divide the vegetables evenly between two 1/2-gallon containers.) Set aside.

To make the brine, in a large saucepan or soup pot, combine the water, vinegar, sugar, peppercorns, fennel and coriander seeds. Bring to a slow boil, stirring to dissolve the sugar. Pour the hot pickling brine over the raw mixed vegetables to cover them completely. Set aside to cool. Cover and refrigerate until ready to use. The giardiniera and pickled onions will keep for up to 2 weeks.

Makes 12 cups; Serving Size: 1/2 cup

V | vg | gf | df | ef | nf

CALORIES: 20; TOTAL FAT: 0 G; CARBOHYDRATE: 5 G; DIETARY FIBER: 1 G; PROTEIN: 1 G

CARAMELIZED THREE-ONION POLENTA

Red and yellow onions and leeks make up this trio of alliums that bring a richly sweet flavor to the creamy polenta. This is an ideal side dish to roasted or braised meats and poultry, including Achiote Chicken (page 294).

1/2 teaspoon Miraval Oil Blend (page 304) or unrefined avocado oil, plus more for greasing the pan

1 1/2 tablespoons thinly sliced red onion

1 1/2 tablespoons thinly sliced yellow onion

1 1/2 tablespoons thinly sliced leek, white portion only, well rinsed

2 1/2 cups Vegetable Stock (page 303), or store-bought vegetable stock, rice milk, or water

3/4 teaspoon fine sea salt

1/2 teaspoon freshly ground black pepper

3/4 cup quick-cooking polenta

In a large saucepan or medium pot set over medium heat, warm the oil. Add the red and yellow onions and cook, stirring constantly, until soft and starting to turn brown, about 2 minutes. Add the leeks and cook, stirring, until soft and brown, 1 minute longer. Add the vegetable stock or liquid of choice, salt, and pepper. Bring to a boil over high heat.

Slowly stream in the polenta, and then turn the heat to medium-slow. Stir constantly until the lumps are gone and the polenta is smooth, about 4 minutes.

Grease an 8-by-8-inch casserole lightly with oil. Spread out the polenta in the casserole to about 1/2-inch thick. Allow to cool to room temperature. As it cools the polenta will set up and become firm (about 25 minutes). When ready to serve, cut the polenta into squares and warm before serving.

Makes 2 cups; Serving Size: 1/2 cup

V | vg | gf | df | ef | nf

CALORIES: 50; TOTAL FAT: 1.5 G; CARBOHYDRATE: 8 G; DIETARY FIBER: 0 G; PROTEIN: 1 G

ANCHO CHILE BUTTERNUT SQUASH PURÉE

A Southwest twist on a classic side dish, this roasted and puréed butternut squash simmers ancho chiles in the vegetable stock for a lively yet subtle flavor boost—an excellent accompaniment to grilled or roasted meats, poultry, or grilled tofu.

....

1/2 large butternut squash, seeds and stringy fibers removed

1 tablespoon unrefined avocado oil

Fine sea salt

Freshly ground white pepper

1/4 dried ancho chile, stemmed and deseeded

1/3 cup diced yellow onion

1/3 cup diced carrot

1 medium garlic clove, crushed with the side of a knife

1/2 cup Vegetable Stock (page 303) or store-bought vegetable broth

2 tablespoons water

Organic cane sugar

Heat the oven to 375°F. Rub the cut side of the squash lightly with a teaspoon or so of the oil. Season with salt and pepper. Roast the squash cut-side down on a rimmed sheet pan until fork-tender, about 30 minutes. Set aside to cool for 10 minutes. Scoop out the flesh and discard the skin. Set the roasted butternut squash aside.

Meanwhile, place the ancho chile in a small dry skillet and toast over medium heat, turning once, until fragrant. Let cool and then tear or crush into tiny pieces.

In a medium saucepan, warm the remaining oil over medium heat. Add the onion, carrot, and garlic. Sauté, stirring frequently, until the vegetables are soft and just beginning to brown, about 5 minutes. Add the toasted ancho chile, vegetable stock, and water. Bring to a simmer and then add the prepared squash. Simmer another 15 minutes.

Use an immersion blender or transfer the squash mixture to the workbowl of a food processor, and blend until smooth. Season to taste with salt and add a little sugar to balance the flavors. Serve immediately or keep warm until ready to serve.

Makes 4 servings; Serving Size: 1/2 cup

V | vg | gf | df | ef | nf

CALORIES: 60; TOTAL FAT: 2.5 G; CARBOHYDRATE: 11 G; DIETARY FIBER: 3 G; PROTEIN: 1 G

BHINDI (OKRA) MASALA

During the summer at Miraval Austin's Cypress Creek Farm, bushels full of red and green okra are harvested, and the chefs cook them in innovative ways, including this Indian-inspired side dish. Bhindi is the Hindi name for okra, a vegetable that often gets a bad reputation for being slimy—but not in this preparation, where it is quickly seared to give it a crisp yet tender texture. While this recipe is meant as a side dish, it would be equally delicious as a vegetarian main course served with rice or quinoa.

Masala Onions

2 tablespoons unrefined avocado oil

2 teaspoons ground turmeric

2 teaspoons ground cumin

1 teaspoon Madras curry powder

1 teaspoon garlic powder

1 teaspoon garam masala

1 large yellow onion, halved lengthwise, cut crosswise into very thin slices

1/2 teaspoon fine sea salt

Okra

3 tablespoons unrefined avocado oil

1 pound okra, halved lengthwise

4 ounces grape tomatoes (about 3/4 cup), halved lengthwise

4 ounces baby spinach

3/4 teaspoon fine sea salt

2 teaspoons garam masala

2 tablespoons chopped fresh cilantro leaves

To make the masala onions, in a medium nonstick sauté pan set over medium-low heat, warm the oil and swirl to coat the bottom of the pan. Add the turmeric, cumin, curry powder, garlic powder, and garam masala. Toast the spices, stirring constantly, until fragrant, about 30 seconds. Add the onions along with 1/2 teaspoon of salt, and sauté, stirring constantly, until the onions are completely softened, about 5 minutes. Set aside and keep warm.

In a large sauté pan set over medium-high heat, warm the oil and swirl to coat the bottom of the pan. Add the okra and cook, stirring occasionally, until the okra is crisp-tender and slightly charred at the edges, about 5 minutes. Add the tomatoes, spinach, and 3/4 teaspoon of salt. Sauté, stirring constantly, until the spinach is wilted and the tomatoes are tender, about 3 minutes. Add the garam masala and cilantro. Stir to blend in and then remove from the heat. Serve immediately along with the masala onions.

Makes 8 servings; Serving Size: 4 ounces

V | vg | gf | df | ef | nf

CALORIES: 120; TOTAL FAT: 9 G; CARBOHYDRATE: 8 G; DIETARY FIBER: 3 G; PROTEIN: 2 G

main dishes

VEGETARIAN

SEAFOOD

MEAT

CHICKPEA & BEET BURGER

Plant-based burgers are a favorite with Miraval Resorts guests. Whether served with a gluten-free bun or not, there are many accompaniments to offer when you make these at home—set out a selection of thinly sliced red onions, sliced or mashed avocado, sliced tomatoes, leafy greens, and Vegan Aioli (page 300).

1 [15oz/430g] can chickpeas, drained and rinsed

2 medium-size raw or roasted beets (if raw, then trimmed and peeled), coarsely chopped

1 medium yellow onion, coarsely chopped

2 garlic cloves

Leaves from one bunch fresh flat-leaf parsley (about 4 cups loosely packed leaves)

1/2 cup gluten-free old-fashioned rolled oats

1/3 cup nutritional yeast

Dash of liquid smoke or use smoked salt (see **Note**)

Fine sea salt

Freshly ground black pepper

Oat flour, if needed

Heat the oven to 400°F. Prepare a rimmed sheet pan lined with a sheet of parchment paper.

In the workbowl of a food processor fitted with the metal blade, pulse the chickpeas, beets, onion, garlic, and parsley until finely chopped. Add the oats, nutritional yeast, liquid smoke or smoked salt, a pinch of sea salt, and freshly ground pepper to taste. Process until everything is well mixed but still has an even chunky texture.

Divide the mixture into 8 portions and shape into patties. If the mixture seems too wet (it won't hold a patty shape), add a couple of tablespoons of oat flour to absorb some of the moisture. Arrange the burgers on the prepared sheet pan. Bake the burgers for 12 minutes on one side, and then flip them over and continue to bake until cooked through, about 12 to 16 minutes longer. Serve immediately with gluten-free buns, if desired.

Note:

If you use liquid smoke, start with 1/2 teaspoon and add more to suit your taste. With smoked salt, add 3/4 teaspoon to start and then taste the mixture. You can skip adding any fine sea salt if you prefer the flavor of the smoked salt. Another alternative is to use a vegan Worcestershire sauce instead of the liquid smoke.

Makes 8 burgers

V | vg | gf | df | ef | nf

CALORIES: 70; TOTAL FAT: 1 G; CARBOHYDRATE: 11 G; DIETARY FIBER: 2 G; PROTEIN: 4 G

BERKSHIRES MUSHROOM SHEPARD'S PIE

This hearty winter dish is Miraval Berkshires' vegetarian version of shepherd's pie, traditionally made with lamb or beef. The mushrooms and lentils are a robust and satisfying substitution for meat. The recipe calls for Puy lentils, a variety of French lentil from the Puy area of France. Look for them in well-stocked grocery stores or online. They have a distinct earthy flavor and hold their shape when cooked, which is important for this recipe.

···

Mashed Potato Topping

2 1/2 pounds Russet potatoes, peeled and cut into small chunks

Fine sea salt

1/2 cup grass-fed unsalted butter, melted

1 cup organic grass-fed whole milk

1/2 cup shredded aged Cheddar cheese

Freshly ground black pepper

Filling

1 cup Puy lentils, well rinsed

1 Bouquet Garni (see **Note**)

4 teaspoons fine sea salt, plus more as needed

1 1/2 teaspoons freshly ground black pepper, plus more as needed

4 tablespoons extra-virgin olive oil

2 pounds assorted mushrooms (maitake, shiitake, cremini, oyster), trimmed and quartered

2 carrots, trimmed, peeled, and cut into 1/2-inch dice

1 parsnip, trimmed, peeled, and cut into 1/2-inch dice

1 medium yellow onion, thinly slice

2 garlic cloves, thinly sliced

2 tablespoons tomato paste

2 cups dry red wine

3 cups Vegetable Stock (page 303) or store-bought vegetable broth plus 1/3 cup for the slurry

1 tablespoon tapioca flour

2 tablespoons chopped fresh rosemary

1/4 cup shredded aged Cheddar cheese

To make the mashed potatoes, place the potatoes in a large saucepan and add enough cold water to cover the potatoes by 2 inches. Bring to a boil over high heat. Add 2 teaspoons of salt, reduce the heat to medium-low, and simmer until the potatoes are fork-tender, 15 to 20 minutes. Drain in a colander, shaking off excess water, and return to the pot. Use a potato masher to mash the potatoes. Stir in the butter, and then stir in the milk. Stir in the cheese. Season to taste with salt and pepper. Cover and keep warm.

While the potatoes are cooking, place the lentils in a medium saucepan, add 4 cups of water, and the bouquet garni. Bring to a boil, reduce the heat so the lentils simmer, and cook until the lentils are tender, 30 minutes. Drain, and discard the bouquet garni. Transfer the lentils to a bowl and season with 2 teaspoons of salt and 3/4 teaspoon of pepper. Set aside.

Arrange a rack in the lower third of the oven and heat the oven to 375°F.

V | gf | ef | nf

CALORIES: 510; TOTAL FAT: 23 G; CARBOHYDRATE: 54 G; DIETARY FIBER: 13 G; PROTEIN: 16 G

In a large Dutch oven, heat 2 tablespoons of the olive oil over medium-high heat. Add the mushrooms and sauté, stirring frequently, until the mushrooms are browned, and all the liquid has evaporated. Season with 1 teaspoon of salt and 1/4 teaspoon pepper. Transfer to a paper towel-lined plate. Add the remaining oil, and then add the diced carrots and parsnip. Sauté, stirring frequently, until just beginning to brown, about 4 minutes. Stir in the onions and garlic and continue to sauté for 2 minutes longer. Season with the remaining 1 teaspoon of salt and 1/2 teaspoon of pepper. Return the mushrooms to the pan, stir in the tomato paste, and sauté 1 minute longer. Add the wine and bring to a simmer. Simmer until the wine has reduced by half. Add the cooked lentils and 3 cups of the vegetable stock and bring back to a simmer.

In a small bowl, whisk together the tapioca flour and 1/3 cup of vegetable stock to make a slurry. When the lentil mixture is simmering, slowly whisk in the slurry, and let the filling cook for another few minutes until the mixture thickens. Stir in the chopped rosemary. Taste the filling and season with salt and pepper, if needed.

Spread the reserved mashed potatoes evenly over the top of the filling. Sprinkle the cheese over the top. Bake the Shepherd's Pie until the filling is hot, the mashed potatoes have a tinge of brown, and the cheese is melted, about 30 minutes. Rest for 15 minutes before serving.

Note:
Bouquet Garni is the French term for a bundle of herbs tied together with kitchen string. The herbs suggested for this dish include: 1 sprig fresh thyme, 1 bay leaf, 2 sprigs fresh parsley, and the leafy top from 1 rib celery.

Makes 8 servings

EDAMAME FALAFEL

A deliciously different take on classic falafel—this version combines edamame and English peas, and a garden variety of fresh herbs along with green onions and garlic. The falafel is served on a bed of lettuce and topped with diced tomato and a spoonful of homemade Tzatziki Sauce. Serve with warm flatbread, if desired. If you can't find fresh peas, use thawed frozen peas instead.

....

2 cups edamame, shelled and blanched

1/2 cup fresh English peas, shelled and blanched (or use frozen)

1/4 cup chopped flat-leaf parsley

1/4 cup chopped fresh dill

1/4 cup chopped fresh cilantro

1/4 cup chopped green onions, including green tops

1 tablespoon minced garlic

1 teaspoon ground cumin

1 teaspoon ground coriander

1 teaspoon fine sea salt

1/2 teaspoon red pepper flakes

Freshly ground black pepper

All-Purpose Gluten-Free Flour (page 303)

Unrefined avocado oil, for frying

1 24-ounce package Mesclun greens

Tzatziki Sauce (recipe follows)

2 large vine-ripened tomatoes, diced

Basic Flatbread (page 227), optional

Drain the blanched edamame beans and peas thoroughly and blot dry with paper towels. It is important that these ingredients be dry.

In the workbowl of a food processor fitted with the metal blade, pulse the edamame, peas, parsley, dill, cilantro, green onions, and garlic until evenly and finely chopped. Scrape down the sides of the workbowl once or twice. Sprinkle the cumin, coriander, salt, red pepper flakes, and freshly ground black pepper over top. Pulse several times to incorporate the spices until the mixture comes together. To test, press mixture together in your hand to see if it clumps together without falling apart.

Transfer the mixture to a bowl. Have ready a large, rimmed sheet pan lined with parchment paper. Use a 2-ounce scoop, or your hands, to form 12 balls about the size of a golf ball. And then press down gently to form into 2-inch-wide patties. (The patties should be about 1/2-inch thick.) Arrange the patties on the sheet pan, and then cover and chill until ready to fry. Chill the falafel for at least 1 hour or up to 8 hours in advance.

When ready to fry the falafel, place the flour in a shallow bowl. Carefully and thoroughly coat the patties all over with the flour, shaking off the excess. Pour 1/2 inch of oil into a heavy skillet, preferably cast-iron, and heat to 375°F. Fry the falafel in batches, delicately turning once, until golden on both sides, 6 to 8 minutes total. Drain on paper towels.

To serve, arrange 2 ounces of Mesclun greens on a plate, top with 2 falafel, spoon 3 tablespoons of Tzatziki sauce over the top and garnish with 2 tablespoons of diced tomatoes. Serve with flatbread, if desired.

Makes 6 servings; Serving Size: 2 falafel

V | gf | ef | nf

CALORIES: 490; TOTAL FAT: 35 G; CARBOHYDRATE: 35 G; DIETARY FIBER: 4 G; PROTEIN: 10 G

TZATZIKI GREEK YOGURT SAUCE

1/2 cucumber, seeded

1 cup low-fat plain Greek yogurt

1 tablespoon finely chopped fresh dill

1 tablespoon finely chopped fresh mint

1 tablespoon fresh lemon juice

1 tablespoon extra-virgin olive oil

1 garlic clove, minced

1/2 teaspoon fine sea salt

Freshly ground black pepper

Grate the cucumber on the coarse side of a box grater. Place the cucumber in a double thickness of paper towels and squeeze out the water. Measure 1/2 cup and place in a medium bowl. Mix in the yogurt and then add the dill, mint lemon juice, olive oil, garlic, salt, and pepper. Cover and refrigerate until ready to serve. The sauce can be made up to 2 days in advance.

Makes about 2 cups; Serving Size: 3 tablespoons

CALORIES: 40; TOTAL FAT: 1.5 G; CARBOHYDRATE: 5 G; DIETARY FIBER: 0 G; PROTEIN: 2 G

LENTIL BOLOGNESE
OR BISON BOLOGNESE

For this recipe, a hearty vegan Bolognese is made with cooked lentils and served over roasted spaghetti squash (which can be substituted with store-bought spiralized zucchini or blanched butternut squash). To turn this recipe into Bison Bolognese, skip cooking the lentils and brown one pound of ground bison in a skillet instead. Use a slotted spoon to remove the cooked bison, and then make the sauce right in that skillet to build a depth of flavor. Add the cooked bison back in and simmer in the sauce before serving. Both versions are delicious, depending on your preferences.

1/2 cup Puy, green, or brown lentils, well rinsed

1 cup Vegetable Stock (page 303) or store-bought vegetable broth

1 tablespoon extra-virgin olive oil

1/4 cup diced fennel bulb

1/4 cup diced carrot

1/4 cup diced yellow onion

1/4 cup diced red bell pepper

2 garlic cloves, minced

1 teaspoon fennel seeds

Fine sea salt

Freshly ground black pepper

1 cup good quality tomato sauce (passata)

Roasted Spaghetti Squash (page 102) or blanched spiralized zucchini or butternut squash

Place the lentils in a small saucepan and add the vegetable stock. Bring to a boil, reduce the heat so the lentils simmer, and cook until the lentils are tender, about 30 minutes. Drain, put the lentils in a bowl, and set aside.

Meanwhile, in a medium sauté pan, warm the olive oil and swirl to coat the bottom of the pan. Add the diced fennel and carrot. Sauté, stirring frequently, until the vegetables are soft but not brown, about 5 minutes. Add the onions, bell peppers, garlic, and fennel seeds. Season with salt and pepper. Sauté 5 minutes longer, stirring occasionally. Add the cooked lentils and the tomato sauce. Cook at a bare simmer, covered, for 2 hours to allow the flavors to meld. Season to taste with salt and pepper.

To serve, arrange 3 ounces of roasted spaghetti squash, or blanched spiralized zucchini or butternut squash, in a warm pasta bowl. Spoon 1/2 cup of the lentil Bolognese over top and serve immediately.

Makes 4 servings; Serving Size: 1/2 cup

gf | df | ef | nf

Lentil Bolognese (over spaghetti squash):
CALORIES: 120; TOTAL FAT: 3.5 G; CARBOHYDRATE: 17 G; DIETARY FIBER: 4 G; PROTEIN: 6 G

Bison Bolognese (over spaghetti squash):
CALORIES: 190; TOTAL FAT: 13 G; CARBOHYDRATE: 7 G; DIETARY FIBER: 2 G; PROTEIN: 12 G

BBQ SPICE-RUBBED BUTTERNUT SQUASH STEAKS

Look for a butternut squash or two with long necks because that is the part of the squash that will be used in this recipe to create "steaks." Use the remainder to make the Butternut Squash Caponata (page 61) or the Ancho Chile Butternut Squash Purée (page 262).

. . . .

Hard Cider Beurre Blanc

1 tablespoon extra-virgin olive oil

1/2 cup finely chopped shallot

1 teaspoon finely chopped garlic

1 teaspoon finely chopped fresh ginger

1 cup hard apple cider

1/4 cup coconut cream

2 teaspoons finely chopped thyme leaves

2 teaspoons finely chopped fresh flat-leaf parsley

1/4 teaspoon fine sea salt

1/4 teaspoon freshly ground black pepper

1 large butternut squash with a long neck

3 tablespoons expeller-pressed grapeseed oil

2 to 3 tablespoons BBQ Dry Spice Rub (page 302)

To make the Beurre Blanc, in a medium saucepan set over medium-low heat, warm the oil and swirl to coat the bottom of the pan. Add the shallot, garlic, and ginger and sauté, just until the aromatics are soft but not brown, about 4 minutes. Add the hard cider, bring to a boil, and then reduce the heat so the liquid just simmers. Cook, uncovered, until the cider is reduced by three-quarters, about 10 minutes. Whisk in the coconut cream, thyme, parsley, salt and pepper. Continue to cook at a low simmer for 10 minutes longer. Taste and add more salt or pepper, if needed. Keep warm.

To prepare the squash, cut off the top stem of the squash and discard it. Peel the squash. Cut the neck portion of the squash crosswise into six 1/2-to-3/4-inch-thick steaks. Rub each steak lightly with grapeseed oil and then coat on all sides with the spice rub. Arrange on a rimmed sheet pan. Save the bottom end of the squash that contains the seeds for another use.

Prepare a medium-hot fire on one side of a charcoal or gas grill. Have the other side set up for indirect grilling. Grill the squash steaks on each side, flipping once, until caramelized and grill marks appear, about 5 minutes per side. Using tongs or a spatula, move the steaks to the cooler side of the grill, cover the grill and finish cooking on indirect heat until the squash is fork-tender. The internal temperature of the grill should be about 375ºF. Alternatively, the squash steaks can be seared in a hot pan on top of the stove and then finished in a 375ºF oven.

To serve, arrange a squash steak on each warmed plate and spoon 2 tablespoons of the sauce around and over the grilled squash. Serve immediately.

Makes 6 servings; Serving Size: 1 (6-ounce) steak

V | vg | gf | df | ef | nf

CALORIES: 170; TOTAL FAT: 9 G; CARBOHYDRATE: 24 G; DIETARY FIBER: 4 G; PROTEIN: 2 G

PASTA ESTATE
SUMMER PASTA

The chefs at Miraval Austin love to use their farm-fresh eggs to make homemade pasta. Our hens' rich diet of vegetable trimmings from the kitchen and insects from the earth give these egg yolks their dark orange color. Head to a farmer's market near you for farm-raised eggs and vegetables to make this seasonal dish. If you have a kitchen scale, weigh the flour for the pasta; otherwise, use just shy of 2 cups of flour to make the dough. Add more if it feels sticky.

Fresh Pasta

2 cups unbleached all-purpose flour

6 large egg yolks

1 large egg

5 tablespoons extra-virgin olive oil

1/2 tablespoon organic grass-fed whole milk

Semolina flour for dusting

Sauce

2 tablespoons extra-virgin olive oil

2 garlic cloves, minced

1 zucchini, ends trimmed, cut into 1/2-inch dice

2 cups heirloom cherry tomatoes, halved

6 small, sweet peppers, seeded and deribbed, cut crosswise into rings

Kernels from 1 ear of corn

1/2 cup white wine

1 tablespoon grass-fed unsalted butter

3/4 teaspoon fine sea salt

10 leaves fresh basil, cut crosswise into thin strips (chiffonade)

To make the pasta, in a stand mixer fitted with the dough hook, combine the flour, egg yolks, egg, and oil. Mix until the dough comes together. Drizzle in the milk and mix until the dough forms a soft ball when you pinch it. Turn the dough out onto a work surface that is lightly floured with semolina flour. Knead the dough until smooth and firm, but still pliable. Wrap the dough tightly in plastic wrap and let sit at room temperature for 30 minutes. This allows the gluten to relax.

To roll out the dough, cut it into 4 equal pieces. Cover the three you aren't working with. Use a pasta machine or roll the dough by hand with a rolling pin, using a generous amount of semolina to keep it from sticking. Roll the dough into long thin sheets. Cut the pasta into wide ribbons (pappardelle) or tear the dough by hand for a rustic look. Repeat with the remaining three portions of dough. Place the cut pasta on a large, rimmed sheet pan dusted with flour until ready to cook. Have ready a large pot of boiling salted water.

To make the sauce, heat the oil in a large sauté pan set over medium heat. Add the garlic and sauté until soft but not brown, about 1 minute. Add the zucchini and sauté, stirring frequently, until crisp-tender, about 1 minute. Add the cherry tomatoes, cook for 1 minute, and then add the peppers and corn. Continue to sauté a few minutes longer until the tomatoes are tender.

While the tomatoes are cooking, add the pasta to the pot of boiling salted water. Cook the pasta for 1 minute, and then drain it in a colander, shaking off any excess water. Divide the pasta among 4 warmed pasta bowls.

To finish the sauce, add the wine and simmer for 1 minute to cook off the alcohol and bitterness. Stir in the butter until melted. Season with salt and toss in the basil. Spoon the sauce over the pasta, dividing it evenly. Serve immediately.

Makes 6 servings; Serving Size: 1/3 cup

V | nf

CALORIES: 440; TOTAL FAT: 24 G; CARBOHYDRATE: 41 G; DIETARY FIBER: 3 G; PROTEIN: 10 G

FIRE ROASTED SALMON
WITH STIR-FRIED BROWN RICE & PINEAPPLE GLAZE

Salmon is such a nutritious and versatile fish to cook. For this recipe, the salmon is grilled for a fire-roasted flavor and placed on a bed of vegetable-flecked brown rice. Quickly cooked baby bok choy adds color to the plate and the dish is finished with a pineapple glaze.

. . . .

Pineapple Glaze

8 ounces fresh pineapple, peeled, cored, and chopped

1/2 red bell pepper, seeded and deribbed, chopped

1 teaspoon finely chopped green onion, white part only

1/2 teaspoon minced fresh ginger

2 tablespoons light brown sugar

1 1/2 cups pineapple juice, plus more, if needed

1 tablespoon rice wine vinegar

2 cups cooked brown rice (recipe follows)

4 (4-ounce) salmon fillets, skin-on and pin bones removed

Fine sea salt

Freshly ground black pepper

2 tablespoons expeller-pressed grapeseed oil

1/4 cup diced red bell pepper

1/4 cup diced celery

1/4 cup thinly sliced green onions, plus more for garnish

1/2 cup Vegetable Stock (page 303) or store-bought vegetable broth

2 tablespoons chopped cilantro

6 baby bok choy, halved lengthwise

To make the pineapple glaze, put the pineapple, bell pepper, green onion, ginger, and brown sugar in the container of a high-speed blender. Blend to finely chop the ingredients. Add 1 1/2 cups of the pineapple juice and vinegar. Blend until smooth. Add additional pineapple juice, if needed, to make a nice sauce consistency. Set aside until ready to use.

Have the rice cooked and cooled so it is ready to stir fry.

Heat the grill to medium-high. Heat the oven to 250°F. Have a wide sauté pan filled two-thirds full with water. Just before grilling, bring the water to a simmer.

Season the salmon fillets with salt and pepper. Place the salmon, flesh-side down, on the hottest part of the grill and sear for 2 to 3 minutes depending on the thickness of the fillets. Turn the fillets and cook the other side for 2 minutes longer. Transfer the salmon to a rimmed sheet pan and place it in the oven to finish cooking, just until medium-rare, about 5 minutes longer.

gf | df | ef | nf

CALORIES: 400; TOTAL FAT: 13 G; CARBOHYDRATE: 42 G; DIETARY FIBER: 6 G; PROTEIN: 30 G

To stir-fry the rice, heat a wok or large skillet over medium-high heat, add the oil and swirl to coat the bottom of the pan. Add the bell pepper, celery, and green onions. Sauté, until barely cooked, 1 minute. Add the rice and sauté for 1 minute. Add the vegetable stock and cook until the vegetable stock is absorbed into the rice, about 3 minutes. Gently stir in the cilantro. Season to taste with salt and pepper.

While the stock is reducing, cook the baby bok choy in the simmering water just until it's bright green and crisp-tender, about 2 minutes. Drain on paper towels.

To serve, spoon the rice onto the bottom of 4 warmed plates or shallow bowls. Place a fillet of salmon on top. Arrange the bok choy around the salmon, and then drizzle 3 tablespoons of the pineapple glaze over the top of the salmon. Garnish with green onions and serve immediately.

Makes 4 servings; Serving Size: 1 fillet

BROWN RICE

3/4 cup medium-grain brown rice

Rinse the rice well and drain. In a small saucepan with a tight-fitting lid, bring the rice and 1 1/2 cups of water to a boil over high heat and cook for 1 minute. Reduce the heat to low, cover, and simmer until the water is absorbed and the rice is tender, about 35 minutes. Remove from the heat and set aside to steam for 10 minutes. Fluff with a fork before serving.

Makes about 2 cups; Serving Size: 1/2 cup

CALORIES: 128; TOTAL FAT: 2 G; CARBOHYDRATE: 26 G; DIETARY FIBER: 2 G; PROTEIN: 2 G

BAKED FLOUNDER
WITH SALSA VERDE

Baking fish inside a foil pouch is one of the easiest and foolproof ways to prepare fish that is moist and flavorful. Flounder, fluke, cod, or halibut are all great choices for this recipe, but there are many other great options depending on what is available at your local fishmonger.

4 [5-ounce] fillets of flounder, or other local white fish

Fine sea salt

Freshly ground black pepper

1 1/2 cup Salsa Verde (page 300), warmed

1 lemon, quartered

Pea shoots or micro greens for garnish

Arrange a rack in the center of the oven and heat the oven to 425°F. Prepare a large, rimmed sheet pan and four (6-inch square) sheets of aluminum foil.

Season the flesh side of the fish fillets with a little salt and pepper. Place a fillet, seasoned-side up, on a piece of foil. Spoon 1/4 cup of the salsa verde on top of each fish fillets. Bring up two sides of the foil and seal them together, and then fold in and seal the other two sides as if you were wrapping a gift. Place the packages on the sheet pan. Bake for 6 minutes.

Carefully open the packets and use a fish spatula, or a wide spatula, to lift each fillet onto a warmed dinner plate. Top each fillet with 2 tablespoons of salsa verde and a squeeze of lemon. Garnish with pea shoots or micro greens and serve immediately.

Makes 4 servings; Serving Size: 1 fillet

gf | df | ef | nf

CALORIES: 170; TOTAL FAT: 7 G; CARBOHYDRATE: 7 G; DIETARY FIBER: 2 G; PROTEIN: 19 G

GULF SHRIMP IN CAULIFLOWER "ALFREDO"
ON SPAGHETTI SQUASH

A blended sauce made from cauliflower, hemp seeds, and plant-based milk steps in for classic Alfredo in this recipe. Roasted spaghetti squash replaces pasta and sautéed Gulf shrimp finishes this seafood main dish. If you can't find Texas Brown Gulf shrimp, look for another wild-caught Gulf or Mexican shrimp.

Spaghetti Squash

1 large spaghetti squash (about 2 to 2 1/2 pounds)

Cauliflower Alfredo

1/4 yellow onion, coarsely chopped

1/2 head cauliflower, base trimmed and leaves removed, coarsely chopped

1 cup hulled hemp seeds

4 cups organic unsweetened oat, soy, or other plant-based milk

1/4 teaspoon freshly grated nutmeg, plus more if needed

3/4 teaspoon fine sea salt, plus more if needed

Shrimp

16 jumbo Texas Brown Gulf shrimp (about 1 1/4 pounds), peeled and deveined

3 tablespoons extra-virgin olive oil

1/2 cup dry white wine

3/4 teaspoon fine sea salt

1/4 cup finely chopped flat-leaf parsley for garnish

Heat the oven to 350°F. Cut the squash in half lengthwise. Use a soup spoon to scoop out the seeds and pith. Arrange the squash halves, cut-side down, on a rimmed sheet pan and bake until fork-tender, about 30 minutes. Set aside to cool and then scoop out the squash strands using a fork. Set aside, covered, at room temperature until ready to finish the dish.

Meanwhile, to make the Cauliflower Alfredo. in a large saucepan or Dutch oven, combine the onion, cauliflower, hemp seeds, and milk alternative. Bring to a simmer over medium-high heat. Reduce the heat to maintain a slow simmer and cook, uncovered, until the cauliflower is very soft, about 30 to 40 minutes. Remove from the heat and set aside to cool for 10 minutes. Blend this mixture in a high-speed blender until you achieve a textured sauce (you may need to do this in batches). Add the nutmeg and salt. Taste, adding more nutmeg and salt, if needed. Set aside.

Just before serving, sauté the shrimp. Pat the shrimp dry with a paper towel to prevent splattering. Heat the oil in a large sauté pan set over medium-low heat. Swirl to coat the bottom of the pan. Carefully add the shrimp and sauté, stirring frequently, until they are barely pink on both sides, about 3 minutes (cooking the shrimp over gentle heat preserves the moisture in the shrimp and keeps the olive oil from smoking). Add the wine and simmer until almost all the wine has reduced and a thick residue remains. Use a slotted spoon to transfer the shrimp to a warm plate. Set aside and keep warm.

Using the same pan, still on medium-low heat, add the Alfredo sauce to the pan and heat through. Add the strands of spaghetti squash and simmer in the sauce until hot. Season to taste with salt. Divide the mixture among 4 warmed pasta bowls. Arrange 4 shrimp on top of each portion. Garnish with chopped parsley and serve immediately.

Makes 4 servings

gf | df | ef | nf

CALORIES: 430; TOTAL FAT: 27 G; CARBOHYDRATE: 21 G; DIETARY FIBER: 5 G; PROTEIN: 34 G

GEORGES BANK SCALLOPS
WITH CAULIFLOWER PURÉE, PEA TENDRILS & PESTO

Scallops are easier to cook than most home cooks believe. The chefs at Miraval Berkshires serve seared scallops sourced from the Georges Bank region on a bed of cauliflower purée. With the purée made and kept warm, and the pesto made in advance, this recipe comes together quickly. When cleaning scallops, look for a piece of muscle on the side of the scallop, referred to as a hinge, and remove it because it is tough to eat. Pea tendrils aren't always easy to find; alternatively, use microgreens or fresh basil as garnish.

12 diver scallops, cleaned, and side "hinge" removed

Fine sea salt

Freshly ground black pepper

3 tablespoons expeller-pressed grapeseed oil

1 tablespoon grass-fed unsalted butter

3 sprigs fresh thyme

4 garlic cloves, peeled

1/2 lemon, seeds removed

1 recipe Cauliflower Purée (recipe follows), hot and ready to serve

4 ounces of pea tendrils for garnish

4 tablespoons Vegan Pesto (page 94), at room temperature

Dry the scallops on both sides with paper towels. Season with salt and pepper and place on a plate.

Heat a large heavy-bottomed sauté pan over high heat. Add the oil and swirl to coat the bottom of the pan. Add the scallops, reduce the heat to medium, and cook the scallops on one side until they start to brown nicely, about 3 minutes. Add the butter to the pan, and then flip the scallops. Add the thyme and garlic. Baste the scallops with the butter and cook until slightly firm, about 2 minutes longer. Remove from the pan and spritz with the lemon juice.

To serve, spoon about 1/2 cup of the cauliflower purée into the bottom of each warmed shallow bowl. Arrange 3 scallops on top. Arrange pea tendrils in the center and drizzle 1 tablespoon of pesto around the purée. Serve immediately.

Makes 4 servings

gf | ef | nf

CALORIES: 270; TOTAL FAT: 19 G; CARBOHYDRATE: 10 G; DIETARY FIBER: 2 G; PROTEIN: 14 G

CAULIFLOWER PURÉE

1 large head of white cauliflower, leaves removed, stem end trimmed

2 teaspoons extra-virgin olive oil

1/2 shallot, thinly sliced

1 small garlic clove, thinly sliced

1/2 cup Chardonnay wine

1 sprig fresh thyme

1 bay leaf

Fine sea salt

Freshly ground black pepper

Cut the cauliflower into medium size florets and do the same for the stem.

In a medium-size saucepan, heat the oil over medium-low heat. Add the shallot and garlic and sauté until softened but not brown, about 1 minute. Add the cauliflower and stir for 1 minute. Add the wine and simmer for 1 minute. Add the sprig of thyme, bay leaf, and season with salt and pepper. Add enough water to just barely cover the cauliflower. Bring to a simmer, cover, and reduce the heat to low. Cook until the cauliflower is fork-tender, about 35 minutes. Remove the bay leaf and thyme.

Using a slotted spoon, transfer the cauliflower to the container of a high-speed blender. Ladle in 1 cup of the liquid. Purée until smooth. Add more liquid, if needed, to make a creamy and smooth purée (it is better to have a thick purée that you can thin, than one that is too thin). Season to taste with salt and pepper. Keep hot until ready to serve.

Makes 6 servings; Serving Size: 1/2 cup

V | vg | gf | df | ef | nf

CALORIES: 104; TOTAL FAT: 3 G; CARBOHYDRATE: 14 G;
DIETARY FIBER: 6 G; PROTEIN: 5 G

NANTUCKET STRIPED BASS
WITH TOMATO NAGE & BABY FENNEL CONFIT

With some planning, this recipe from Miraval Berkshires can be easy to make at home. All three component recipes can be made a day or two in advance of serving this dinner-party-worthy dish. Read through the recipe completely before you begin. Substitute branzino or rockfish if you can't find striped bass. Keep in mind that you'll need cheesecloth, kitchen twine, parchment paper, and a blender to make this recipe.

· ·

4 (5-ounce) fillets striped bass, skin on

Fine sea salt

Freshly ground black pepper

4 tablespoons expeller-pressed grapeseed oil

4 teaspoons grass-fed unsalted butter

4 sprigs fresh thyme

4 garlic cloves, peeled and pressed with the side of a chef's knife

Juice of 1/2 lemon, seeds removed

1 recipe Baby Fennel Confit (recipe follows)

2 cups Tomato Nage, warmed (recipe follows)

1/2 cup thinly sliced radishes

1/4 cup loosely packed fennel fronds

4 ounces baby sorrel leaves or mesclun greens

Extra-virgin olive oil

Flaky sea salt

Dry the bass on both sides with paper towels. With a sharp knife, score the skin side of each fillet twice. Season the fillets with salt and pepper.

Heat a large heavy-bottomed sauté pan over high heat until hot. Add the oil and swirl to coat the bottom of the pan. Add the fillets, skin-side down, and reduce the heat to medium-high. Cook the fillets on one side, without fussing with the fish, until the skin no longer sticks to the bottom of the pan, about 5 minutes.

Swirl in the butter, and then flip the fillets. Allow the butter to brown and add the thyme sprigs and garlic. Baste the fish with the butter and cook until the fish is firm, about 3 to 4 minutes longer. Remove the pan from the heat. Spritz each fillet with a little lemon juice.

To serve, arrange 2 fennel bulbs on the bottom of each warmed shallow bowl. Place a fish fillet on top. Pour 1/2 cup of the warmed Tomato Nage around each fillet. In a medium bowl, quickly toss the radishes with the fennel fronds and greens. Drizzle in olive oil, and a sprinkling of flaky sea salt and pepper. Toss with tongs and mound a portion on top of each fillet. Serve immediately.

Makes 4 servings; Serving Size: 1 fillet

gf | df | ef | nf

CALORIES: 570; TOTAL FAT: 39 G; CARBOHYDRATE: 19 G; DIETARY FIBER: 8 G; PROTEIN: 35 G

BABY FENNEL CONFIT

8 bulbs baby fennel or 2 bulbs of fennel, quartered (save the fronds for garnish)

2 cups extra-virgin olive oil

1 tablespoon sea salt

Strips of peel from 1 lemon

1 sprig fresh thyme

1 bay leaf

Arrange the fennel in a sauté pan large enough to hold them in one layer. Add the olive oil, salt, lemon peel, thyme, and bay leaf. Bring to a simmer over medium heat and then reduce the heat to low. Cut a circle of parchment about the size of your pan. Cut a small circle in the center of the pan-sized parchment and place it on top of the fennel in the pan. (In culinary terms this is called a cartouche). Simmer the fennel bulbs until tender, about 30 minutes. Remove cartouche with tongs. Serve immediately or cool to room temperature and store in oil up to 1 week.

Makes 4 servings; Serving Size: 2 bulbs

V | vg | gf | df | ef | nf

CALORIES: 100; TOTAL FAT: 7 G; CARBOHYDRATE: 9 G; DIETARY FIBER: 4 G; PROTEIN: 1 G

TOMATO NAGE

2 tablespoons extra-virgin olive oil

1/2 yellow onion, diced

2 garlic cloves, thinly sliced

1/4 to 1/2 teaspoon red chili flakes

1/2 fennel bulb, cored, cut into small dice, tops removed (save the fronds for garnish)

1/2 rib of celery, trimmed and thinly sliced

Pinch saffron

1/2 cup white wine, such as Chardonnay

1/2 teaspoon tomato paste

4 cups cored, peeled, and diced plum tomatoes (see **Note**)

1/2 cup water

1 long (1-inch-wide) strip orange peel

1 sprig fresh thyme

1 bay leaf

1 teaspoon whole coriander seeds, toasted

1 star anise

1/4 cup freshly squeezed lemon juice

Pinch fine sea salt

Pinch freshly ground black pepper

In a large saucepan, warm the olive oil over medium heat. Add the onion, garlic, and chili flakes. Sauté, stirring frequently, until soft but not brown, about 3 minutes. Add the diced fennel and celery. Sauté until translucent, 3 to 4 minutes. Stir in the saffron, and then add the wine. Reduce the wine by half, and then stir in the tomato paste, diced plum tomatoes, and water. Bring to a simmer.

Meanwhile, place the orange peel, thyme, bay leaf, coriander, and star anise in a cheesecloth bundle tied with kitchen twine. Add to the pot. Simmer the mixture on low heat for 45 minutes. Set aside to cool for 10 minutes.

Remove the herb bundle. Purée the mixture in a high-speed blender until smooth. Add the lemon juice. Season to taste with salt and pepper. Pass the tomato mixture through a fine-mesh sieve into a clean bowl or container with a tight-fitting lid. Use immediately or cover and refrigerate for up to 2 days. Heat before serving.

Note:
Ideally, this recipe works best starting with fresh, vine-ripened plum tomatoes, but sometimes using canned diced tomatoes can be a timesaver. Buy both a 28-ounce and 14.5-ounce can of tomatoes to measure out 4 cups of diced tomatoes after you drain the liquid from the can.

Makes 6 servings; Serving Size: 1/2 cup

V | vg | gf | df | ef | nf

CALORIES: 120; TOTAL FAT: 5 G; CARBOHYDRATE: 13 G; DIETARY FIBER: 3 G; PROTEIN: 3 G

ELOTE TROUT

Steelhead trout is the centerpiece of this playful recipe that takes inspiration from elote, the fabulous grilled Mexican street corn. Two easy-to-make sauces add layers of flavor to this colorful dish. After tossing a cupful of the Avocado Poblano Dressing with the cabbage, there will be some left over. Spoon the rest into a bowl and serve it like a dip with crudités and tortilla chips.

....

Chili Lime Aioli

1/4 cup mayonnaise

1 1/2 teaspoons fresh lime juice

1/2 teaspoon chili powder

Avocado Poblano Dressing

1 poblano chile

1 ripe avocado, halved and pitted

2/3 cup lightly-packed fresh cilantro leaves

6 tablespoons fresh lime juice

3/4 teaspoon fine sea salt

1 recipe Basic Jasmine Rice (page 306)

About 1 cup fresh corn kernels, from 2 ears corn

4 (4-ounce) fillets of steelhead trout

Fine sea salt

Expeller-pressed grapeseed or unrefined avocado oil

2 cups finely shredded cabbage

2 ounces crumbled queso fresco cheese

Minced fresh cilantro for garnish

To make the Chili Lime Aioli, in a small bowl stir together the mayonnaise, lime juice, and chili powder. Cover and refrigerate until ready to serve. The aioli can be made 1 day in advance.

To make the Avocado Poblano Sauce, place the chile over a gas flame or under the broiler and char the skin, turning the chile until all sides are blackened and the pepper is soft. Wrap in damp paper towels and set aside for 5 minutes to cool. Using the paper towels, wipe away all the charred skin, slit the chile in half, and remove the core and seeds. Transfer to the workbowl of a food processor and add the avocado, cilantro, lime juice, and salt. Process to make a smooth, thick, and creamy sauce. Add a tablespoon or two of water to thin it out, if needed. Salt to taste. Transfer to a bowl, cover, and set aside until ready to serve. The sauce can be made up to 8 hours in advance. Refrigerate until needed.

Heat the oven to 425°F.

Make the Basic Jasmine Rice and keep warm.

Place the corn in a large dry skillet over medium-high heat. Toast the corn, stirring constantly, until golden in spots, 4 to 5 minutes. Set aside and keep warm.

gf | nf

CALORIES: 630; TOTAL FAT: 36 G; CARBOHYDRATE: 56 G; DIETARY FIBER: 6 G; PROTEIN: 31 G

To sear the fish, season the flesh side of each fillet with salt. Place a large ovenproof skillet over medium-high heat, add enough oil to coat the bottom of the pan. Add the fillets, seasoned-side down, and sear on one side until golden and cooked halfway through, about 3 minutes. Carefully turn the fillets over and transfer the pan to the oven. Bake the fish until cooked through, about 4 minutes longer.

While the fish is baking, place the shredded cabbage in a large bowl. Toss with 1 cup of the dressing.

To serve, spoon 1/2 cup of jasmine rice in the center of each warmed plate or shallow bowl. Portion the cabbage slaw and place it on top of the rice. Lay a fillet of trout over the top. Divide and scatter the corn and cheese around the fish. Spoon 1 tablespoon of the chili lime aioli over the top. Garnish with cilantro and serve immediately.

Makes 4 servings; Serving Size: 1 fillet

MISO-GLAZED SEA BASS
WITH JASMINE RICE & SUGAR SNAP PEAS

The best way to coordinate the cooking of this meal so everything is hot and ready to serve, is to make the rice and glaze first and keep it warm. Have everything prepared for the sugar snap peas before you start cooking the fish, and then once the fish is in the oven, sauté the sugar snap peas. The meal will come together in a snap!

· ·

Glaze

1 tablespoon extra-virgin olive oil

1/4 cup chopped fresh lemongrass

1 tablespoon chopped fresh ginger

1 cup [4 ounces] peeled and diced Yukon Gold potatoes

6 tablespoons red miso paste

2 cups Vegetable Stock (page 303) or store-bought vegetable broth

1 tablespoon minced fresh cilantro

4 [4-ounce] sea bass fillets

1/8 teaspoon fine sea salt

1/8 teaspoon freshly ground black pepper

2 tablespoons Miraval Oil Blend (page 304) or expeller-pressed grapeseed oil

1 recipe Jasmine Rice (recipe follows)

1 recipe Sugar Snap Peas (recipe follows)

Heat the oven to 425°F. Have ready an ovenproof skillet large enough to hold the fillets in a single layer.

To make the glaze, place a medium heavy skillet over medium-high heat, add the oil and swirl to coat the bottom of the pan. Add the lemongrass and ginger and sauté, stirring constantly, until fragrant, 1 minute. Add the potato and cook, stirring, for 1 minute. Add the miso and stir well to break up the paste and cook for 30 seconds. Add the vegetable stock or broth and bring to a boil. Reduce the heat to low, and simmer until the potatoes are tender, about 9 minutes.

Transfer the mixture to the container of a high-speed blender and blend until smooth. Strain into a clean bowl, and then stir in the cilantro. Keep warm until ready to use.

Season the fillets on both sides with salt and pepper.

Place the skillet over medium-high heat, add the oil and swirl to coat the bottom of the pan. Add the seasoned fish and sear on one side for 1 minute. Carefully turn the fillets over, and then transfer the skillet to the oven and roast the fish for 5 minutes.

Remove the pan from the oven, turn each filet and let them rest in the pan on top of the stove while assembling the remaining components.

To serve, spoon 1/4 cup of cooked rice on to each of 4 large plates and angle the fillets on top of the rice. Place the peas to the side of the rice and drizzle the sauce over the fillets. Serve immediately.

Makes 4 servings; Serving Size: 1 fillet

gf | df | ef | nf

CALORIES: 330; TOTAL FAT: 8 G; CARBOHYDRATE: 35 G; DIETARY FIBER: 5 G; PROTEIN: 28 G

JASMINE RICE

1/2 teaspoon Miraval Oil Blend (page 304)

1/4 cup diced carrots

2 cup Basic Jasmine Rice (page 306)

1/4 cup Vegetable Stock (page 303) or store-bought vegetable broth

1/8 teaspoon fine sea salt

1/8 teaspoon freshly ground black pepper

Heat the oil in a medium saucepan set over medium heat. Add the carrots and cook, stirring frequently, until soft, about 2 minutes. Add the cooked rice and stir well for 15 seconds. Add the stock, salt, and pepper and cook, stirring, until the rice is hot and the liquid has evaporated, about 2 minutes. Remove from the heat, cover, and keep warm until ready to serve.

Makes 8 servings; Serving Size: 1/4 cup

SUGAR SNAP PEAS

1/4 teaspoon Miraval Oil Blend (page 304)

2 cups sugar snap peas

Pinch fine sea salt

Pinch freshly ground black pepper

1/2 cup Vegetable Stock (page 303) or store-bought vegetable broth

Heat the oil in a large heavy skillet over medium-high heat. Add the sugar snap peas, salt, and pepper. Sauté, stirring constantly, for 1 minute. Add the stock and cook, stirring, until the peas are bright green and tender, but still retain their crunch, about 2 minutes. Remove from the heat and serve immediately.

Makes 4 servings; Serving Size: 1/2 cup

V | vg | gf | df | ef | nf

CALORIES: 60; TOTAL FAT: 0 G; CARBOHYDRATE: 13 G; DIETARY FIBER: 0 G; PROTEIN: 1 G

V | vg | gf | df | ef | nf

CALORIES: 30; TOTAL FAT: 0 G; CARBOHYDRATE: 5 G; DIETARY FIBER: 1 G; PROTEIN: 1 G

MUSSELS
WITH WINE, TOMATOES & HERBS

A fine meal for those who love mussels—steamed in white wine and seasoned with fresh herbs, aromatics, cherry tomatoes, and portobello mushrooms. Serve with toasted pita chips or a slice of grilled bread.

3 pounds Black mussels, scrubbed and debearded

3 tablespoons all-purpose flour

3 tablespoons Miraval Oil Blend (page 304) or unrefined avocado oil

1/4 cup minced shallots

3 large garlic cloves, minced

2 (4-ounce) portobello mushroom, wiped clean, stemmed, gills removed, chopped

3 cups halved cherry tomatoes

1 tablespoon minced fresh oregano

1 tablespoon minced fresh flat-leaf parsley

1 tablespoon minced fresh thyme leaves

2 1/2 cups dry white wine

2 teaspoons grass-fed unsalted butter

1 teaspoon fine sea salt

1/4 teaspoon freshly ground black pepper

1/2 lemon, seeds removed

Submerge the mussels in a large bowl full of clean, cold water and add the flour. Swish it around and leave the mussels for 20 minutes. This way they spit out any sand and grit within the shells. Drain well and set aside.

Heat a large, deep skillet or sauté pan over medium heat. Add the oil and swirl to coat the bottom of the pan. Add the mushrooms and cook, stirring until the mushrooms give off liquid, 2 minutes. Stir in the shallots and garlic. Cook, stirring, until fragrant and the shallots start to turn golden brown, about 2 minutes. Stir in the tomatoes and cook for 15 seconds.

Add the herbs, salt, and pepper. Stir well to incorporate and cook for 10 seconds. Add the wine, stir well, and bring to a boil. Add the butter and stir to incorporate. Add the mussels. Reduce the heat to medium, cover the pan, and cook until the mussels open, about 5 minutes.

Remove the pan from the heat. Divide the mussels and the wine and tomato sauce between four warmed shallow bowls. Discard any mussels that did not open. Squeeze a bit of lemon juice over each bowl. Serve immediately.

Makes 6 servings

gf | ef | nf

CALORIES: 420; TOTAL FAT: 16 G; CARBOHYDRATE: 20 G; DIETARY FIBER: 2 G; PROTEIN: 29 G

ROGHAN GHOSHT

Gosht or ghosht refers to tender meat that has been cooked for a long time. This delicious aromatic lamb curry dish comes from Kashmir. Seek out black cardamom pods and Kashmiri chili powder at a spice store or order online. This is one of those savory stews with warm spices that you'll crave in the colder months and make repeatedly. Serve with basmati rice and garnish with freshly chopped cilantro.

4 tablespoons expeller-pressed grapeseed oil

1 yellow onion, diced

2 pounds lamb stew meat, cut into 1 1/2-inch cubes

2 cinnamon sticks

8 whole cloves

10 black peppercorns

4 black cardamom pods

1 tablespoon Kashmiri chili powder

2 teaspoons fennel seeds

1 tablespoon ground ginger

4 cups water

2 cups plain lowfat Greek yogurt

Fine sea salt

Freshly ground black pepper

3 cups cooked basmati rice

Chopped fresh cilantro for garnish

In a Dutch oven set over medium-high heat, warm the oil and swirl to coat the bottom of the pan. Add the onion and sauté until soft but not brown, about 5 minutes. Add the lamb along with the cinnamon sticks, cloves, peppercorns, and cardamom pods. Sauté, stirring frequently, to brown the lamb on all sides. The lamb will release liquid; cook until all the liquid has evaporated.

Add the chili powder, fennel seeds, ground ginger, and water. Bring to a simmer, and then reduce the heat and braise the lamb, partially covered, until the lamb is tender, about 1 1/2 hours. Remove the pan from the heat. Stir in the yogurt. Season to taste with salt and pepper. Serve with 1/2 cup basmati rice and garnish with cilantro.

Makes 6 servings; Serving Size: 1 cup

gf | ef | nf

CALORIES: 450; TOTAL FAT: 19 G; CARBOHYDRATE: 27 G; DIETARY FIBER: 1 G; PROTEIN: 41 G

BRAISED LAMB SHANKS
WITH MILLET POLENTA & MEYER LEMON GREMOLATA

This is a deeply satisfying winter or early-spring main course to make for a family gathering or dinner with friends. The lamb shanks can be roasted 1 to 2 days in advance. While the millet polenta is cooking, the Meyer Lemon Gremolata can be made and that leaves a quick steaming of broccolini to finish the dish. Meyer lemons are a seasonal specialty and not all markets carry them. Use the common "Eureka" lemon if you can't find Meyer lemons.

· ·

Lamb Shanks

2 (1-pound) lamb shanks

Fine sea salt

Freshly ground black pepper

3 tablespoons expeller-pressed grapeseed oil

1 cup button mushrooms, wiped clean, quartered

1 yellow onion, quartered

2 garlic cloves, smashed

1 carrot, trimmed, peeled, and cut into 1/2-inch dice

1/2 fennel bulb, cored and thinly sliced, tops removed, fennel fronds saved for garnish

1 rib celery, trimmed, peeled, and cut into 1/2-inch dice

2 tablespoons tomato paste

2 cups full-bodied red wine, such as Cabernet Sauvignon

1 long (1-inch-wide) strip orange peel

1 sprig fresh thyme

1 sprig rosemary

1 bay leaf

6 cups Vegetable Stock (page 303) or store-bought vegetable broth

Millet Polenta

1 teaspoon extra-virgin olive oil

1/2 cup millet

2 1/2 cup Vegetable Stock (page 303) or store-bought vegetable broth

Zest of 1/2 lemon

Fine sea salt

Freshly ground black pepper

2 tablespoons grass-fed unsalted butter, at room temperature

1/4 cup freshly grated Parmesan cheese

1/4 cup freshly grated pecorino cheese

3 tablespoons Meyer Lemon Gremolata (recipe follows)

4 stems broccolini, steamed

4 sprigs fennel fronds for garnish

Season the lamb shanks with salt and pepper and set aside for 20 minutes to allow the seasonings to penetrate the meat.

Arrange a rack in the lower third of the oven and heat the oven to 325°F. Have ready a 6-quart Dutch oven.

Place the Dutch oven over medium-high heat, add the oil, and swirl to coat the bottom of the pan. Brown the lamb shanks on all sides, about 8 minutes. Once brown, remove them from the pan and transfer to a plate.

Add the mushrooms and sauté, stirring frequently until brown, about 5 minutes. Add the onion and garlic, sauté for 1 minute. Add the carrots, fennel, and celery, and sauté for 2 minutes longer. Stir in the tomato paste and sauté for 1 minute longer. Add the red wine and reduce by half, about 10 to 12 minutes.

Meanwhile, place the orange peel, thyme, rosemary, and bay leaf in a cheesecloth bundle and tie with kitchen twine.

Once the wine is reduced, add the herb sachet to the pot along with the vegetable stock. Season with salt and pepper. Bring to a boil. Return the lamb shanks to the pot. Cover and transfer to the oven to braise for 3 hours. The lamb shanks can be served immediately, or you can cool them and then transfer them to a covered container and refrigerate for up to 2 days.

gf | ef | nf

CALORIES: 654; TOTAL FAT: 48 G; CARBOHYDRATE: 36 G; DIETARY FIBER: 10 G; PROTEIN: 30 G

While the lamb is braising make the Millet Polenta and the Meyer Lemon Gremolata.

To cook the Millet Polenta, place a medium, heavy-bottomed saucepan over medium-high heat. Add the oil and swirl to coat the bottom of the pan. Add the millet and stir to toast the millet until golden brown. Add the vegetable stock, lemon zest, and season with salt and pepper. Bring to a boil. Simmer, uncovered, stirring occasionally, until the millet is tender, and the stock is absorbed, about 25 minutes. Stir in the butter and grated cheeses. Cover and keep warm.

While the polenta is cooking, make the Meyer Lemon Gremolata.

To serve, remove the lamb from the bones and divide into 4 portions. Divide the millet polenta among 4 warmed shallow pasta bowls. Portion the lamb over the top. Garnish each plate with lemon gremolata and steamed broccolini. Top with a sprig of fennel and serve immediately.

Makes 4 servings

MEYER LEMON GREMOLATA

1/2 cup chopped flat-leaf parsley

1/4 cup finely chopped tarragon leaves

Zest of 2 Meyer lemons or 1 "Eureka" lemons

1 garlic clove, minced

2 teaspoons extra-virgin olive oil

Fine sea salt

Freshly ground black pepper

In a small bowl, stir together the parsley, tarragon, lemon zest, and garlic. Stir in the olive oil. Season with salt and pepper. Set aside.

Makes 4 servings

HERB-ROASTED CHICKEN BREAST
WITH QUINOA PILAF & GRAPEFRUIT MARMALADE

A special addition to this lovely main course is a homemade grapefruit marmalade. Make it a weekend project if you like or skip this step and buy a store-bought grapefruit marmalade to serve as the accompaniment.

Cranberry Quinoa Pilaf

2 tablespoons extra-virgin olive oil

1/4 cup diced yellow onion

1/4 cup diced carrots

1/4 cup diced celery

2 tablespoons finely chopped shallots

1 1/2 teaspoons minced garlic

1 teaspoon fine sea salt

1/4 teaspoon freshly ground black pepper

1/4 cup dry white wine

1/2 cup organic white quinoa, rinsed and well drained

1 1/2 cups Vegetable Stock (page 303) or store-bought vegetable broth

2/3 cup dried cranberries, preferably unsweetened

1 sprig fresh thyme

1 bay leaf

Herb-Roasted Chicken Breast

4 (6-ounce) boneless, skin-on chicken breasts, trimmed of excess fat

Fine sea salt

Freshly ground black pepper

3 tablespoons grass-fed unsalted butter

3 tablespoons extra-virgin olive oil

1/4 cup mixed chopped fresh herbs, such as thyme, rosemary, and parsley

16 baby heirloom carrots, tops trimmed and scrubbed

1/2 cup store-bought or homemade Grapefruit Marmalade (recipe follows), heated so it spoons like a sauce

Arrange one rack in the center of the oven and a second rack in the lower third. Heat the oven to 425°F.

In a stovetop-to-oven casserole with a tight-fitting lid, heat the oil over medium-low heat, and swirl to coat the bottom of the pan. Add the onion, carrot, celery, shallots, and garlic. Sauté, stirring frequently, until soft but not brown, about 4 minutes. Season with the salt and pepper and then add the wine and reduce slightly. Add the quinoa along with the stock, cranberries, thyme and bay leaf. Bring to a boil, and then cover and transfer to the lower shelf of the oven. Bake for 30 minutes until the liquid is absorbed and the quinoa is tender. Remove from the oven. Fluff with a fork, and then remove the thyme and bay leaf. Keep hot.

While the quinoa is baking, prepare the chicken and carrots. Pat the chicken dry with paper towels, and then season the chicken on both sides with salt and pepper.

In a large heavy-bottomed ovenproof sauté pan set over medium heat, melt 2 tablespoons of the butter and 2 tablespoons of the oil. Swirl to coat the bottom of the pan. Arrange the chicken breasts, skin-side down, and sear until the skin is golden. Avoid moving the chicken until the skin easily releases from the pan. (This step may take as long as 7 minutes in order to get a beautiful golden crust on the skin.) Flip the chicken and sear the other side for 2 minutes. With the chicken breasts skin-side up, scatter the herbs over their tops and baste with the pan drippings. Transfer the pan to the middle shelf of the oven and bake, uncovered, until the chicken is cooked through, and the internal temperature of the meat is 165°F on an instant-read thermometer, about 8 minutes.

gf | ef | nf

CALORIES: 560; TOTAL FAT: 29 G; CARBOHYDRATE: 36 G; DIETARY FIBER: 6 G; PROTEIN: 38 G

While the chicken is baking, heat a medium-sized sauté pan over medium heat. Add the remaining tablespoon of butter and oil. Swirl to coat the bottom of the pan. Add the carrots and sauté, using tongs to turn the carrots, until brown spots appear, about 4 minutes. Season with salt and pepper. Cover and cook until the carrots are tender, about 4 minutes longer.

To serve, spoon 1/2 cup of the cranberry quinoa pilaf onto the bottom of 4 warmed plates or shallow bowls. Lay a chicken breast across the top. Arrange 4 carrots on each plate. Spoon 2 tablespoons of the warmed grapefruit marmalade over top and serve immediately.

Makes 4 servings

GRAPEFRUIT MARMALADE

2 large (about 1 1/2 pounds) organic grapefruits, some pith removed, peel cut into thin strips, flesh chopped

1 2/3 cups honey

1/2 cup bittersweet botanical liqueur (amaro)

1 tablespoon chopped fresh rosemary

1 1/2 cups water

Combine the grapefruit, honey, bittersweet botanical liqueur, rosemary, and water in a large, heavy-bottomed saucepan. Bring to a boil over medium-high heat, stirring occasionally. Reduce the heat so the mixture simmers gently and then cook, stirring frequently, until the mixture is reduced and thickens to a lovely marmalade consistency, about 30 to 40 minutes. The best way to test is to freeze several soup spoons on a plate. When the marmalade is thick, dip one of the spoons into the marmalade and tap some onto the frozen plate. If you can run your finger through the marmalade and it stays separated, then the marmalade is done. If not, cook it a little longer and test again.

Remove from the heat and set aside to cool to room temperature. Transfer to covered jars and refrigerate for up to 2 months.

Makes 4 cups; Serving Size: 2 tablespoons

V | gf | df | ef | nf

CALORIES: 60; TOTAL FAT: 0 G; CARBOHYDRATE: 15 G; DIETARY FIBER: 0 G; PROTEIN: 0 G

ACHIOTE CHICKEN

MIRAVAL RESORTS · GUEST FAVORITE

A delicious dish doesn't always require a long list of ingredients. This main course is one of those, so consider it your back-pocket recipe for a quick weeknight meal. The orange-achiote sauce can be made several days ahead and refrigerated or frozen in small containers. Look for achiote (annatto) paste, a South and Central American condiment, in well-stocked supermarkets or order it online. Serve with Ancho Chile Butternut Squash Purée (page 262), or Caramelized Three-Onion Polenta (page 261), or Jasmine Rice (page 306).

Orange-Achiote Sauce

4 cups homemade or store-bought low-sodium chicken broth

2 cups freshly squeezed orange juice

1 tablespoon achiote paste

4 (6-ounce) boneless, skin-on chicken breasts (see ***Note***)

Fine sea salt

Freshly ground black pepper

Expeller-pressed grapeseed oil

2 tablespoons grass-fed unsalted butter

To make the Orange-Achiote Sauce, whisk together the chicken broth, orange juice, and achiote paste in a large saucepan. Bring to a boil over high heat. Reduce the heat so the mixture gently simmers and cook until it is reduced by half, yielding 3 cups of sauce. Remove from the heat and keep warm, or cool to room temperature, transfer to a covered container, and refrigerate for up to 5 days (the sauce can be divided and frozen in small containers for up to 1 month).

Heat the oven to 400ºF. Season the chicken breasts on both sides with salt and pepper.

In a large ovenproof sauté pan, add just enough oil to coat the bottom of the pan. Heat the oil until hot but not smoking, and add the chicken breasts, skin-side down. Sear until the chicken is deeply golden brown and then flip the chicken over. Place the pan in the oven and cook until the breasts are cooked through, and the internal temperature reads 165ºF on an instant-read thermometer, about 8 minutes.

Remove the pan from the oven. Transfer the chicken to a warm platter and let the chicken rest for 4 minutes. Using the same pan (and being careful because the handle is hot), place the pan over medium-high heat. Add 2 cups of the orange-achiote sauce and simmer until reduced by one-quarter, about 5 minutes. Swirl in the butter. Place a chicken breast in a warmed shallow bowl and spoon the sauce over the top. Serve immediately.

Note:

The chefs at Miraval Austin use "airline chicken breasts" for this recipe. These are skin-on, boneless chicken breasts with the drumette attached. Unless you have a butcher who will cut these for you, the best option is to use skin-on, boneless chicken breasts, which will work perfectly.

Makes 4 servings

gf | ef | nf

CALORIES: 410; TOTAL FAT: 21 G; CARBOHYDRATE: 13 G; DIETARY FIBER: 0 G; PROTEIN: 39 G

FLANK STEAK BOWL

Build a satisfying, protein-packed meal in a bowl with slices of grilled steak arranged over a bed of chopped romaine lettuce. Add layers of flavor with Pickled Onions (page 260), roasted corn, diced tomato, cilantro leaves, and drizzle it all with chimichurri.

. . . .

Marinade

1/2 cup freshly squeezed orange juice

1 1/2 tablespoons freshly squeezed lime juice

1 1/2 tablespoons extra-virgin olive oil

1 1/2 tablespoons tamari or gluten-free soy sauce

1 tablespoon chipotle chiles in adobo

1/4 bunch fresh cilantro leaves

3 garlic cloves

1 tablespoon chili powder

1 tablespoon organic cane sugar

2 teaspoons ground cumin

1 teaspoon ground coriander

1 teaspoon fine sea salt

2 pounds grass-fed flank steak

1 recipe Chimichurri (page 37)

6 ounces Pickled Red Onions (page 260)

2 heads of romaine lettuce, cut crosswise into thin strips

3 ears corn, grill-roasted and then kernels removed from the cob

4 vine-ripened tomatoes, cored, halved, seeded, and diced

8 ounces crumbled queso fresco

1/4 bunch fresh cilantro leaves

To make the marinade, combine the orange and lime juice, olive oil, tamari, chipotle chiles, cilantro, garlic, chili powder, sugar, cumin, coriander, and salt in the container of a high-speed blender. Blend to make a smooth sauce.

Place the steak in a 9-by-13-inch glass baking dish, or other container of comparable size, pour the marinade over the top. Turn the steak over to evenly coat both sides. Cover and refrigerate for at least 3 hours, but no more than 5 hours. (Alternatively, place the flank steak in a gallon-size lock-top plastic bag and pour the marinade into the bag. Distribute the marinade so it covers all of the meat and squeeze out all the air. Seal the bag, place on a rimmed sheet pan, and refrigerate.)

While the meat is marinating, make the chimichurri, pickled red onions, and chop and have ready all the toppings for the bowl. (You can grill-roast the corn and cut the kernels from the cobs just before grilling the steak).

When ready to grill, remove the steak from the marinade and discard the marinade. Prepare a hot fire in a charcoal or gas grill. Grill the flank steak on high, turning occasionally, until the steak is beautifully charred on the outside and the internal temperature registers 120°F on an instant-read thermometer, about 7 to 10 minutes total. Transfer the steak to a carving board and allow to rest for 5 minutes. Slice across the grain into thin strips.

To assemble each bowl, divide the lettuce among 8 bowls. Place strips of steak (about 4 ounces) on top. Scatter the corn, tomatoes, and cheese over the top. Drizzle with chimichurri and garnish with cilantro leaves. Serve immediately.

Makes 8 servings

gf | ef | nf

CALORIES: 520; TOTAL FAT: 31 G; CARBOHYDRATE: 27 G; DIETARY FIBER: 3 G; PROTEIN: 33 G

LAMB LOIN CHOPS
WITH GOAT CHEESECAKE & ROSEMARY GREMOLATA

To serve this main course at home, you need a game plan, and we have a simple one for you. Make the garlic purée and the blackberry compote 1 to 2 days in advance; the rosemary gremolata and the filling for the chevre cheesecakes can be made up to 8 hours in advance and refrigerated; that leaves searing the lamb chops and baking the cheesecakes right before serving. The recipe calls for a silicone muffin pan for the cheesecakes; it will make releasing them easy, and it's a useful pan to have for other muffin recipes.

....

Garlic Purée

16 garlic cloves, peeled

3/4 cup to 1 cup Vegetable Stock (page 303) or low-sodium chicken broth

2 tablespoons grass-fed unsalted butter

Fine sea salt

Blackberry Compote

8 ounces fresh or frozen blackberries

1/2 cup confectioners' sugar

1 tablespoon minced fresh rosemary

1 tablespoon minced fresh thyme leaves

Rosemary Gremolata

1/2 cup panko bread crumbs

1 tablespoon finely chopped fresh flat-leaf parsley

1 tablespoon lemon zest

1 tablespoon minced garlic

1/2 teaspoon finely chopped rosemary

1/2 teaspoon fine sea salt

Freshly ground black pepper

Goat Cheesecakes

2/3 cup panko bread crumbs

1/3 cup grated Parmesan cheese

2 tablespoons grass-fed unsalted butter, melted

2 teaspoons finely chopped fresh rosemary

8 ounces soft goat cheese (chevre)

1 large egg, beaten

2 tablespoons all-purpose flour

1 tablespoon organic grass-fed milk

1 1/2 teaspoons chopped fresh flat-leaf parsley

1 teaspoon chopped thyme leaves

1 1/2 teaspoons snipped chives

1/2 teaspoon fine sea salt

Several grinds of freshly ground black pepper

8 bone-in lamb loin chops, about 4 ounces each

Fine sea salt

Freshly ground black pepper

ef | nf

CALORIES: 650; TOTAL FAT: 33 G; CARBOHYDRATE: 42 G; DIETARY FIBER: 3 G; PROTEIN: 44 G

To make the Garlic Purée, put the garlic and vegetable stock or broth in a small saucepan set over medium heat, and simmer, partially covered, until the garlic is very tender, about 15 minutes. (Add up to 1/4 cup more broth, if needed.) Add the butter and melt completely. Blend using an immersion blender or process in a mini-chop food processor until smooth. Season with salt to taste. Set aside and keep warm, or transfer to a covered container and rewarm just before serving.

To make the Blackberry Compote, combine the blackberries, confectioners' sugar, rosemary, and thyme in a small saucepan. Cook over low heat, stirring occasionally, until the mixture thickens, about 20 minutes. Set aside and reserve until ready to use.

To make the Rosemary Gremolata, combine the panko, parsley, lemon zest, garlic, rosemary, salt, and a few grinds of black pepper in a medium bowl. Set aside in a covered container until ready to use.

To make the Goat Cheesecakes, first make the crust. Heat the oven to 350ºF. In the workbowl of a food processor fitted with the metal blade, pulse to combine the panko, Parmesan, unsalted butter, and rosemary. Divide the mixture evenly on the bottom of 8 standard-size silicone muffin cups. Press lightly and then bake for 10 minutes. Set aside.

Meanwhile, make the filling. First, simply wipe out the workbowl of the food processor to get rid of the crumbs. Add the goat cheese, egg, flour, milk, parsley, thyme, chives, salt, and pepper. Process until evenly smooth. Transfer to a bowl (use immediately or cover and refrigerate until ready to bake the cheesecakes). To bake the cheesecakes, scoop 2 ounces of the filling into each muffin cup. Bake the cheesecakes until set, about 20 minutes. Keep warm.

When ready to cook the lamb, season the lamb chops on both sides with salt and pepper. Place the loin chops bone-side down in a large, heated cast-iron skillet set over medium-high heat. Cook on the bone for 5 minutes. Lay the loin chop on one side and cook until well seared, about 4 minutes. Flip and cook on the other side until well seared, about 4 to 5 minutes longer for medium rare, 125ºF on an instant-read thermometer.

To serve, spread 2 tablespoons of the warm garlic purée onto the base of each warmed dinner plate. Place 2 lamb loin chops on top and a goat cheesecake next to the lamb chops. Spoon some of the blackberry compote onto the cheesecake. Garnish the plate with the rosemary gremolata. Serve immediately. You will end up with 3 to 4 extra cheesecakes; serve them, or reheat them later for delicious leftovers.

Makes 4 servings

basics & accents

SALSA VERDE

A favorite condiment at Miraval Arizona is the Salsa Verde. Look for firm and plump tomatillos in the produce section of your local grocery store. Use the salsa as an appetizer with toasted chips, spooned over enchiladas or burritos, or as a condiment for grilled seafood. We pair it with the Baked Flounder (page 278).

10 ounces tomatillos

1/2 cup coarsely chopped white onion

2 serrano chiles, stem end removed (halved, seeded, and deribbed for less heat)

2 garlic cloves

2 tablespoons chopped cilantro leaves

1 tablespoon organic expeller-pressed canola oil

1 teaspoon fine sea salt

Remove the papery husks from the tomatillos and rinse to remove the sticky residue. Cut each tomatillo into quarters.

In a medium saucepan, combine the tomatillos, onion, chiles, and garlic. Add just enough water to cover the vegetables. Bring to a boil and then reduce the heat and simmer for 10 minutes.

Using a high-speed blender, add all the vegetables, including the liquid in the pot to the container of the blender. Add the cilantro and blend until smooth.

Using the same pot, warm the oil over medium heat. Add the tomatillo mixture and simmer for 20 minutes. Stir in the salt. Remove from the heat and cool to room temperature. Use immediately, or transfer to a covered container and refrigerate for up to 5 days.

Makes 8 servings; Serving Size: 1/4 cup

V | vg | gf | df | ef | nf

CALORIES: 30; TOTAL FAT: 2 G; CARBOHYDRATE: 3 G;
DIETARY FIBER: 1 G; PROTEIN: 1 G

VEGAN AIOLI

The classic aioli is recreated in a vegan version with soy milk replacing the egg yolks, giving the garlicky sauce as smooth and creamy a texture as the original. Add chopped fresh herbs to flavor the aioli, use Garlic Confit (page 302) in place of the raw garlic, or toss in a tablespoon or two of charred lemon instead of the fresh lemon juice to make a more boldly flavored lemon aioli.

2 garlic cloves

3 tablespoons fresh lemon juice

1 1/2 teaspoons Dijon mustard

1/2 teaspoon fine sea salt

1/8 teaspoon freshly ground white pepper

1/2 cup organic unsweetened soy milk

1/4 cup extra-virgin olive oil

3/4 cup organic expeller-pressed canola oil

In the container of a high-speed blender, combine the garlic, lemon juice, Dijon mustard, salt, pepper, and soy milk. Blend until smooth. With the machine running, drizzle in the olive oil, followed by the canola oil, until the sauce is emulsified. Taste and add more salt and pepper, if needed. Transfer to a covered container and refrigerate until ready to use. The aioli will keep refrigerated for up to 5 days.

Makes 12 servings; Serving Size: 2 tablespoons

V | vg | gf | df | ef | nf

CALORIES: 169; TOTAL FAT: 19 G; CARBOHYDRATE: 1 G;
DIETARY FIBER: 0 G; PROTEIN: 0 G

QUICK NAPA CABBAGE KIMCHI

Incorporating fermented foods, like kimchi, into our diet can help support gut health and digestion. It can be easy to make kimchi at home and has become popular as a weekend cooking project. For this recipe, it helps to have a kitchen scale for weighing the cabbage, salt, ginger, garlic, and onion. Also, wearing disposable gloves to mix together the kimchi protects your hands from the peppers.

1 head (about 2 pounds) napa cabbage, halved lengthwise and cored, chopped into 1-inch pieces

1/4 cup fine sea salt

2 tablespoons coarsely chopped yellow onion

8 garlic cloves

1 tablespoon peeled fresh ginger, coarsely chopped

2 kiwi, peeled and quartered

1/4 cup rice wine vinegar

2 tablespoons Korean chile flakes or Aleppo pepper

2 tablespoons Espelette (Piment d'Espelette) or red pepper flakes

1/4 cup kombucha

In a large bowl, toss together the cabbage and salt. Set aside for one hour, and then rinse it thoroughly and squeeze dry. Return it to a large clean, dry bowl.

In a food processor fitted with the metal blade, process, the onion, garlic, and ginger until finely minced. Add the kiwi and process until puréed. Add the vinegar, Korean chile flakes, and Espelette pepper and process until incorporated. Pour this mixture into the cabbage in the bowl and mix thoroughly. Now stir in the kombucha.

Pack the kimchi into a large fermenting crock or quart-size glass jars with tight-fitting lids. Leave at room temperature for 24 hours, and then move it to the refrigerator. It is best to wait 3 to 4 days for it to develop more flavor before serving.

Makes 16 servings; Serving Size: 1/4 cup

V | vg | gf | df | ef | nf

CALORIES: 15; TOTAL FAT: 0 G; CARBOHYDRATE: 3 G; DIETARY FIBER: 1 G; PROTEIN: 1 G

BBQ DRY SPICE RUB

Created by the chefs at Miraval Berkshires, this flavorful spice blend is terrific on fruits, vegetables, grilled meats, and seafood. If you have a coffee grinder, it's best to grind the coffee fresh for this fragrant spice rub.

1/4 cup finely ground dark-roast coffee

3 tablespoons light brown sugar

2 tablespoons coarse sea salt

2 tablespoons smoked paprika (pimentón de la Vera)

1 tablespoon ground cumin

1 tablespoon ancho chile powder

1 tablespoon granulated garlic

1 tablespoon granulated onion

2 teaspoons dry mustard powder

1 teaspoon freshly ground black pepper

1 teaspoon freshly ground white pepper

1 teaspoon ground coriander

1 teaspoon dried Mexican oregano

1 teaspoon ground Guajillo pepper, seeds removed

1/2 teaspoon ground cinnamon

In a medium bowl, whisk together all the ingredients. Store, away from light, in a tightly sealed container at room temperature. The spice rub may keep for up to one month.

Makes 1 cup

V | vg | gf | df | ef | nf

CALORIES: 17; TOTAL FAT: 0 G; CARBOHYDRATE: 3 G; DIETARY FIBER: 1 G; PROTEIN: 0 G

GARLIC CONFIT

Use garlic confit in vinaigrettes, marinades, and to baste vegetables for roasting or grilling. Store it in an airtight container in the refrigerator for up to 2 weeks or freeze it along with the infused oil in silicone ice cube trays for easy retrieval.

Peeled garlic from 3 heads of garlic

1 1/2 cups (or more) expeller-pressed grapeseed oil

Heat the oven to 250°F. Place the garlic in a small ovenproof baking dish or heatproof saucepan with a lid. Pour the oil over top, making sure the garlic is submerged. Add more oil, if needed.

Cover and bake until the garlic cloves are golden and tender, about 2 hours. Uncover and let cool. Transfer the garlic and oil to an airtight container, preferably glass, and refrigerate until ready to use.

Makes 1 1/2 cups

V | vg | gf | df | ef | nf

CALORIES: 90; TOTAL FAT: 9 G; CARBOHYDRATE: 1 G; DIETARY FIBER: 0 G; PROTEIN: 0 G

ALL-PURPOSE GLUTEN-FREE FLOUR

The chefs at Miraval Austin created their own gluten-free flour blend. Grab your kitchen scale and make a batch to have on hand for baking.

20 ounces white rice flour

9 ounces brown rice flour

9 ounces potato starch

5 ounces chickpea (garbanzo bean) flour

4 ounces tapioca flour

In a large bowl, whisk together all the ingredients. Transfer to a sealed container and store at room temperature, for up to 6 months, until ready to use.

Makes 10 1/2 cups; Serving Size: 1/2 cup

V | vg | gf | df | ef | nf

CALORIES: 240; TOTAL FAT: 1 G; CARBOHYDRATE: 52 G; DIETARY FIBER: 2 G; PROTEIN: 4 G

VEGETABLE STOCK

Making vegetable stock at home is easy and a basic recipe that every home cook should try to master. This stock is used in so many of this book's recipes. Make a batch, or a double batch, and keep it on hand in the freezer.

3 cups roughly chopped, peeled yellow onion

2 cups roughly chopped tomato

1 1/2 cups roughly chopped celery

1 1/2 cups roughly chopped carrots

1/2 cup roughly chopped cremini or shiitake mushrooms

2 teaspoons black peppercorns

5 sprigs fresh thyme

8 cups water

In a stockpot or Dutch oven, combine all the vegetables, along with the mushrooms, peppercorns, and thyme. Add the water and bring to a boil. Reduce the heat and simmer, uncovered, for 2 hours.

Remove from the heat and strain through a fine-mesh strainer, or a colander lined with cheesecloth into a clean container that has a tight-fitting lid. Let cool, uncovered, to room temperature. Refrigerate until ready to use. The stock may keep refrigerated for up to 5 days and frozen for up to 1 month.

Makes 3 cups; Serving Size: 1/2 cup

V | vg | gf | df | ef | nf

CALORIES: 25; TOTAL FAT: 0 G; CARBOHYDRATE: 6 G; DIETARY FIBER: 1 G; PROTEIN: 1 G

MIRAVAL OIL BLEND

We use this blended oil regularly in the Miraval Resorts kitchens, and we call for it in many of this book's recipes. The unrefined avocado oil can withstand high cooking temperatures, and the olive oil adds flavor.

3/4 cup unrefined avocado oil

1/4 cup extra-virgin olive oil

Combine the oils and transfer to a mister or spray bottle, which will allow you to dispense small amounts.

Makes 1 cup; Serving Size: 1 tablespoon

V | vg | gf | df | ef | nf

CALORIES: 124; TOTAL FAT: 14 G; CARBOHYDRATE: 0 G;
DIETARY FIBER: 0 G; PROTEIN: 0 G

CLARIFIED BUTTER
OR GHEE

Clarifying butter removes the milk solids, leaving only the pure butterfat so it can withstand higher cooking temperatures without burning. Make a batch and store it in the refrigerator to have on hand for sautéing. A wide-mouth, cup-size canning jar works well for storing the butter.

1/2 cup grass-fed unsalted butter

Cut the butter into small chunks and place in a 1-cup glass measuring cup. Microwave the butter until completely melted and it foams on top, being careful that it doesn't bubble over. Remove from the microwave and set aside for 2 minutes. The butter will have settled into three layers: foam on the top; clarified butter in the middle; and milk solids on the bottom. Using a small spoon, carefully remove the foam from the top. Slowly pour the clarified butter into a small jar, being careful to leave all the milk solids behind. Use immediately or cover and refrigerate until ready to use. Clarified butter may keep for several months in the refrigerator.

Makes 1/2 cup; Serving Size: 1 tablespoon

V | gf | ef | nf

CALORIES: 130; TOTAL FAT: 15 G; CARBOHYDRATE: 0 G;
DIETARY FIBER: 0 G; PROTEIN: 0 G

CARAMELIZED ONIONS

Make a batch and know that caramelized onions can be refrigerated for a few days or frozen for up to 2 months.

1 tablespoon grass-fed unsalted butter

1 tablespoon extra-virgin olive oil

1 1/2 pounds yellow or white onions, thinly sliced

1/2 teaspoon fine sea salt

In a large skillet over medium heat, melt the butter along with the olive oil. Add the onions along with the salt and sauté, stirring frequently, for 15 minutes. Reduce the heat to low if the onions are browning too quickly. The onions should be soft and beginning to turn golden. Continue to cook over low heat, stirring occasionally, until the onions are meltingly soft and caramel in color, about 25 minutes longer. If any brown bits have clung to the bottom of the skillet, add water, a tablespoon at a time, to release them. Remove the skillet from the stove and let the onions cool to room temperature. Use immediately or refrigerate in a covered container.

Makes 2 cups; Serving Size: 1/4 cup

V | gf | ef | nf

CALORIES: 63; TOTAL FAT: 3 G; CARBOHYDRATE: 8 G; DIETARY FIBER: 1 G; PROTEIN: 1 G

BASIC JASMINE RICE

Did you know you can freeze cooked rice? If you are cooking for just 1 or 2 people, make a batch and freeze the extra for up to 6 months.

1 1/2 cups Vegetable Stock (page 303), store-bought vegetable broth, or water

3/4 cup jasmine rice

Combine the vegetable stock or water, and the rice in a medium saucepan and bring to a boil over high heat. Reduce the heat to low, cover, and simmer until the rice is tender and all the liquid is absorbed, 10 to 12 minutes. Remove the pan from the heat and let stand, covered, for at least 5 minutes. Fluff with a fork and serve.

Makes 2 cups; Serving Size: 1/2 cup

V | vg | df | gf | ef | nf

CALORIES: 102; TOTAL FAT: 0 G; CARBOHYDRATE: 22 G; DIETARY FIBER: 0 G; PROTEIN: 2 G

BASIC BLACK BEANS

2 cups dried black beans, picked over for broken beans and pebbles, rinsed well

8 cups Vegetable Stock (page 303), or store-bought vegetable broth, or water

Place the beans in a large saucepan, add the vegetable stock or water, and bring to a simmer. Cook, stirring occasionally, until the beans are tender but still retain their shape, about 2 hours. Remove from the heat and serve or use as directed in a recipe that calls for black beans.

Makes 1 quart; Serving Size: 1/2 cup

V | vg | gf | df | ef | nf

CALORIES: 114; TOTAL FAT: 1 G; CARBOHYDRATE: 20 G;
DIETARY FIBER: 7 G; PROTEIN: 7 G

Plant-Based Specialty Butters

Make a batch of butters for a Sunday brunch to smear on toast or serve with pancakes or waffles. Once made, the nut butters keep best when stored in a covered container in the refrigerator. Think about making these as holiday food gifts.

MATCHA CASHEW BUTTER

2 cups toasted cashews

1 1/2 teaspoons matcha powder

1 1/2 teaspoons raw organic agave syrup

Water, as needed

In the workbowl of a food processor fitted with the metal blade, process the cashews, matcha powder, and agave until smooth, scraping down the sides of the bowl once or twice. Add water only if needed. Transfer to a covered container. Use immediately or cover and refrigerate until ready to use. The nut butter may keep refrigerated for up to 1 month.

Makes 1 cup; Serving Size: 2 tablespoons

CALORIES: 180; TOTAL FAT: 15 G; CARBOHYDRATE: 9 G; DIETARY FIBER: 1 G; PROTEIN: 5 G

COCOA ALMOND BUTTER

2 cups almond butter

1 1/2 teaspoons unsweetened cocoa powder

1 1/2 teaspoons raw organic agave syrup

Water, if needed

In the workbowl of a food processor fitted with the metal blade, process the almond butter, cocoa powder, and agave until smooth, scraping down the sides of the bowl once or twice. Add water only if needed. Transfer to a covered container. Use immediately or cover and refrigerate until ready to use. The nut butter may keep refrigerated for up to 1 month.

Makes 2 cups; Serving Size: 2 tablespoons

MAPLE PECAN BUTTER

2 cups toasted pecans

1 1/2 teaspoons real maple syrup

1 1/2 teaspoons ground cinnamon

Water, if needed

In the workbowl of a food processor fitted with the metal blade, process the pecans, maple syrup, and cinnamon until smooth, scraping down the sides of the bowl once or twice. Add water only if needed. Transfer to a covered container. Use immediately or cover and refrigerate until ready to use. The nut butter may keep refrigerated for up to 1 month.

Makes 1 cup; Serving Size: 2 tablespoons

V | vg | gf | df | ef

CALORIES: 194; TOTAL FAT: 17 G; CARBOHYDRATE: 6 G; DIETARY FIBER: 3 G; PROTEIN: 7 G

CALORIES: 210; TOTAL FAT: 21 G; CARBOHYDRATE: 5 G; DIETARY FIBER: 3 G; PROTEIN: 3 G

desserts

GINGER SPICE COOKIES

Ginger is a spice that refreshes and satisfies the palate, especially after a meal. These cookies are delicate and perfectly petite. No wonder they are so popular at Miraval Arizona. The recipe makes a lot of cookies. This can be great for a house full of guests, a bake sale, or a cookie exchange. You could also freeze half of the cookie dough to bake at a later time.

3 1/4 cups unbleached all-purpose flour

2/3 cup whole-wheat pastry flour

2 teaspoons baking soda

1 teaspoon ground ginger

1/2 teaspoon fine sea salt

1/2 teaspoon ground cinnamon

1/8 teaspoon ground cloves

1/2 cup grass-fed unsalted butter, at room temperature

1 3/4 cups turbinado sugar

1/2 cup unsulfured dark molasses (not blackstrap)

6 large egg whites

Arrange one rack in the center of the oven and another in the lower third. Heat the oven to 375°F. Lined two sheet pans with parchment paper. Set aside.

In a medium bowl, whisk together the two flours, baking soda, ginger, salt, cinnamon, and cloves. Set aside.

In a stand mixer fitted with the paddle attachment, or in a large bowl using a handheld mixer, cream the butter until light and fluffy, about 2 minutes. Add the sugar and molasses and beat until well incorporated, about 2 minutes longer. Beat in the egg whites, stopping the mixer once to scrape down the sides of the bowl. On low speed, add half of the flour mixture and beat just until the flour disappears. Add the remaining flour and mix just until incorporated, scraping down the sides of the bowl, if needed.

Spoon the dough by the heaping tablespoonful, or use a #30 cookie scoop, onto the prepared sheet pans, spacing the cookies 2 inches apart. Bake the cookies until the edges are crisp and the centers are still chewy, about 12 to 14 minutes. For even baking, at the midpoint, switch the pans between the racks and rotate them front to back. Remove from the oven and transfer the cookies to wire racks to cool. Repeat to bake additional batches.

Store the cookies between sheets of waxed or parchment paper in a sealed container at room temperature for up to 5 days or frozen for up to 2 weeks.

Makes about 50 (1-ounce) cookies; Serving Size: 1 cookie

V | nf

CALORIES: 90; TOTAL FAT: 2 G; CARBOHYDRATE: 17 G; DIETARY FIBER: 0 G; PROTEIN: 1 G

VEGAN SNICKERDOODLES

Soft and chewy, with an irresistible cinnamon-sugar coating, snickerdoodles bring back childhood memories of lunchbox favorites and holiday cookie exchanges. Here is a vegan version using mashed ripe bananas in the dough.

3 cups unbleached
all-purpose flour

1 tablespoon baking powder

1 teaspoon fine sea salt

1 cup vegan butter, at room
temperature

2 cups organic cane sugar

3 large ripe bananas, mashed
(about 2 cups)

1 teaspoon vanilla bean paste

Snickerdoodle Sugar

1/2 cup organic cane sugar

2 tablespoons ground
cinnamon

In a medium bowl, whisk together the flour, baking powder, and salt. Set aside.

In a stand mixer fitted with the paddle attachment, or in a large bowl using a handheld mixer, cream the butter and sugar until light and fluffy, about 2 minutes. Mix in the bananas and vanilla bean paste, scraping down the sides of the bowl once or twice. On low speed, add half of the flour mixture and beat just until the flour disappears. Mix in the rest of the flour, stopping the mixer once to scrape down the sides of the bowl.

Portion the dough into balls, using a one-ounce scoop or your hands to form balls about 3/4 the size of a golf ball, and freeze before baking. Bake as many as you want and keep the rest in the freezer to bake later. Frozen cookie dough keeps well for up to 2 months.

When ready to bake the cookies, arrange 1 rack in the center of the oven and another in the lower third. Heat the oven to 375°F. Line two sheet pans with parchment paper.

Make the snickerdoodle sugar: In a small bowl, stir together the sugar and cinnamon.

Roll the frozen balls of dough in the cinnamon-sugar mixture and arrange the balls 2 inches apart on the prepared pans. Bake the cookies for 8 minutes, and then switch the pans between the racks and rotate them front to back. Continue to bake until the bottoms are lightly browned, about 10-12 minutes longer. Remove from the oven and transfer the cookies to wire racks to cool. Repeat to bake additional batches.

Store the cookies between sheets of waxed or parchment paper in a sealed container at room temperature for up to 5 days or frozen for up to 2 weeks.

Makes about 48 (1-ounce) cookies; Serving Size: 1 cookie

V | vg | df | ef | nf

CALORIES: 100; TOTAL FAT: 3.5 G; CARBOHYDRATE: 16 G; DIETARY FIBER: 0 G; PROTEIN: 1 G

BLACK BEAN BROWNIES

A guest-favorite precisely because the unexpected ingredient—black beans—makes these chocolaty treats high in fiber and deliciously nutritious. Look for pure coffee extract in the baking aisle of specialty markets or online. And for those choosing a dairy-free diet, know that lots of popular chocolate brands sell dairy-free chocolate chips; read the label to make certain. This recipe utilizes a standard-sized food processor to purée the black beans and smooth the batter. An alternative would be to use an immersion blender.

6 large eggs

1/4 cup + 3 tablespoons cold-pressed canola oil

2 cans black beans, drained and rinsed

1 cup organic cane sugar

1/2 cup unsweetened cocoa powder

1 teaspoon baking powder

1/2 teaspoon fine sea salt

2 1/4 teaspoons pure vanilla extract

1/2 teaspoon pure coffee extract, optional

Generous 1/3 cup dairy-free mini chocolate chips

1 1/4 cups chopped walnuts

Position a rack in the center of the oven and heat the oven to 350°F. Lightly coat the bottom and sides of a 9-by-13-inch glass baking pan with nonstick cooking spray (or rub it all over with a little neutral oil). Line the pan with a sheet of parchment paper. Set aside.

In a medium bowl, whisk together the eggs and oil.

In the workbowl of a food processor fitted with the metal blade, process the black beans until puréed. (They won't be smooth at this point.) With the machine running, stream in the egg mixture and process until smooth. Add the sugar, cocoa powder, baking powder, salt, vanilla, and coffee extracts, if using. Process until combined. Add the chocolate chips and pulse just until incorporated.

Pour the batter into the prepared pan and smooth the top. Evenly scatter the walnuts over the top. Bake until the edges start to crack and the middle bounces back, about 35 to 45 minutes. (The edges should be puffed and the center should not be jiggly.) Cool in the pan on a wire rack. Cut into 24, approximately 2-inch-square brownies. (If desired, freeze for 30 minutes to 1 hour first to cut neater squares.) Store the brownies in the refrigerator between sheets of waxed or parchment paper in a sealed container. The brownies keep well refrigerated in a sealed container for 5 days or in the freezer for 2 months.

Makes 24 (approximately 2-inch-square) bars; Serving Size: 1 bar

V | gf | df

CALORIES: 143; TOTAL FAT: 8 G; CARBOHYDRATE: 15 G; DIETARY FIBER: 3 G; PROTEIN: 4 G

COWGIRL COOKIES

In this recipe, the classic cowgirl cookie is delightfully reimagined as both vegan and gluten-free. A mixture of flax meal and water replaces the egg and vegan butter is substituted. All the terrific textural crunch of the original cookie is included with the addition of rolled oats, chocolate chips, coconut flakes, and sunflower seeds. Plan ahead, as these cookies hold their shape best when formed into balls and frozen before baking.

....

2 tablespoons flaxseed meal

1/3 cup water

1 1/3 cups All-Purpose Gluten-Free Flour (page 303) or store-bought GF flour

1 1/2 teaspoons baking soda

1 1/2 teaspoons baking powder

2 teaspoons fine sea salt

1 cup vegan butter, at room temperature

1 cup organic cane sugar

1 cup light brown sugar

1 teaspoon pure vanilla extract

2 1/4 cups gluten-free old-fashioned rolled oats

1 1/3 cups vegan chocolate chips

1 1/2 cups unsweetened coconut flakes

Generous 3/4 cups sunflower seeds

In a small bowl, stir together the flaxseed meal and water. Set aside.

In a medium bowl, whisk together the flour, baking soda, baking powder, and salt. Set aside.

In a stand mixer fitted with the paddle attachment, or in a large bowl using a handheld mixer, cream the butter, sugar, and brown sugar until light and fluffy, about 2 minutes. Mix in the flax meal mixture and vanilla extract. On low speed, add the flour mixture and beat just until the flour disappears. Mix in the oats, stopping the mixer once to scrape down the sides of the bowl. Remove the bowl from the mixer.

Using a rubber spatula, mix in the chocolate chips, coconut flakes, and sunflower seeds until evenly distributed. Portion the dough into balls, using a one-ounce scoop or your hands to form balls about 3/4 the size of a golf ball. Arrange close together, but not touching, on a rimmed sheet pan and freeze for at least 3 hours before baking. (Once frozen, pack the balls of dough into a freezer bag and keep frozen until ready to bake.)

When ready to bake the cookies, arrange one rack in the center of the oven and another in the lower third. Heat the oven to 350°F. Line two sheet pans with parchment paper. Arrange the frozen balls of dough 3 inches apart on the prepared pans. Bake the cookies until the cookies are thin, lace-y crisp, and beautifully brown, about 14 to 16 minutes. For even baking, at the midpoint, switch the pans between the racks and rotate them front to back. Remove from the oven. Let the cookies cool on the pans for 10 minutes before transferring them to wire racks to cool. Repeat to bake additional batches.

Store the baked cookies between sheets of waxed or parchment paper in a sealed container at room temperature for up to 5 days.

Makes about 42 cookies; Serving Size: 1 cookie

V | vg | gf | df | ef | nf

CALORIES: 180; TOTAL FAT: 8 G; CARBOHYDRATE: 24 G; DIETARY FIBER: 3 G; PROTEIN: 4 G

CHOCOLATE PECAN BAR

Guests at Miraval Arizona give these vegan chocolate pecan bars a thumbs up. The crust has an intriguing herbal note with the addition of minced fresh rosemary, and that plays beautifully with the chocolate and pecans. The bottom crust is an easy pat-in-the-pan dough, and it is forgiving. If any cracks appear after it is baked, gently push the dough back together. Keep an eye on the sugar syrup as it boils, stir as it thickens, and turn down the heat if it begins to sputter. It is a luscious filling worth the time to prepare. This recipe utilizes both a mixer and a food processor. A blender will also work for the preparation of the filling.

Crust

2 1/2 cups unbleached all-purpose flour

1/2 cup organic cane sugar

1 1/2 teaspoons finely minced fresh rosemary

1 1/2 teaspoons fine sea salt

1 cup coconut oil, melted (see **Note**)

Filling

12 ounces firm tofu, well drained and blotted dry

1/2 cup organic unsweetened oat or soy milk

1/4 cup cornstarch

1 1/2 teaspoons fine sea salt

1 cup raw cane (turbinado) sugar

1/2 cup light brown sugar

1/2 cup real maple syrup

1/2 cup vegan butter, cut into cubes

4 cups pecan halves

2 cups vegan chocolate chips

Arrange an oven rack in the center of the oven and heat the oven to 375°F. Line a 13-by-18-inch rimmed sheet pan (half sheet pan) with parchment paper. Set aside.

To make the crust, combine the flour, sugar, rosemary, and salt, in the bowl of a stand mixer fitted with the paddle attachment, or in a large bowl using a handheld mixer. Mix on low speed, and then slowly pour in the melted coconut oil to form a dough. Once the dough comes together and looks uniform, stop the mixer. Transfer the dough to the prepared sheet pan. Pat out the dough to evenly cover the bottom of the pan. Bake until lightly golden brown, about 10 to 14 minutes. Gently transfer the pan to the wire rack to cool while you make the filling. (If any cracks appear, gently press the dough while still warm to seal it back together.)

To make the filling, combine the tofu, oat or soy milk, cornstarch, and salt in the workbowl of a food processor fitted with the steel blade. Process until smooth. Alternatively, use a blender.

In a 3-quart saucepan, stir together the raw cane sugar, brown sugar, and maple syrup. Bring to a boil over medium heat, stirring frequently with a heatproof spatula, until thick bubbles appear and the syrup thickens. (This would be just below 235°F (soft-ball stage) on a candy thermometer.)

V | vg | df | ef

CALORIES: 313; TOTAL FAT: 21 G; CARBOHYDRATE: 31 G; DIETARY FIBER: 2 G; PROTEIN: 4 G

Meanwhile, place the pecans and chocolate chips in a large heatproof bowl.

When the sugar syrup is thick, remove it from the heat. Whisk in the butter, and then whisk in the tofu mixture until smooth. Pour this mixture over the pecans and chocolate in the bowl. Stir and fold the ingredients until all the chocolate is melted. Evenly pour the filling over the baked crust and spread with an offset spatula to smooth the filling.

Bake for 20 minutes and then rotate the pan. Continue to bake for 12 to 15 minutes longer, until the filling bubbles at the edges. Transfer to a wire rack to cool. Once cool, refrigerate overnight before cutting into 36 bars, roughly 1 1/2-by-3 1/2-inches in size.

Store the bars at room temperature between sheets of waxed or parchment paper in a sealed container. The chocolate pecan bars keep well in a sealed container for 5 days or in the freezer for 2 months.

Note:
If needed, add additional melted coconut oil, 2 tablespoons at a time, if the crust is not coming together, but only enough to form a dough that is not sticky.

Makes 36 (1 1/2-by-3 1/2-inch) bars; Serving Size: 1 bar

HONEY CRÈME BRÛLÉE

Traditionally, the cream of a baked custard is infused with vanilla; but this version, created by the pastry chefs at Miraval Austin, infuses the cream with a deeply caramelized local honey, and a touch of spiced rum is added at the end. Watch closely when you cook the honey, you want it to bubble and turn a lovely amber color, but not burn. When you add the cream, step back a bit as you stir because the honey will sizzle and steam as the cream is added. Plan to make this dessert one day ahead of serving to be sure the custard sets, and the dessert is deliciously cold.

As you'll see in the accompanying photograph, the custards are garnished with a curvy ribbon of Dulce Chantilly (page 320), a dusting of Vanilla Rose Powder (page 320), and a few roasted cocoa nibs. Make these garnishes if you have time and your inner pastry chef wants to play in the kitchen. Otherwise, a few berries clustered on top make a lovely and simple garnish.

· ·

3 1/2 tablespoons honey

3 cups heavy (whipping) cream, at room temperature

4 large egg yolks (see **Note**)

3 tablespoons organic cane sugar

3/4 teaspoon fine sea salt

1 teaspoon spiced rum

Optional Garnishes:

Dulce Chantilly (recipe follows)

Vanilla Rose Powder (recipe follows)

Roasted cocoa nibs (see **Note**)

Pour the honey into a small saucepan and cook over medium heat until it turns a deep amber color and is fragrant, being careful to not let it burn, 3 to 4 minutes. Remove from the heat. Using a silicone spatula, carefully stir in the cream. Place the pan back on the heat and, stirring frequently, bring the cream to just below a boil. Remove from the heat.

Meanwhile, in a large bowl, whisk together the egg yolks, sugar, salt, and spiced rum.

Whisk 1 cup of the hot-cream mixture into the egg mixture to combine. Gradually whisk in the rest of the hot-cream mixture. Strain through a fine-mesh strainer into a clean container. Cover and refrigerate overnight.

Heat the oven to 350°F. Arrange 8 (4-ounce) ramekins in a large baking pan.

Whisk the egg mixture as it will have separated overnight. Ladle the egg mixture into each ramekin, dividing evenly. Pour hot water into the baking pan to come halfway up the sides of the ramekins. Bake until the custards are set, about 45 to 55 minutes. The custards should look set with a slight jiggle in the center. Remove the pan from the oven and let the custards cool in the water bath, set on a wire rack. Remove the custards from the water bath, place on a sheet pan and refrigerate at least 3 to 4 hours before serving. (If storing longer, up to 2 days, before serving, cover each ramekin tightly with plastic wrap before refrigerating.)

Makes 6 to 8 individual servings

Honey Crème Brûlée continued on the next page

V | gf | nf

CALORIES: 420; TOTAL FAT: 39 G; CARBOHYDRATE: 17 G; DIETARY FIBER: 0 G; PROTEIN: 4 G

Honey Crème Brûlée continued

....

To roast cacao nibs, heat the oven to 350°F. Scatter a handful of cacao nibs on a small, rimmed sheet pan and roast until they smell like brownies, about 10 to 15 minutes. Set aside to cool.

Spoon or use a pastry bag to pipe the Dulce Chantilly on top of each custard to garnish. Use Vanilla Rose Powder to dust the tops of the custards just before serving. Garnish with cacao nibs.

Note:

Don't toss those egg whites! They can be used to make the Turkey Sausage and Egg White Frittata on page 223 or the Ginger Spice Cookies on page 312. Store the leftover egg whites in a covered container in the refrigerator for up to 4 days. They may also be frozen for up to 2 months. Always date and label the container with the number of egg whites inside.

DULCE CHANTILLY

3 1/4 ounces Valrhona Dulce White Chocolate, chopped

1 cup heavy (whipping) cream

Place the white chocolate in a small heatproof bowl. In a small saucepan set over medium heat, bring the cream to a simmer. Pour the cream over the chocolate and whisk together until fully combined. Cover and refrigerate the mixture overnight. Once cold, transfer the mixture to a stand mixer fitted with the whisk attachment. Whip to form soft peaks.

....

VANILLA ROSE POWDER

1/2 ounce vanilla bean, cut into 1-inch lengths

1 ounce food-grade dried rose petals

Heat the oven or a toaster oven to 250°F. Place the vanilla bean in a small heatproof dish and bake to dry out the vanilla bean, 20 to 30 minutes. Cool slightly.

Transfer the vanilla bean and rose petals to a spice grinder and blend to form a powder.

COCOA DATE PIE

A favorite of guests at Miraval Austin, this vegan and gluten-free, no-bake pie has a press-in-the-pan crust that is sweetened with dates and is full of nuts. The entire pie is frozen before being served, making it ideal for entertaining.

Crust

2 cups Medjool dates, pitted

1/2 cup unsalted, roasted almonds

1/2 cup unsalted, roasted cashews

1/2 cup unsalted, roasted pecans

2 teaspoons pure vanilla extract

Filling

1 cup pitted and chopped dates

1 cup organic unsweetened soy milk

1 cup almond butter

1/2 cup unsweetened cocoa powder

1 teaspoon pure vanilla extract

1 teaspoon almond extract

To make the crust, combine the dates, almonds, cashews, pecans, and vanilla in the workbowl of a food processor fitted with the metal blade. Process until all the nuts are evenly and finely chopped.

Place the mixture between two sheets of parchment paper and roll out the crust slightly larger than a 9-inch pie plate. Lift off the top sheet of parchment and flip the crust over and onto the pie plate. Lift off the remaining sheet of parchment. Press the crust evenly into the bottom and up the sides of the pie plate. Place the pie plate with the crust in the freezer while you make the filling.

To make the filling, place the dates in a medium heat-proof bowl. In a small saucepan set over medium heat, bring the soy milk to just below a boil. Remove from the heat and pour the soy milk over the dates to soften them. Let cool briefly and then transfer the mixture to a food processor. Process until completely smooth, 1 to 2 minutes, scraping down the sides of the bowl once. Add the almond butter, cocoa powder, and the vanilla and almond extracts. Process until smooth.

Spread the filling in the prepared crust and smooth the top with an offset spatula. Freeze the pie for at least 8 hours or overnight. Once frozen, cover tightly with plastic wrap or foil and freeze for up to 3 weeks. To serve, cut into 16 slices.

Makes 1 (9-inch) pie; Serving Size: 1 slice

V | vg | gf | df | ef

CALORIES: 270; TOTAL FAT: 17 G; CARBOHYDRATE: 28 G; DIETARY FIBER: 5 G; PROTEIN: 7 G

CHOCOLATE CHAI CUPCAKES

Festive and fun, these gluten-free and dairy-free chai cupcakes are decadent and special enough for a celebratory occasion yet cute enough for a child's birthday party. To decorate these cupcakes, you'll need to make the Vegan Espresso Ganache Truffles (page 323). Making a chocolate ganache is easier than the name implies, as all you need to do is melt chocolate and coconut oil together and stir in the rest of the ingredients—it's like magic. You can leave out the coffee liquor, if desired. Make your own Gluten-Free Flour for this recipe (page 303) or use store-bought.

1/3 cup organic expeller-pressed canola oil plus more for greasing the muffin tins

4 chai tea bags

3/4 cup boiling water

2 tablespoons flaxseed meal

1/4 cup water

1 1/2 cups All-Purpose Gluten-Free Flour (page 303) or store-bought GF flour

1 cup organic cane sugar

1/4 cup unsweetened cocoa powder, sifted

1 1/2 teaspoons baking powder

1 teaspoon baking soda

Pinch fine sea salt

1 cup rice milk

2 teaspoons pure vanilla extract

1/2 recipe Vegan Espresso Ganache Truffles (page 323)

Arrange a rack in the center of the oven and heat the oven to 375°F. Lightly coat a standard 12-cup muffin pan with canola oil, or line the pan with paper liners. Set aside.

Place 4 chai tea bags in a large mug or heatproof measuring cup. Add 3/4 cup boiling water. Set aside to steep for 10 minutes. Remove and discard the tea bags. Cool to room temperature.

In a small bowl, stir together the flaxseed meal and 1/4 cup water. Set aside.

In a medium bowl, whisk together the flour, sugar, sifted cocoa powder, baking powder, baking soda, and salt.

In a large bowl, whisk together the rice milk, canola oil, vanilla, steeped chai tea, and the flax meal mixture until evenly combined. Using a silicone spatula, fold in the dry ingredients just until the flour disappears.

Divide the batter evenly among the muffin cups, filling each about three-quarters full. Bake until the cupcakes are puffed and brown and a cake tester or toothpick inserted in the center comes out clean, about 20 to 25 minutes. Transfer the pan to a wire rack. Allow the cupcakes to cool for 10 minutes before removing them from the pan. Cool completely on a wire rack before decorating.

To decorate the cupcakes, make a half batch of the chocolate ganache recipe on page 323, following the first two steps in the recipe. Instead of refrigerating the ganache, as directed in the second step of the recipe, you have two options to consider for decorating the cupcakes: To achieve a high-gloss smooth chocolate top, dip the top of each cupcake in warm ganache and then set aside until the chocolate sets. Alternatively, place cooled, but not refrigerator-cold, ganache in a pastry bag fitted with a fluted piping tip and decorate each cupcake.

Store the cupcakes at room temperature in a sealed container for 2 days or in the freezer for up to 1 month.

Makes 12 cupcakes

V | vg | gf | df | eg | nf

CALORIES: 303; TOTAL FAT: 15 G; CARBOHYDRATE: 40 G; DIETARY FIBER: 3 G; PROTEIN: 2 G

VEGAN ESPRESSO GANACHE TRUFFLES

When all you want is one small bite of great chocolate after a meal to satisfy that craving for something sinfully rich and sweet, these espresso ganache truffles will meet that need. Make a batch and keep them on hand in the freezer.

....

4 1/2 ounces vegan dark chocolate (70% cacao), finely chopped

2 tablespoons coconut oil

1/4 cup + 2 tablespoons canned coconut milk

1 tablespoon organic raw agave syrup

2 tablespoons coffee liqueur, such as Kahlua

1/2 teaspoon fine sea salt

Unsweetened cocoa powder for rolling the truffles

In a medium microwave-safe bowl, melt the chocolate, uncovered, on 50 percent power. Heat in 30 second increments, stirring each time, until the chocolate is melted. (The amount of time it takes is very dependent on the microwave. A slow and steady melt is better than scorching the chocolate.) As an alternative, place the chocolate in a metal bowl set over a saucepan of simmering water. Stir until the chocolate melts, being careful not to let any water touch the chocolate. Stir in the coconut oil until it is completely melted.

In a small saucepan, combine the coconut milk and agave syrup. Bring to a boil over medium heat. Remove from the heat and pour over the chocolate. Let the mixture sit on top of the chocolate for 1 minute. Using a silicone spatula, stir the mixture, from the outer edge of the bowl towards the center, until smooth. Stir in the coffee liqueur and salt until completely smooth. Refrigerate until set, at least an hour or overnight.

Place a few tablespoons of cocoa powder in a small bowl. Using a melon baller, scoop truffles up the mixture and roll with your hands to form uniform balls. Cover and chill, if needed. Roll in the cocoa powder until evenly coated. Transfer to a sealed container. Store the truffles in the refrigerator for 5 days or in the freezer for up to 1 month.

Makes 12 truffles; Serving Size: 1 truffle

V | vg | gf | df | ef | nf

CALORIES: 99; TOTAL FAT: 7 G; CARBOHYDRATE: 9 G; DIETARY FIBER: 1 G; PROTEIN: 1 G

rituals

FOR A LIFE IN BALANCE

CREATE A CULINARY SOUNDTRACK

Our Miraval Austin mixologist of all things—from beverages to songs—often talks about how creating a soundtrack for a meal can enhance its sensory experience. A playlist takes you on a journey, and when you pair it with a culinary quest, it can become a wild ride of discovery. From soul music to ska, a playlist can mix familiar components with new finds to evoke memories and ignite curiosity.

. . . .

"Music makes you think about what matters and how you express that. For some people, it's art, writing, or cooking. A playlist can be a catalyst, and my hope is that you hear something new and use it as an opportunity to continue to learn more about it. It's what we do at Miraval Resorts—we learn new ideas and use them to dive into a new way of being."
- Miraval Austin Colleague

Try adding one heaping teaspoon of curiosity and all five of your senses to your most open mind to create a personalized playlist for any meal with these simple steps.

- *Set an intention and the table:*
  Visualize your hopes for the meal or recipe with calm, peaceful, centering, or ambient-sounding songs. Consider how you will present the meal through lighting, colors, and setting. Are you sitting formally around a table or having a picnic outside? Are you lighting it up with candles, moonlight, or lanterns?

- *Prepare your food:*
  Gather ingredients, chop, dice, or marinate with slightly more upbeat songs. Notice the textures of the food and the sounds your knives and tools make. What is the rhythm of your prep?

- *Fire it up:*
  Begin cooking the meal with high-energy songs for a fun yet focused state of mind. Inhale the aromas you create and think about who or what they recall.

- *Eat mindfully:*
  Bring the energy back down to chill vibes and select background songs that engage your sense of hearing to enhance the meal.

- *Honor the experience:*
  Relax peacefully and hang out with a loved one or yourself after a great meal, taking time to appreciate each other and the moment with music like rhythm & blues or jazz that elevates the vibe and keeps the energy chill and mellow.

People come to the Miraval Resorts bar and make a choice—fruit smoothie or smooth mezcal? K-Pop or Hip Hop? Sometimes, removing judgment and making space for curiosity and conscious exploration nudges people to make better decisions.

> **"**Some guests turn it into an opportunity to exercise more self-control, and some people need to ease up a little or let themselves indulge. Sometimes you want the structure and familiarity of a classic country song, and sometimes you want to feel the thumping beat of techno. The important thing is to tune into your intention and remember that you are making conscious choices every day.**"**
>
> — MIRAVAL AUSTIN COLLEAGUE

CRYSTALS & THE CULINARY EXPERIENCE

Crystals are minerals that come out of the ground; a subterranean rainbow of colors that can illuminate our natural connections and help us explore the nature of our intentions.

Each stone carries different qualities and colors, and we can use them to set the scene for our intentions. Developing a relationship with crystals can be a form of spiritual nourishment and can symbolically support any quest for balance and beauty in daily life. This includes using them in our kitchens to inspire us and, by suggestion, infuse our meals with our best intentions.

....

Use this chart to explore suggested properties associated with a selection of popular crystals:

Mental clarity	fluorite, sodalite, citrine, smoky quartz, chevron amethyst
Energetic cleansing	clear quartz, amethyst, larimar, aqua aura
Grounding	labradorite, black tourmaline, shungite, black onyx
Energetic renewal	blood stone, carnelian, jasper, citrine, garnet
Emotional relief	rose quartz, citrine, blue lace agate, aquamarine, opal
Empowerment	yellow jasper, citrine, rose quartz, carnelian
Self-love	rhodonite, rhodochrosite, rose quartz, amazonite turquoise

Crystal arts specialists at Miraval Resorts offer these tips:

Harness the Energy of Crystals

Because crystals come from the earth, many contain contaminants that should not contact food or water directly. When using crystals alongside your beverages or food, stick to basic, non-toxic, non-porous stones like rose quartz, amethyst, clear quartz, smoky quartz, or natural citrines. Keep them adjacent to, but not touching, your food or beverages.

- Select your crystal to match your intention and say it out loud. It can even be one word: nourishment, compassion, or gratitude.

- Separate your stones and the liquid you plan to drink. You can do this with a purchased double-chambered glass or pitcher or by placing your stones next to a pitcher of water.

- Use this water for drinking or for washing fruits and vegetables.

- Make your leftovers sparkle by placing a crystal next to the container with the intention for your food to stay vibrant and beautiful. It can be a touchstone to remind you to slow down and be grateful.

- A clear quartz crystal in your refrigerator can reflect your intention to keep it clean and full of positive energy.

Crystals can also offer a way to elevate our everyday practices:

Reading a Recipe

Put a tiger's eye in your pocket or around your neck to inspire you to focus on your recipe or ingredient list.

In the Kitchen

Add citrine to your cooking space to remind yourself to not be attached to how it's going to turn out. The process of creating food includes curiosity, compassion, and creation. Citrine, with its lemony hue, can evoke feelings of prosperity and joy.

Crystals help us find beauty in little moments. Even simple tasks like washing produce can become a ritual of reciprocal intentions: we nourish our fruits and vegetables with loving energy so they can return that love to our bodies in the form of nutrients.

Selecting a Centerpiece for a Meal

Consider the type of energy you want to hold for a meal. If you use a stone or crystal as a centerpiece, remember to keep it physically separate from your food and beverages.

- Birthday celebrations: Decorate with a birthstone or one that reflects the celebrated person's favorite color.

- Ritual or regular meals: Select a stone like rose quartz or green aventurine that honors a meal ritual, like Sunday dinners. You can designate a stone that is present on each weekly dinner table and serves as a literal touchstone for everyone to share something at the beginning of the meal.

- Social time: Blue chalcedony, a communication stone, encourages us to cultivate kind, conscious, articulate, fun-loving conversation with everyone. It has beautiful ribbons of coloring and creates a lovely centerpiece for harmonious, loving conversation.

- Party favors: Offer your guests a special stone to take home with them.

Recharging

Did you know that crystals, like mushrooms, can be recharged? Putting mushrooms in the sunlight for 30 minutes enhances the vitamin D in the mushrooms. In a similar way, you can recharge your crystals by bringing them home to the elements that produced them: earth, air, fire*, and water.

- Rinse them in bioavailable water, like rain. Refrain from cleansing stones that end in "ite" in water since they are more delicate and can deteriorate.

- Leave them in natural light (gentle sunlight, moonlight) for several minutes.

- Bathe them in sound waves (metal sound bowls, tuning forks, crystal bowls, tingshas, vocal toning).

- Smudge them by burning white or blue sage, sweetgrass, palo santo, or incense.

- Mist or diffuse pure essential oils over them.

- Bury them in the earth, sea salt, or Himalayan salt for 24 hours.

> *Note:* Never put crystals directly in your water. Many crystals can be toxic when immersed in water. If you are going to use a crystal-infused bottle, be sure the crystals are in a separate chamber and don't touch the water. Check that the company doesn't use adhesive, glue, or wire to secure the crystal in place. Never replace medical care with crystals.

Do not leave flames unattended; keep out of reach of children.

LIVE AN ANTI-INFLAMMATORY LIFESTYLE

Inflammation is a natural immune response to injury or infection. It isn't inherently bad—it's the body's natural way of repairing itself. Acute or short-term inflammation occurs when you get sick with a cold or injured. But when you're in a state of chronic inflammation—which can be triggered by eating certain foods that may stimulate an inflammatory response in the blood—it can lead to a series of health issues.

Most processed foods can contribute to inflammation by altering the bacteria that live in our gut, and that alteration can interact with our immune system and trigger it in a way that may lead to chronic inflammation.

One of our most popular classes is called Tame the Flame, a workshop that teaches guests how to live an anti-inflammatory lifestyle. Here are a few ways you can integrate this approach to support your health.

Remove & Replace	Review your pantry, refrigerator, and freezer items. Only keep things whose ingredients you recognize as food.
Strive for 5	Strive for 5 or more servings of non-starchy vegetables a day. Variety is key.
Find the Fiber	Choose 3 to 5-gram servings of fiber-rich whole grains, bread, and cereals more often.
Pump up the Pulses	Pulses (chickpeas, beans, lentils) are rich in protein, iron, fiber, potassium, folate, and antioxidants. Add crunchy chickpeas to a salad, sip bean soup, or dip your veggies in hummus.
Ditch the Chips	Support your energy levels with a handful of nuts instead of chips. Each nut has unique properties, so consider varying types daily.
Promote Plants	Make plants (instead of animal proteins) the star and center of the meal.
Swap the Fat	Cheese, butter, ghee, and coconut oils are all rich in saturated fat. Use them sparingly and replace with unsaturated fats (avocado, nuts, seeds, olive oil).
Season Liberally	Combined, all herbs and spices have over 2000 different anti-inflammatory compounds, and using them can also help you reduce your sodium intake.
Minimize Added Sugar	Read ingredient labels and opt for foods with little or no added sugar. Don't be concerned with the sugar found in fruit.
Ground Yourself	Anchor yourself and absorb the earth's limitless supply of inflammation-decreasing antioxidants by walking barefoot outside. Hang out without shoes for 20 to 30 minutes on natural outdoor surfaces like grass, sand, or stone.

MORNING CACAO RITUAL

Cultivating a daily ritual with cacao can help us practice self-connection regularly. Cacao is an ancient medicinal plant native to the indigenous peoples of South America. Its delicious and sacred pods can help us drop into our hearts and connect to the wisdom within.

....

Ceremonial Cacao Ingredients

1 cup of brewed rose tea or steeped rose petals (see **Note**)

4 tablespoons of chopped ceremonial cacao

Sweetener of choice, such as 1 teaspoon honey

Pinch of Himalayan salt

A splash of nut or seed milk, optional

1 to 2 teaspoons coconut oil for creaminess, optional

Additional rose petals for garnish, optional

Optional additives:

A splash of nut or seed milk of your choice

1 to 2 teaspoons coconut oil to make it extra creamy

Note:

Use a consciously sourced rose powder or food-grade rose petals. Brew the recommended tea for about 3 minutes. Steep food-grade rose petals in barely simmering but not boiling water for 10 minutes.

"I deeply cherish Cacao and her ability to assist us in opening our hearts to become more authentically ourselves, to awaken the seeds of love and joy in us, and the very real grounding that takes place when we drink this ancient plant medicine."
- Miraval Berkshires Colleague

We use cacao that comes from a collective of women in Ecuador who nourish and sing songs to the cacao trees and ask them to open the hearts of anyone who touches them. The plant's caretakers gather pods, open them, and dry and ferment them in the sun for three days. They hand-shell and roast the seeds over an open fire and then grind them with a mortar and pestle into a thick paste which gets formed into bricks and exported. The lineage of cacao is passed down from grandmother to mother to child. They hold the wisdom of this plant in their family tree.

Using a sweetener depends on your taste; use more, less, or none. Traditionally, ceremonial cacao is served with no sweetener (it's an acquired taste – meet your body where it is).

Instructions:

- Allow your heart and mind to still, tune into your intention, and feel gratitude and love in your heart for the sacred cacao tree.

- Consider lighting a candle or burning sweet incense to honor this ritual and set a sacred space.

- From a centered place, combine all the ingredients in a pot on low heat, and let the cacao melt while constantly stirring it (don't let it boil).

- Pour the cacao into a cup that feels special. As an option, add rose petals on top.

- Holding it in front of your heart, express your intention and gratitude to open you up to receiving its gifts.

....

Cacao Ritual:
Holding the cacao with your eyes closed, say aloud or silently in your head:

*Thank you to the heart of the **Sky**, vast and wide.*

*Thank you to the heart of the **Earth**, the heartbeat,*
minerals, crystals, and stones.

*Thank you to the heart of the **Fire**, warmth, knowledge, wisdom, and light.*

*Thank you to the heart of the **Water**, flowing purely like rivers of light.*

I give thanks to everyone who brought this cacao to me/us and
the elements that nourished its roots and seed.

I give thanks to my own heart for showing up and being open
to receiving the messages I'm meant to receive.

Mama Cacao, Mama Cacao, Mama Cacao,
Come fly with me.

Feel the green energy of the trees around you and the sun's warmth. A path appears before you, and you walk down it. In front of you is a beautiful cacao tree full of pods. You go to the tree, place your hand on it, honor it, and give thanks. State your intention, gather it, and blow it into your cup. Imagine you are pouring this cup onto the tree and into the earth. Reach cups to the sky, greet the new day, bring it to your heart, and take a sip.

Play ceremonial music and listen to the messages that come through. Write them down in your journal or express them through movement, art, or music.

A PILLOW FOR SUMMONING DREAMS

Dream pillows have been used for centuries to calm bad dreams, encourage good ones, protect, and carry out a specific intention.

· ·

2 or 3 tablespoons of herbs

Natural cotton batting

1 small bag (muslin or linen works well)

Essential oils

1 bowl

1 mixing spoon

Paper

Pen/pencil

Select 2 to 3 calming herbs and combine with 1 essential oil. *Chamomile and Lavender are both herbs and essential oils.*

Herbs	Essential Oils	Properties
DRIED HOPS FLOWERS		sleep, nightmare prevention, psychic development
MUGWORT		
ROSE PETALS		love, divination, protection, beauty, feminine energy
ROSEMARY		strength, protection, memory
MARIGOLD		purity, divinity, connection between life and death
CHAMOMILE	CHAMOMILE	wealth, peace, love, tranquility, purification
LAVENDER	LAVENDER	sleep, peace, cleansing, joy, clarity
	CLARY SAGE	feminine health, psychic ability
	SANDALWOOD	wishes granted, peace
	CEDARWOOD	wealth, purification

Directions:

Meditate or take a walk in nature to choose an intention, then write it down on a small piece of paper to add to your pillow. Choose herbs and oils based on this intention and stir them together with 2 drops of essential oil in a bowl, keeping your intention at your heart's center. Line the bag with cotton batting to keep the herbs contained within the cotton batting, then spoon herbs into the bag. Add your intention before tying the bag tightly. Place it under your pillow while you sleep.

YOUR SALON APOTHECARY
HERBAL SCALP TREATMENT

Did you know you have a spa apothecary in your kitchen? The ingredients in your refrigerator and pantry are not just for one purpose; they can nourish your skin and hair as well as your insides. Don your Miraval Resorts Spa robe, read the message on the cuff that says breathe, and whip up your own spa pantry treatment, created by our Life in Balance Spa estheticians.

••

Equipment

Spice grinder

1 medium bowl

1 spoon

1 pint-size glass jar with a tight-fitting lid

1 small bowl

2 large hand towels or dishtowels

1 large heat-safe bowl

1 color applicator brush (can substitute with a basting brush or popsicle stick)

2 large hair clips + 1 shower cap

Weighted blanket, optional

Ingredients

4 tablespoons dried herbal blend (½ cup lavender, ¼ cup each: dried rosemary, chamomile, ground ginger, rose hip)

Jojoba or grapeseed oil

5 tablespoons carrier oil mixed with 3 drops lavender essential oil (or chosen oil)

Boiling water

Lavender (a super-flora that may have some anti-inflammatory and anti-microbial properties) creates our herbal base. Other power herbs include hair-growth-supporting rosemary, calming chamomile, stimulating ginger, and rosehip, which helps break down dead skin cells. This treatment cleanses your scalp and soothes your senses, creating a space of total relaxation. It works best on freshly washed hair.

Choose between scalp-smoothing jojoba oil (closest to our natural sebum), which helps repair breakage, can regulate oil production, and washes out easily, and antioxidant grapeseed oil, a natural DHT (a common hair loss component) blocker, which is anti-microbial, anti-inflammatory, penetrates quickly, and supports hair growth.

Instructions:

- Using a spice grinder, make the dried herbal blend by first grinding each herb individually into a powder. Measure and place each herb in a medium-sized bowl. Stir with a spoon to blend the mixture. Transfer 4 tablespoons of the dried herbal blend to a small bowl and stir in 4 tablespoons of either the jojoba or grapeseed oil. It will have the consistency of a pesto! Place the remainder of the dried herb blend in a sealed glass jar for later use. Store away from heat or light.

- Now start your treatment by brewing a pot of tea and setting an intention.

- Drip the essential oil mixture into a hand towel, roll it, and place it in a large heat-safe bowl. Wrap a second towel around your shoulders to catch any falling herbs.

- Rub 1 to 2 tablespoons of additional oil into your scalp in a circular motion.

- Pour boiling tea over the rolled hand towel, sitting close to allow the steam to open the hair cuticles, aiding in moisture absorption and hair shaft penetration.

- Using an applicator brush, apply the oil-herb blend directly onto your scalp. Massage the herbal blend into your scalp for 15 minutes to break down dead skin cells and product build-up while regulating pH and stimulating blood flow.

- Clip your hair up after giving yourself a gentle scalp massage. Squeeze out any remaining hot water from your hand towel and wrap it around your head. Place a shower cap over the hot towel, steaming herbs, and oils. Sip your tea under a weighted blanket, if using, while the flora penetrates. Dim the lights, let the treatment sit for 30 minutes, then wash out with shampoo and conditioner.

- Proper hair care will keep your scalp clean and build-up-free for up to 5 weeks.

Note: *Avoid open wounds, cuts, sores, or abrasions. Do not use if allergic to herbs or oils. Use caution with heat and hot water. If contact with eyes, flush with water.*

Quick Rosemary Rinse:

Prepare this simple hair rinse ahead of time for busier days when time is scarce.

- Boil 1 quart of water and 1 cup dried rosemary, and then simmer for 30 minutes. Set aside off the heat to steep for 4 to 5 hours (the longer, the better).

- When the water is cool, add 4 drops of essential oils. Pour into a spray bottle and mist into the scalp as needed.

Note: *Rosemary rinse blocks DHT, stimulates and refreshes the scalp, may have anti-fungal and anti-inflammatory properties, and may promote healthy hair growth and scalp strand retention.*

A WIN FOR SKIN
DRY BRUSHING + ABHYANGA

Dry brushing is a service you can give yourself at home with one simple tool before you step into your morning shower. It is a great morning ritual on its own but even better when paired with a basic self-massage with oil called Abhyanga. Brushing your skin before it gets wet lets you exfoliate without depleting moisture. Additionally, it can increase circulation and stimulate the lymphatic system to get rid of toxins in the body.

....

Did you know that the Sanskrit word for oil (Sneha) is the same word for love? Self-massage (or Abhyanga) is revered in Ayurveda, a healing system developed in ancient India. It is an ancient practice that lets you envelop your body in oil while you surround it with love.

Benefits of Dry Brushing & Abhyanga:
- Stimulates the lymphatic system and expels toxins
- Warms the body, supports blood flow and circulation, and reduces muscle stiffness
- Improves energy and mental alertness
- Exfoliates, encourages cellular renewal, and revives skin tone and texture

Dry brushing and oil massage activate lymphatic drainage, which helps reduce symptoms like bloating, fatigue, sinus problems, and swelling. Our skin is our first line of defense against bacteria and keeping it clean and clear helps it function better.

Pairing these two techniques is a winning recipe for smooth, hydrated, radiant skin. It can even make you feel like you are glowing inside. Dry brushing stimulates muscle fibers and helps keep your skin toned and tight. Abhyanga (oil massage) hydrates and stimulates your skin with a gentle touch so you can start your day with a brush with greatness.

What you need for Dry Brushing:
This invigorating technique uses a dry, stiff-bristled brush to slough off dead skin, priming it to expel toxins and absorb moisturizer more efficiently. If a dry brush is too harsh, you can use raw silk or silicon mitts that give you the same effect but do not feel quite so prickly. If you prefer a traditional brush, look for medium to soft bristles made of natural materials like cactus or agave bristles called sisal.

Note: Dry brushing should be avoided by people with severely dry, irritated, or inflamed skin, eczema, or psoriasis.

What you need for Abhyanga:

Choose the oil based on your skin type:

- **DRY SKIN:** Heavy oils like almond, sesame, or avocado oil
- **SENSITIVE SKIN:** Neutral oils like ghee or sunflower oil
- **OILY SKIN:** Light oils like safflower, sweet almond, or flaxseed oil

Technique:

Morning rituals that are a win for skin.

- Find a dry brush or glove that suits your skin.
- Stand in the shower with your brush in hand before turning on the water.
- Grip the head of the brush and massage your dry body using light, upward strokes, starting with your feet, and moving to your calves, thighs, hips, and beyond.
- Hold the long arm of the brush to access harder-to-reach back areas.
- Warm a small amount of oil in your hands and massage it into your body, using straight, long motions on your arms and legs and circular motions on your joints.
- Enjoy your shower. With the shower still running, clean your brush with soap and water.

A LETTER FROM OUR GUEST
To the Chef

Your Texas Shrimp and Artichoke dish was the most wonderfully tactile dish I've ever experienced.

> "*It invited me to lean in, put my elbows on the table, and reach in with both hands. As the meal evolved, I devolved into an exquisite experience of not wiping my hands; I stopped wiping my mouth, and even let an artichoke leaf dangle for a moment so I could continue to experience its texture and abandon anything held back in polite decorum.*"

For good measure, I finished it off by washing my hands in my water glass.

I suppose this is, in part, what you intended (although I suspect I took it all further than most).

Thank you for the "invitation."

Well done.

ENDNOTES

1. Menu and recipes created by Miraval Arizona Chef Matthew Demery, Director of Food and Beverage Jonathan Rosenthal, and Registered Dietitian Nancy Teeter. *(page 24)*

2. Ritual created in collaboration with Miraval Resorts nutritionists and dietitians. *(page 43)*

3. Recipes and menu created by Miraval Berkshires Chefs Justin Taylor and Andrea Pang. *(page 56)*

4. Ritual created in collaboration with Farm & Garden Specialists Hunter Coberly at Miraval Austin and Sarah Duprey at Miraval Berkshires. *(page 75)*

5. Recipes and menu created by Chefs Ben Baker at Miraval Austin, Matthew Demery at Miraval Arizona, and Justin Taylor at Miraval Berkshires. *(page 88)*

6. Ritual created in collaboration with Miraval Austin Wellbeing Specialist Lori Burdick. *(page 111)*

7. Menu and recipes created by Miraval Berkshires Program Chef Adrian Bennett and Ayurvedic Specialist Bart Staub. Beverage recipe created by Miraval Berkshires Cultural Connoisseur Nick Grimaldi. *(page 126)*

8. Ritual created by Miraval Berkshires Spiritual Guide and Energy Worker Raya Buckley. *(page 149)*

9. Ritual created in collaboration with Miraval Berkshires Ayurvedic Specialist Bart Staub. *(page 150)*

10. Menu and recipes created by Miraval Austin Chef Ben Baker. *(page 162)*

11. Ritual created in collaboration with Miraval Austin Astrologer Lynn Carroll-Rivera. *(page 189)*

12. Special thanks to Miraval Arizona Registered Dietitians Nancy Teeter and Makenna Baum. *(page 206 - 211)*

13. Ritual created in collaboration with Miraval Austin Mixologist Alhaji Abubakbar (HAAJi). *(page 326)*

14. Ritual created in collaboration with Miraval Arizona Crystal Arts Specialist Lindsey Banis and Miraval Arizona Yoga and Meditation Supervisor Alysa Volpe. *(page 328)*

15. Ritual created in collaboration with Miraval Arizona Registered Dietitians Nancy Teeter, Makenna Baum, and Miraval Berkshires Registered Dietitian Jenae Halstead. *(page 330)*

16. Ritual created by Miraval Berkshires Spiritual Guide and Ceremonialist Dayla Robinson. *(page 332)*

17. Ritual created by Miraval Austin Multimedia Artist Jayne Wick. *(page 334)*

18. Ritual created in collaboration with Miraval Arizona Ayurvedic Specialist Clinton Horner and Miraval Arizona Life in Balance Spa Manager Heidi Smith-Mullen. *(page 336)*

19. Ritual Created by Miraval Berkshires Master Stylist Bridget DesRosiers. *(page 338)*

ACKNOWLEDGMENTS

Miraval Team: Susan Santiago, Brian Contreras, Dina Niekamp, Heather David, Mark Stebbings, Sheri Morgan Muskin, Gilbert Santana, Neil McLeod, Tasha Britton, Luke Bloom, Dan Loehr, Charlie Barnett, Kendra Bolton, Christine Mariconti, Maura Staunton, Heidi Smith-Mullen, Kayla Fournerat

Chefs and beverage specialists: Ben Baker, Justin Taylor, Adrian Bennett, Andrea Pang, Matthew Demery, Jon Rosenthal, Nick Grimaldi

Nutritionists and Registered Dietitians: Nancy Teeter, Makenna Baum, Jenae Halstead

Miraval Berkshires Colleagues: Raya Buckley, Bridget DesRosiers, Sarah Duprey, Bart Staub, Dayla Robinson

Miraval Austin Colleagues: Alhaji Abubakbar (HAAJi), Lori Burdick, Lynn Carroll-Rivera, Hunter Coberly, Jayne Wick

Miraval Arizona Colleagues: Lindsey Banis, Clinton Horner, Noel Patterson, Alysa Volpe

Miraval Resorts family and friends: Jennifer English, Laura Faulkner, Lauren Landwerline, Bobbin Mulvaney

Helpers, tasters, and testers: Katelin Narlow, Meri Kemp, Andrea Slonecker, Adam Hilsinger, Gabriel Royster, Grady Rajagopalan, Joanie Simon

Creatives and consultants: Elizabeth Ann Moser, Heather Hryciw, Daria Maneche, Amy Treadwell, Ken DellaPenta

INDEX